Radio Active

Lester Beall, *Radio*. 1937. Used by permission of the Archives
and Special Collections, Wallace Library, Rochester Institute
of Technology.

Radio Active

Advertising and Consumer Activism, 1935–1947

Kathy M. Newman

UNIVERSITY OF CALIFORNIA PRESS

Berkeley / Los Angeles / London

University of California Press
Berkeley and Los Angeles, California
University of California Press, Ltd.
London, England

© 2004 by the Regents of the University of California

Library of Congress Cataloging-in-Publication Data
Newman, Kathy M. 1966–
    Radio active : advertising and consumer activism, 1935–1947 / Kathy M.
Newman.
        p.   cm.
    Includes bibliographical references and index.
    ISBN 0–520–22372–1 (cloth : alk. paper) — ISBN 0–520–23590–8 (pbk :
alk. paper)
    1. Radio advertising — United States — History.   2. Consumer
behavior — United States — History.   3. Boycotts — United States —
History.   4. Consumer protection — United States — History.   I. Title.
HF6146.R3 N48   2004
659.14'2'097309043 — dc21   2003014270

Manufactured in the United States of America
13   12   11   10   09   08   07   06   05   04
10   9   8   7   6   5   4   3   2   1

Contents

List of Tables   vii

Acknowledgments   xi

Introduction. The Dialectic between Advertising
and Activism   1

PART I. CULTURAL CRITICS IN THE AGE OF RADIO

1. The Psychology of Radio Advertising: Audience
   Intellectuals and the Resentment of Radio Commercials   17

2. "Poisons, Potions, and Profits": Radio Activists
   and the Origins of the Consumer Movement   52

PART II. CONSUMERS ON THE MARCH: CIO BOYCOTTS,
ACTIVE LISTENERS, AND 'CONSUMER TIME'

3. The Consumer Revolt of "Mr. Average Man": Boake Carter
   and the CIO Boycott of Philco Radio   81

4. Washboard Weepers: Women Writers, Women Listeners,
   and the Debate over Soap Operas   109

5. "I Won't Buy You Anything But Love, Baby": NBC,
   Donald Montgomery, and the Postwar Consumer Revolt   139

   Conclusion. High-Class Hucksters: The Rise and Fall
   of a Radio Republic   166

   Notes   193

   Bibliography   213

   Index   229

Tables

1. Results of Lux Study, 1934   18
2. Responses of 1,100 St. Louis Residents to Different Forms of Advertising, 1950   41
3. Audience Recognition of Products by the Programs That They Sponsored, 1950   44
4. Economic Stratification of the Radio Audience, 1940   47
5. Composition of Total Program Audiences by Income Group, 1940   48
6. Audience Tastes in Programming and Advertising by Education Level, 1946   49
7. Survey Respondents' Answers to Questions about Whether They Would be Willing to Pay Directly for Radio to Avoid Advertisements, 1935   50
8. Radio Advertising as a Percentage of All Advertising, 1934–1955   183

Dedicated to my grandmother —
Louise Renshaw Smith

Acknowledgments

I have done my best thinking and writing work in the company of others. This project began as a dissertation in the American Studies program at Yale. I thank my classmates, advisors, and co-workers at Yale for their generous support: Jean-Christophe Agnew, Debby Applegate, Ingrid Baumgartner, Hazel Carby, Nancy Cott, Michael Denning, Ann Fabian, Christina Klein, Timothy Marr, Trip McCrossin, David Montgomery, Stephen Rice, Corey Robin, Scott Saul, Michelle Stephens, Debra Thurston, Thomas Thurston, and Eve Weinbaum.

I also thank my comrades in the organizations I have been a part of — both intellectual and political. I thank the Payne-Whitney American Studies Reading Group; Graduate Employees and Students Organization (GESO), Locals 34 and 35; the Hotel Employees and Restaurant Employees International (HERE); the Center for Cultural Analysis; the Center for Arts and Society; the CMU Junior Faculty Collective; the Steel City Chess Club; the Highland Park Vegetarian Alliance; the Reservoir Track Team; and the Pittsburgh Chapter of the Labor Party.

Special thanks to Jean-Christophe Agnew and Hazel Carby for teaching the courses that inspired this project and for their work as members of my dissertation committee. Special thanks also to Michael Denning for advising this project and for holding out the utopian possibilities of intellectual work. Susan Douglas and Michele Hilmes read the entire manuscript several times for UC Press; they have been the best readers and role models imaginable. Lizabeth Cohen supported this project from its earliest beginnings; Elizabeth Fones-Wolf has shared invaluable research information; Elena Raslagova has been a terrific research partner; Dana Frank was enthusiastic about an early draft and was the first to teach me about "purchasing power." Other colleagues who have offered crucial commentary on this project in its conference presentation and manuscript form include the fellows of the 1999–2000 Charles Warren Center at Harvard University, James L. Baughman, Stuart Ewen, Lawrence Glickman, Joshua Gregson, Daniel Horowitz, Tera Hunter, Roger Lancaster, George Lipsitz, Jason Loviglio, Margaret McFadden, Annelise Orleck, Kimberly Phillips, Kellie Robertson, Barry Shank, Carol Stabile, Peter Stearns, Jennifer Trainor, and Michael Witmore.

I thank my colleagues in the English Department at Carnegie Mellon University for their unwavering support, especially Marian Aguiar, Stephanie Batiste, Jane Bernstein, Jim Daniels, Sharon Dilworth, Barbara Johnstone, David Kaufer, John Klancher, Peggy Knapp, Chris Neuwirth, David Shumway, Erwin Steinberg, and Kristina Straub. Special thanks to the English Department staff, Stephanie Dickie, Danny Josephs, and Vickie Makel, for making things work. I have received the generous support of several research funds at CMU, including the Berkman Faculty Fund, the FALK fund, and the Faculty Development Fund. I have also benefited from a team of top-notch graduate research assistants, including Neeta Bhasin, Ratnapriya Das, Douglas Davis, Adam Vrbanian, and Mary Zimmerlee. Special thanks to John Trenz, who spent one year checking references and reordering my files. He has been a great assistant and is on his way to becoming a great film scholar.

I thank the helpful staff members at the Wisconsin Historical Society, the archives at Oregon State University, the Walter P. Reuther Library, the Archive Service Center at the University of Pittsburgh, and the Archives and Manuscript Collection at Columbia Library. I also thank the families of Frederic Wakeman (Frederic Wakeman Jr. and Sue Farquhar), Ruth Brindze (Anne and Eugenie Fribourg), and Peter Morell (Valdi Morell) for sharing their time, photographs, and family histories. I thank Eric Smoodin, my first editor at UC Press, for his boundless enthusiasm. I thank Monica McCormick, my second editor, for making me finish.

Finally, I thank my best friends/colleagues/family members: to Christina Klein for reading multiple drafts and for always expecting more; to Amy Greenberg and Richard Doyle for sharing their truck, their home, and their enthusiasm; to Eve Weinbaum for teaching me the importance of failure; to Kellie Robertson for making Pittsburgh into the place we've always wanted to live; to Michael Witmore for knowing exactly what to say; to Tera Hunter for being such a good friend and mentor; to Christopher Robinson for helping me lighten my load; to Jennifer Trainor for becoming my neighbor and for Ligonier; and to Joshua Gregson, for giving me the two things I have always wanted more than anything. To my mother, Ann Panush, my stepfather, Larry Panush, and my sister, Brenda Newman, for their love, time, and money. Lastly, I thank my grandmother, Louise Renshaw Smith, for being the real intellectual in the family and for keeping the faith. It is to her that this book is dedicated.

The Dialectic between Advertising and Activism

In 1937 Bill Phillips, an information officer for the Department of Agriculture, hired a graphic designer named Lester Beall to make a series of posters for the Rural Electrification Administration (REA). The REA planned to use Beall's posters to "communicate the benefits of electricity to citizens in regions such as Appalachia." Beall used the silk-screening process to create six posters that promoted radio technology, electric light, washing machines, running water, farm machinery, and heat generation as among the benefits of electricity. He used bold colors — dark blue, crimson red, black, white, and lemon yellow — over large areas, with little text, and directional arrows to show the flows of light, electricity, and radio waves. The poster for radio, for example, illustrated three white radio waves, like bolts of lightening, moving downward from the upper right-hand corner of the poster toward a black house on a red hill. In 1937 these posters not only promoted electricity, they also promoted Beall's career, earning him the first-ever one-man show for a graphic designer at the Metropolitan Museum of Modern Art (see frontispiece).[1]

Beall had some links to what Michael Denning has called the "Cultural Front" of the 1930s, but he was just as comfortable designing a promotional brochure for CBS (as he did in 1936) as he was designing the cover of the progressive daily *PM* or a series of posters advocating the anti-Fascist movement in Spain (as he did in 1937).[2] At the same time, his work reflected the tension between advertising and activism that was evident in other American cultural forms — particularly radio — from the Depression era to the end of World War II. His poster for radio was meant to inspire rural Americans to act: to embrace electricity and to welcome it into their homes. The image, however, was vaguely threatening: the radio waves angled in on the rural residents from a vague point in space, seemingly as if they might invade or shock the inhabitants. Was radio a force for good? or would it bring an oppressive edict from the gods in the form of a lightening bolt, pinning humans between heaven and earth?

This book had its beginnings in my quest to prove that radio was not a force for evil, and, more specifically, that it did not merely "passify" its listeners. Dissatisfied with the cultural studies practice of "reading" resistance into narrative texts, I wanted to search out clearly documented and unmistakable forms of radical social activity. Moreover, I wanted to see if a specific mass cultural form, such as radio, might have helped such radical social activity come into being. I wanted to explore the ironic and counterintuitive possibility that radio might have helped to produce the very consciousness among radio listeners which they needed to fight radio itself. My interest in this question stemmed from a curiosity about the applicability of a Marxist labor framework to the realm of culture. I wanted to see whether or not Marx's intuition about the engine of revolution — the idea that oppressive working conditions stimulate the resistance of the worker — could be extended to the realm of leisure. Might oppressive "cultural" conditions — such as excessive radio advertising — stimulate the resistance of the listener?

The simple answer to this question is: yes. From the beginning of network radio, virtually any advertisement broadcast over the airwaves was considered by some listeners to be "excessive"; indeed, listeners fought against the commercial sponsorship of radio for nearly twenty years — from the mid-1920s to the mid-1940s. However, as my research deepened, my dream of finding a specifically "working-class" rebellion against radio advertising evaporated; I searched in vain for a massive movement of worker-led boycotts against radio sponsors and/or working-class manifestos against the evils of mass culture. Workers, as Elizabeth Fones-Wolf has shown, fought hard to get *on* the radio, and workers were certainly part of the coalition of activists who made up the "consumer movement" — one of the forces fighting radio advertising. In one spectacular case workers did use their consumer power, successfully, to quell an anti-labor radio commentator. But for the most part, Americans with the lowest income and least education were the most likely to appreciate radio in the 1930s and 1940s — advertising and all.

And thus the "radio activity" that I document in this book does not always measure up to the "radical social activity" that practitioners of cultural studies are often keen to identify. At times, the radio activity that I examine is positive — as in the case of listeners who wrote letters of thanks to product sponsors. Thus, the documentation of such "activity" — the various ways in which radio listeners acted in response to radio — became more important than to establishing, in every case, the "radical" nature of that activity. However, I have discovered that there is a dialectical relationship between advertising and activism. Specifically, in the 1930s there was a dialectical relationship between radio advertising and an emerging consumer movement. Radio advertising helped to provoke a negative reaction on the part of consumers who objected to it, and, at the same time, radio helped the consumer movement to adopt a positive notion of what it meant to be a consumer through programs, like *Consumer Time* (1935–47), sponsored by the U.S. Department of Agriculture. Radio advertisements told listeners that they possessed a new form of individual power: the power to consume. However, when consumers began to use this power collectively, they used it both to fight radio advertising and to argue for rights and privileges that would increase their power as consumers.

Why focus on radio? Certainly, there were other forms of advertising that were both influential and under attack. But, as Susan Douglas has argued, "Radio has been the mass medium through which the struggles between rampant commercialism and loathing of that commercialism have been fought over and over again. . . . Listeners both acquiesced to and rebelled against how radio was deployed by the networks."[3] As Douglas makes clear, the cyclical backlash against advertising is almost as certain in American culture as advertising itself. Douglas also pokes holes in the persistent belief that mass culture renders us "passive." She argues that while "we can passively hear . . . we must actively listen," and that this active listening often leads to the formation of imagined communities: "Orality fosters a strong collective sensibility. . . . The fact that we hear not only with our ears but also with our entire bodies . . . means that we are actually feeling similar sensations in our bodies at the same time when we listen as a group."[4]

Building on Douglas's insights, I argue that the imagined communities produced by radio listening in the 1930s and 1940s were also consuming communities: radio helped Americans imagine themselves, collectively, as a nation of consumers. However, listeners and advertisers alike saw consumption, like listening, as an active rather than a passive process. And thus, ironically, radio advertising helped to provoke the very movement of consumers which became intent on its destruction. And even when the consumer movement failed to eliminate radio advertising, it offered a positive and sometimes radical definition of what it meant to be a consumer in a time of scarcity.

This study also draws, in part, on the media theories of the Marxist communications theorist Dallas Smythe. Though he did not become known for his media criticism until the 1960s, Smythe was himself a product of the radio age. He was born in Canada in 1907, received a Ph.D. in economics from the University of California at Berkeley in 1937, and worked as a statistician for the U.S. Department of Labor. Later, he became the first Chief Economist for the Federal Communications Commission, from 1943 to 1948, helping to author one of the most controversial reports on "excessive advertising" in the FCC's history. In the 1960s he emerged as an important scholar of the political economy of communications in North America.[5] One of his most provocative insights for the Marxist study of communications is the idea that the real "commodity" in communications is the audience itself. This "audience commodity," he explains, is also a collective:

What [advertisers] buy are the services of audiences with predictable specifications which will pay attention in predictable numbers and at particular times to a particular means of communication (television, radio, newspapers, magazines, billboards, and third-class mail) in particular market areas. As collectivities these audiences are commodities. As commodities they are dealt with in markets by producers and buyers (the latter being advertisers). . . . The audience commodities bear specifications known in the business as "the demographics." The specifications for the audience commodities include age, sex, income level, family composition, urban or rural location, ethnic character, ownership of home, automobile, credit card status, [and] social class.[6]

While advertisers discovered the "audience commodity" prior to the 1930s, it was under the regime of commercial radio that a new class of intellectuals emerged whose primary job it was to study, rate, and value that audience commodity. For this new class of "audience intellectuals," the process of rating the audience commodity became an industry in and of itself.

The concept of the audience as a commodity is a simple insight, virtually intuitive, and yet it has been relatively unexplored by media historians and cultural critics. This oversight, which Dallas Smythe called the "blind spot" in Western Marxism, has allowed practitioners of cultural studies to emphasize the role that audiences play as "consumers" of mass-cultural texts while overlooking the role these same audiences play as "commodities" that are created, rated, and sold by networks and advertisers. This confusion arises in part because the cultural texts we have become accustomed to interpreting — novels and films — are more like commodities than are the narratives produced for radio and television. Novels and films are cultural narratives, but they are also consumer goods, which consumers purchase directly, at bookstores and movie theaters. The narratives on radio and television, in contrast, are *not* purchased directly by the consumer. They are produced by broadcasters using the profits made from selling airtime to advertisers. The programs themselves are not for sale; the attention of the audience is.[7]

Under the circumstances, we might assume that audiences, therefore, are hopelessly commodified — that we are produced, packaged, and peddled like so much sausage. But Smythe argues that the production of the audience commodity is only one side of the story. The audience commodity, he argues, engages in active resistance to the process of commodification: "Monopoly capital has produced its principal antagonist in the core area: people commodified in audience markets who are consciously seeking noncommodified group relations."[8] Using Smythe, and the historical case study of radio in the 1930s and 1940s, I argue that while radio audiences were created, packaged, and sold by broadcasters and advertisers, those same audiences, "seeking noncommodified group relations," banded together to form the consumer movement. And while the consumer movement did not reject the terms of the market, it did represent an attempt on the part of ordinary people to situate themselves within an emerging consumer economy. Consumers refused, simply, to be produced; they actively engaged in the struggle to define what it meant to be a consumer. And, ironically, though the leaders of the consumer movement were not all "radical" or politically left-wing, the consumer movement was perceived by the business establishment of the late 1930s and early 1940s as hell-bent on the destruction of capitalism.

This study, in addition to drawing on Smythe, builds on the pioneering work that has been done in the field of radio history: Susan Smulyan's *Selling Radio: The Commercialization of American Broadcasting, 1920–1934*, and Robert McChesney's *Telecommunications, Mass Media, and Democracy: The Battle for the Control of U.S. Broadcasting, 1928–1935*. These authors conclude that our current system of advertising-sponsored mass culture was not inevitable; they show how advertisers, educators, government officials, and consumer activists battled for control of the airwaves.[9] In this book, I extend their study of the debate over commercial radio to show that even after advertisers successfully conquered broadcasting in 1934, listeners continued to resent, and resist, advertisers' control of radio.

Both Smuylan and McChesney have shown that a coalition of educators, labor leaders, and women's groups organized against the commercial control of radio starting in the late 1920s. At the same time, the movement we know today as "the Consumer Movement" was also emerging, spurred on by the muckraking classics, *Your Money's Worth: A Study in the Waste of the Consumer's Dollar,* by Stuart Chase and Fred Schlink (1926), and *100,000,000 Guinea Pigs: Dangers in Everyday Foods, Drugs, and Cosmetics,* by Arthur Kallet (1933). The simultaneous rise of these two movements was not a coincidence. In fact, they were connected in two ways: (1) at the level of leadership and constituency, both movements drew on many of the same organizers, written materials, and grassroots organizations; and (2) at the level of discourse, both movements imagined consumers as active and potentially powerful — that is, if they were willing to become educated about consumer economics.

Radio advertisements contributed to both a positive and a negative sense of what it meant to be a consumer. On the one hand, as Charles McGovern has argued, "radio restored the crucial element of personal contact between seller and buyer."[10] Thus, the new aural salesmen addressed the radio audience as "friends" and told consumers that they had new forms of personal power — assuring them that they could be more beautiful, taller, more popular, and more successful with the products advertised over the air. On the other hand, radio commercials were annoying — they were the first form of electronically transmitted oral advertising — and consumers rejected the form and the content of many ads. And so the personal power promised by radio advertisements was transformed into a new form of social power when listeners realized they were not alone. The "you" addressed by the radio advertisement was always an individual "you" but it had the potential to become a collective "you" — an audience commodity, to use Dallas Smythe's term, "seeking noncommodified group relations."

In extreme cases, listeners registered their dissatisfaction with a radio program or advertisement by organizing a boycott of the program and/or product sponsor. Though this was a relatively rare occurrence, advertisers worried that consumers were constantly about to launch an attack on the products advertised over the air. In particular, they worried that consumers might protest something *about* the advertising itself. And here their concern was not unfounded: consumer activists, long before they organized boycotts of specific products, were moved to act by irritating, offensive, and untruthful advertisements. Advertising and activism first met on the playing field of *anti-advertising* activism.

Meg Jacobs makes a parallel argument about the relationship between the federal government and consumer activism in the 1930s and 1940s. She argues that the federal government fostered a new sense of consumerism during the Depression, and that consumerism provided a way for working-class Americans to engage class politics:

> In the United States, during the first half of the twentieth century, issues of mass consumption provided the idiom for class politics. Absent a strong socialist or labor party, or even a mass union movement, consumption politics served as a vehicle for a social-democratic agenda. The rise of consumerism as an "ism" was not synonymous with the triumph of an individualist atomistic political culture.[11]

The federal government, however, was not the only force that helped working-class Americans to become self-conscious consumers. In the 1930s radio played a major role in shaping an emerging consumer consciousness. Likewise, the consumer movement played a major role in articulating a powerful critique of radio itself. This dialectic between radio advertising and consumer activism was one of the products of the radio age.

From the 1930s to the mid-1950s radio was the dominant mass medium in the United States.[12] Radio was also the most important form of advertising, economically. As Stephen Fox has shown, "In 1938 . . . radio passed magazines as a source of advertising revenue, and the gap kept widening."[13] Radio reached the greatest number of people, but also the most demographically diverse groups of people. More Americans had a radio than a telephone, phonograph, or a newspaper/magazine subscription.[14] As a result, radio was heralded as a great democratizer — at the same time that its powers were also feared. Hitler's use of radio in Nazi Germany lurked behind the scathing critiques of the medium developed by the Frankfurt School, and Theodor Adorno, in particular. It was radio and the sound films — not television — that resulted in the first critique of the "culture industry," in the seminal essay by Theodor Adorno and Max Horkheimer published in *The Dialectic of Enlightenment* in 1947.[15]

Along with the dominance of radio came the dominance of the sponsor: in this period the product sponsor had more control over the actual content of programming than at any time in American history. Station representatives, and, more importantly, advertising agencies, produced both the shows *and* the advertisements:

The agency created not only the ads but also the programs, contracted for talent and studio facilities — often from the networks — to produce programs, and then presented the finished program, with integrated commercials, to the network. In effect, the agencies bought time in large chunks from the networks and a few of the largest independent stations. Stations got the popular show, networks provided the facilities and collected the money — and Madison Avenue had all but total control over network prime-time and daytime programming.[16]

The radio age was thus an age in which capital, in the form of the product sponsor, had the most direct control over the content of mass culture.

This new age also demanded the creation of a caste of "audience intellectuals" whose job it became to target, study, rate, activate, and pacify radio's audience commodities. These audience intellectuals — the men and women who worked as advertisers, broadcasters, sociologists, psychologists, and market researchers — were often sneered at by academic intellectuals of the same period. But, as advertising historian Michael Schudson has argued, these marketers and advertisers generally saw themselves as the "democrats of the business world" — the professionals who believed they could give the audience "what it wanted," because the audience was their object of relentless examination.[17]

But what were the larger cultural and political effects of radio? There were three general forms of listener activity during the 1930s and 1940s. Most commonly, the great mass of listeners responded to a specific radio program by writing a letter to the show's sponsor, the network, or the show's author, expressing positive or negative feelings about the show and/or the sponsor. The second form of response was more limited to writers, activists, and intellectuals. Radio critics writing for newspapers and magazines, consumer activists, and university professors published their commentaries in newspapers, magazines, consumer bulletins, and in full-length books. The last form of listener response, and, admittedly, the most rare, focused directly on an individual sponsor and could include the boycott of a product associated with an offensive advertisement or program. In these moments, the audience commodity became a self-conscious and active audience, aware of the tricks of the audience intellectuals, highly critical of radio and advertising, and organized. The radio age helped to produce this articulate, self-conscious, and active audience: it made them "radio-active."

The most active of the "radio-activists" were women. In the radio age, the popular discourse about mass culture was deeply connected to the discourse of gender. Radio was often depicted as a feminized medium, designed to "seduce" the unwitting consumer into sitting through the salesman's routine. If the medium itself was not depicted as feminine, then the recipients of the broadcast were positioned metaphorically as female. Finally, as Michelle Hilmes has shown, women played a crucial role as audiences *for* and as producers *of* radio programming in the radio age.[18] Throughout this period women made 85 percent of all consumer purchases in the United States. When advertisers had a message to deliver, their most important audience consisted of the people doing the bulk of the purchasing: women.

This relationship between women, mass culture, and consumption was not merely a twentieth-century innovation: historians have shown that women have been associated with mass culture and consumption under capitalism since at least the eighteenth century.[19] As Ann Douglas has argued for the nineteenth century, and Andreas Huyssen has argued for the "modern" era, mass culture itself has often been associated with women, "while real, authentic culture remains the prerogative of men."[20] Throughout the twentieth century women have been associated with mass culture in part because they have constituted one of the most important consumer audiences for mass culture — including daytime vaudeville shows, magazines, radio, and television. As women have done the bulk of the purchasing, so then have advertisers struggled to reach them. And therefore corporations helped to create a variety of entertainment forms, sponsored by advertising (or linked to shopping as an activity, in the case of vaudeville), that have appealed directly to women.[21]

Radio performed this cultural task better than any other medium had before: it allowed women to listen to daytime dramas while they did their household chores, while at the same time they were being exhorted to buy the products they needed to cook and clean. Radio was the ideal medium for the busy housewife. Because it was dependent on "ear-attention" rather than "eye-attention," the listener could be influenced by mass culture while still performing her unpaid labor in the home. Then, in the afternoon, she could go to the store and perform yet another task for the economy: she could purchase the goods she heard advertised on the radio. It seemed a perfect system for the management of desire, and, thus, for the management of distribution.

However, though women became the objects of radio advertising, they were not rendered completely passive in the process. Historical studies by Jacqueline Dirks, Dana Frank, and Sylvie Murray have argued that women consumers, far from being passive recipients of a consumer identity, have aggressively shaped their role in the market, often combining their consuming power in the form of consumer leagues, trade unions, and housewife associations. Historians of the consumer movement, including Lawrence Glickman, Charles McGovern, and David Katz, have also emphasized the role of women.[22] In the work of these historians, we are beginning to see that consumer activism is a rich, complicated, and understudied aspect of American feminism.[23]

Radio was one of the forces that helped to organize housewives. In some cases, the organization was quite literal: networks like NBC employed women like Dorothy McFadden to organize listener clubs around the country. In other ways, housewife organizations emerged as a byproduct of new trends in radio listening. Listeners banded together, sometimes to praise and other times to protest, their favorite and/or least favorite programs. At the same time, previously existing women's organizations like the Women League of Shoppers and the General Federation of Women's Clubs often took on radio as their object of reform. And so, at the same time that radio was bringing some women together in new ways, as listeners and as fans, radio was also becoming an object of female concern. After all, these women argued, radio had invaded their homes and was thus deserving of their scrutiny.

While broadcasters looked upon some women's organizations as relatively benign, they became anxious when they observed women organizing against radio or using their newfound consumer power to demand better working conditions for laborers or lower prices for food. It is not a coincidence that the radio age paralleled the emergence of the consumer movement. The consumer movement, which was founded in the 1920s and 1930s, exploded after World War II; the experience of war rationing — while it left people hungry and anxious to spend — also left them wary. When price caps established during the war by the Office of Price Administration were lifted and the price of coveted goods like meat, milk, and butter increased, consumers did not simply rush to buy. Organized through veterans' groups, trade unions, neighborhood and housewife associations, consumers staged "buyers strikes" in an attempt to bring back the price constraints of the OPA, or, at the very least, bring down the price of food, housing, and clothing.

The fact that boycotts were called "buyers strikes" should make us question the separation we generally make between the spheres of production and consumption. Is shopping a form of labor? Is a consumer boycott a "buyers strike"? How is production linked to consumption? If the "blind spot" of the commodity audience has plagued the fields of cultural studies and advertising history, the blind spot for American labor history is the boycott. Many labor historians have overlooked this form of grassroots protest, leaving the stories of secondary boycotts, pickets, protests, and sit-ins for lower prices, lower rent, or fair employment practices woefully unsung.[24] Moreover, without these stories, we cannot see how working people have sought to reconcile the power they have as consumers with the power they have as producers of consumer goods. It is conventional wisdom to assume that production is the realm of pride and power, whereas consumption is the realm of leisure, escape, distraction, and disempowerment.

Scholars who study the history of leisure have argued against this conventional wisdom, showing how the time for leisure has been hard won by working-class movements, dating back to the "eight-hour" movement of the late nineteenth century. Historians like Roy Rosenzweig, David Nasaw, Richard Butsch, and John Kasson have helped to explain how the very concept of "leisure" evolved from something that was reserved for the "leisure class" to something that could be purchased by a member of the working class on the weekends. In addition, historians such as Steven J. Ross, Nathan Godfried, and Elizabeth Fones-Wolf have looked at the ways workers have been represented by mass culture, as well as how they have used cultural forms to their tactical advantage. Ross's study of workers and early cinema, Godfried's book on the labor radio station WCFL, and Elizabeth Fones-Wolf's work on the CIO and radio have set the standard in the field. This scholarship has helped us to see that struggles over access to leisure have been as important as class struggles on the factory floor.[25]

Like Ross, Godfried, and Fones-Wolf, I am interested in the relationship between workers and mass culture. More specifically, I am interested in the unintended consequences of radio for labor — the ways in which radio inadvertently reminded working-class consumers that their power could be strategically deployed, both on the job and in the marketplace. Thus, in the course of this study, I will be advocating a number of revisions of the consumer/producer dichotomy. First, consumers have to be "produced." Though the commodity audience is not a traditional "product" wrapped up in a package with a label, industry insiders think of their work in industrial terms and often talk of "welding" or "molding" a consumer audience. Second, consumption is a form of work. Consumption may not be a form of "productive labor" in Marxian terms, but consumption is more akin to labor than it is to leisure. The labor involved in consuming has been underexamined by economists because it constitutes part of the unpaid, invisible labor done by women. And, finally, workers have used their power as consumers to improve their working conditions, often in the form of union-led boycotts. Militant housewives, in a similar way, have employed the tactic of the boycott and the rent strike to fight for improvements in the quality of life for themselves and their families. These boycotts demonstrate that workers and consumers understand that their power is not limited to the realm of production.

This book is divided into two parts. Part I examines the history and theory of the audience commodity and the consumer boycott, describing the work that was involved in producing that commodity for the radio and the "radio-active" audience which resulted. Chapter 1 examines the first node of the dialectic, the inner life of what I call the "audience intellectuals," who theorized both the form of the radio advertisements and the reactions of the radio audience. In Chapter 2 I look at the "consumer intellectuals" — their writings, organizations, and ideologies. Both sets of intellectuals were involved in theorizing the new role of the consumer under the influence of radio, but each had distinct agendas and spheres of influence.

Part II provides detailed case studies of three kinds of radio programming and the activism they provoked. In Chapter 3, I examine a CIO-led boycott of the Philco company, which sponsored news broadcaster Boake Carter, and the ways in which workers used the vulnerability of the sponsor to further their labor cause. In Chapter 4, I examine the prewar and postwar controversy over the radio soap opera and the forms of radio activity this controversy produced. Finally, in Chapter 5, I examine the radio program *Consumer Time*, which was produced by Donald Montgomery under the auspices of the U.S. Department of Agriculture, as well as the postwar consumer protests Montgomery helped to organize after he was fired by the government. In the Conclusion, I look at the best-selling novel which spoofed radio, *The Hucksters*, whose publication in 1946 brought anti-advertising attitudes to a cacophonous crescendo.

In each of these case studies, I examine a different moment in the dialectic between radio advertising and radio activism. In the case of Boake Carter and the militant CIO members that boycotted Philco — Carter's sponsor — I argue that workers brought their struggle over working conditions into the realm of mass culture. Their boycott of Philco shows their sophisticated understanding of the vulnerability of the single-sponsor structure of radio programming. Advertising did not provoke their activism, but advertising became the target in their activist struggle for control over the workplace. In the case of radio soap operas, I examine the distinct forms of radio activity generated by soap operas and soap ads. I look at the boycotts of soap operas organized by middle-class housewives, the criticism of this radio form produced by mostly male newspaper columnists, the defensive activity of one of the premier soap opera authors, Irna Phillips, and at letters written by ordinary listeners. The fan letters show that listeners believed their pleas would be heeded. Finally, in the case of Donald Montgomery and *Consumer Time,* I show that the consumer movement could use radio for its own purposes. Radio activity was not always negative, nor was it always directed at radio; in fact, in the case of Donald Montgomery, who was consumer counsel for the United Auto Workers during World War II, radio activity could be directed — in the form of massive consumer boycotts — against industries that had little to do with radio advertising at all.

At the same time that this book traces various moments in the dialectic between advertising and activism, it also looks at the roots of cultural studies itself. Many of the "audience intellectuals" who examined radio advertising and radio audiences pioneered the methods of interpretation and criticism used by academic intellectuals who study mass culture today. This book examines the history of the fight between intellectuals and the producers of mass culture over its control. Needless to say, the intellectuals lost. It is tempting to speculate that this loss is one of the reasons that progressive intellectuals are still grappling with mass culture. While many of us will admit to indulging in it, and even enjoying writing about it, most of us have eschewed advertising-sponsored mass culture as a realm for practical intervention, seeing it either as morally bankrupt or as economically imbedded in a system we wish to transcend. And thus the production of mass culture has been almost entirely ceded to the people who really like capitalism, or at least who don't mind it very much. At this point, then, the question becomes not a negative one, as in "How do we move beyond good and evil in our discussions of mass culture?" but, rather, "Can mass culture be of any use to progressive politics?" If mass culture, like capitalism, isn't going away any time soon, do we shun it, or do we try to intervene?

In the end, the stories in this book are meant to inspire us to think about ways we might want to use, protest, and/or produce mass culture for ourselves. They are meant to help us imagine a world in which mass culture might play a role in making the world a better place: a world in which we all might become "radio-active."

PART ONE

Cultural Critics
in the Age of Radio

The Psychology of Radio Advertising

Audience Intellectuals and the Resentment of Radio Commercials

---

In 1934 the makers of Lux soap hired the social scientist Paul Lazarsfeld to conduct a study on the effect of one of their soap advertisements. Lux worried that the ad might create the idea in the mind of consumers that cosmetics were harmful. Lazarsfeld's study confirmed Lux's worst fears: "Thirty-eight per cent of the women, when they were asked directly, replied that they thought the advertisement meant that cosmetics are harmful." In a related and even more surprising result, Lazarsfeld asked the women respondents to agree or disagree with the statement, "Nowadays, the consumer needs legal protection against the manufacturer of cosmetics," and discovered that more than three-quarters of women, or 76 percent, agreed that consumers "definitely" or "probably" needed legal protection against cosmetics manufacturers (see Table 1).

It is unlikely that these numbers, which reflect a high degree of suspicion of the cosmetics industry, were the mere result of cosmetic advertisements. A burgeoning consumer movement which produced a coherent literature, an educational outreach program, and received publicity from the mainstream press had helped the average consumer to become wary of false claims made by advertisers and products that were proven to be harmful (see Chapter 2). Still, it is significant that advertisers worried that their own advertising copy might create the impression that cosmetics were harmful. Advertisements often implied that competing prod-

TABLE I. Results of Lux Study, 1934

Female responses to the statement: *"Nowadays, the consumer needs legal protection against the manufacturer of cosmetics."*

Definitely Yes	58%
Probably Yes	18%
Doubtful	7%
Probably No	4%
Definitely No	13%

SOURCE: Series I, box 27, folder 5, BASR Papers.

ucts were harmful, but in doing so, they raised the suspicion that their own brands were potentially harmful as well.[1]

This chapter examines the "advertising" half of the dialectic between advertising and activism. Radio advertisements anticipated, and generated, listener resentment. This resentment was then studied, catalogued, and theorized by what I call "audience intellectuals" — a new class of intellectuals that emerged in the radio age. Audience intellectuals, with their studies of listener attitudes, helped broadcasters design strategies to overcome the listeners' resistance to advertising. In this chapter, I will sketch a brief history of these audience intellectuals. Next, I will look at the form and content of the radio advertisements themselves, focusing on the question of why early radio advertising was so negative in its rhetoric. Then, I will look at how listeners expressed their resentment toward radio advertisements. Finally, I will look at the strategies devised by audience intellectuals to overcome the resistance to advertising on the part of the listener.

In the 1930s a new caste of professionals, the "audience intellectuals," played a unique role in producing, appealing to, and studying audiences for radio broadcasting. They helped to shape the audiences for radio programs through advertising, marketing, program selection, and product distribution. Audience intellectuals were made up of two sub-groups of professionals who often worked together: advertisers/marketers, including copywriters, who worked at advertising agencies and academics who worked as professors of advertising and economics at universities; and university-affiliated social scientists, especially psychologists and sociologists, who specialized in quantitative and psychological interview techniques.

Trade magazines like *Advertising Age, Broadcasting, Printer's Ink,* and

Tide constituted the publishing nexus for most advertising professionals. The collective lore of the trade magazines was often repackaged and disseminated by advertising professionals who wrote the advertising textbooks used in college classrooms and radio stations. One such writer was Charles Wolfe, whose comprehensive *Modern Radio Advertising* (1949) included chapter introductions from well-known radio personalities such as Kate Smith and Fred Allen. The earliest advertising textbooks of the radio age included Orrin E. Dunlap Jr.'s *Radio in Advertising* (1931), Neville O'Neill's *The Advertising Agency Looks at Radio* (1932), and Herman S. Hettinger's *A Decade of Radio Advertising* (1933).

The second group of audience intellectuals — sociologists, psychologists, and audience raters — also wrote textbooks for college courses and industry professionals. Paul Lazarsfeld was one of the key leaders of this influential caste; three of his studies involving radio in the 1940s were crucial to the field: *Radio and the Printed Page* (1940), *The People Look at Radio* (1946), and *Radio Listening in America* (1948). Also important was Lazarsfeld's series of volumes entitled *Radio Research and Communications Research*, which were published as part of his work with the Office of Radio Research (funded by the Rockefeller Foundation), and which included articles by such Frankfurt School critics as Theodor Adorno and Leo Lowenthal. It is likely that Theodor Adorno, who worked closely with Lazarsfeld at the Office of Radio Research, began to formulate his critique of American mass culture, known today as "The Culture Industry," in response to the radio audience studies in which he participated. The radio age, in addition to producing a new caste of industry professionals, also helped to produce the nascent practice of cultural studies.

Lazarsfeld is especially important to this history because he was one of the most active of the audience intellectuals to study radio audiences during 1930s and 1940s. In addition, Lazarsfeld was one of the early theorists of radio activity. He provided a theoretical framework for thinking about consumption as an active rather than a passive process. And, while his left-leaning political background did not make him a "radical" in the American context, it is interesting to think about the fact that European Socialism influenced the development of American marketing research. The Harvard professor Gordon Allport and his Ph.D. student Hadley Cantril, who together wrote *The Psychology of Radio* (1935), were also key figures in the new science of audience investigation. They explained how radio, with its unique aural form, capitalized on the time habits of a nation — making it one of the most powerful advertising/political media ever devised. As Timothy Glander has argued, *"The Psychology of Radio* was in many ways a groundbreaking work, and it accurately recognized many of the social changes radio was creating."[2]

Susan Smulyan has shown that the earliest textbooks on radio advertising were written by audience intellectuals with close ties to both the advertising and radio industries. She notes that Orrin Dunlap, who wrote *Radio in Advertising* (1931), studied radio and electronics during World War I and worked in advertising after the war. Dunlap was an effective promoter of radio advertising because he had experience in radio, advertising, and print journalism. According to Smulyan, the audience intellectual Herman Hettinger had a more traditional academic background. His first radio textbook, *A Decade of Radio Advertising* (1933), was a revised version of his dissertation, and he taught at the Wharton School of Finance and Commerce at the University of Pennsylvania before becoming the director of research for the National Association of Broadcasters.[3] In spite of his academic background, however, Hettinger had important ties to the broadcast industry. In the introduction to *A Decade of Radio Advertising,* Hettinger thanks Dr. Leon Levy, who, besides being a dentist, was president of the influential CBS affiliate in Philadelphia, WCAU, and brother-in-law to the president of CBS, William Paley.[4]

The second group of audience intellectuals, the sociologists and psychologists who worked simultaneously for universities and the broadcast industry, were structurally more distant from — and more critical of — the commercial broadcasting system. While they studied the attitudes of radio listeners, in part to help broadcasters understand what listeners did not like about radio, they often had criticisms of their own. Cantril and Allport, for example, suggested that radio should be "removed from the dictatorship of private profits." These were strong words, especially from a study that was funded in part by CBS as well as by several Boston-area radio stations.[5]

Before Cantril received his Ph.D. at Harvard in social psychology, he had received a B.A. from Dartmouth (class of 1928) and had studied for two years in Berlin. While at Dartmouth, he had roomed with Nelson Rockefeller. Years later, after Cantril had published *The Psychology of Radio,* a representative of the Rockefeller Foundation asked him if he would be interested in becoming the director of a new institute for the study of mass communications. Cantril turned down the offer, suggesting that the Rockefeller Foundation offer the job to Paul F. Lazarsfeld instead. Lazarsfeld accepted the job and became the head of the newly created Office of Radio Research — a post that established Lazarsfeld as one of the founders of communications research in America.[6]

Paul F. Lazarsfeld was born in Vienna in 1901. His unique educational and political background — a mix of Austro-Marxism, socialism, mathematics, statistics, physics, psychology, and sociology — led to his interests in social stratification, the relationship between different kinds of choices (such as shopping and voting), and consumer psychology. His first application of the technique of "audience research" was for a political cause; he was active in the Socialist Student Movement and he designed a questionnaire to examine the problem of movement morale:

We were concerned with why our propaganda was unsuccessful, and wanted to conduct psychological studies to explain it. I remember a formula I created at the time: a fighting revolution requires economics (Marx); a victorious revolution requires engineers (Russia); a defeated revolution calls for psychology (Vienna).[7]

Though Lazarsfeld later became a sociologist, psychology had a powerful influence on the development of his early career. His mother was a student of the psychologist Alfred Adler, who, according to Lazarsfeld, practiced a kind of psychology whose "opposition to Freud had a strong sociological tinge."[8]

While a graduate student at the University of Vienna, Lazarsfeld worked as a camp counselor in a socialist children's camp. Lazarsfeld credited his political experience in the Socialist Youth movement in Austria with his success as an institution builder in the United States: "In part it was due, I believe, to the fact that I and many of my collaborators had team experience in the Socialist Party and in the youth movement; in my case, I would guess that this style of work was partly a psychological substitute for political activities."[9] In the late 1920s he received his doctorate in mathematics and started teaching math and physics at the high school level. He continued, however, to be interested in psychology. He taught some statistics classes for the Bühlers — Charlotte and Karl — who started the Psychological Institute at the University of Vienna. The clients of the Institute included the "Frankfurt Institut" headed by Max Horkheimer. Lazarsfeld helped Horkheimer conduct a "series of inquiries," which were later reported in the Frankfurt Institute's study on "Authority and the Family." Eventually, Lazarsfeld gave up his teaching post and started to work full time for the Psychological Institute. He was skilled at finding grant money. Early on in Lazarsfeld's career, clients of the Psychological Institute included soap and shoe companies. Lazarsfeld found that he could study consumer choice as a methodological substitute for voting behavior because it was both politically safer and easier. He found that as models for the psychology of choice, shopping and voting had a lot in common: "Such is the origin of my Vienna market research studies: the result of the methodological equivalence of socialist voting and the buying of soap."[10]

For Lazarsfeld, voting and buying had one thing in common: they were both representative of a certain kind of "action," or — in the German — *handlung,* a concept which, according to Lazarsfeld, had "great sanctity in the European humanistic tradition." Lazarsfeld believed that if he could discover why people bought, then he could discover why they voted. In Lazarsfeld's view, studying choice could lead to a better understanding of political action — even if the choice under scrutiny was the choice between one brand of soap and another. Importantly, Lazarsfeld was interested in the similarities between voting and shopping not because he wanted to reduce the act of voting to the act of shopping, but because he wanted to *elevate* shopping to the level of voting. He saw the decision to buy one thing over another, or one brand instead of another, as part of a "politicized" process, as influenced by custom, family, income, class, region, discussion, and persuasion as was choosing a political candidate.

Thus, Lazarsfeld was interested in issues of class and social stratification in the early studies he made of workers, youth, and the unemployed. And, though he worked well with corporations in the United States, he maintained his concern for the "proletarian consumer" throughout his career. This interest, as well as a suggestion by the head of the Austrian Socialist Party, Otto Bauer, led Lazarsfeld to conduct a study of the "leisure problems" faced by workers in times of "severe unemployment" in the Austrian town of Marienthal.[11] The study was subsidized, in part, by a local trade union, and the researchers offered donations of clothing and food to the participants who agreed to be interviewed.[12] Lazarsfeld's study of Marienthal, which became a kind of Austrian "Middletown," helped launch his career as an American academic and market researcher. His success with the study attracted the attention of *Middletown*'s author Robert Lynd and helped Lazarsfeld get a Rockefeller traveling fellowship in 1933. One year later, when the Socialist Party was outlawed in Austria and many of his family members were imprisoned, Lazarsfeld was able to get his fellowship extended so that he could stay in the United States.

After creating a statistical research center in Newark, New Jersey, from 1935 to 1937 Lazarsfeld was asked to head the Office of Radio Research. His appointment as the director of this project (which was later transferred to Columbia) launched his long career as a sociologist, radio expert, political theorist (especially in the realm of voting behavior), and commentator on mass culture and the masses. Throughout his career, however, Lazarsfeld never lost interest in the idea of "action." In all of his studies, no matter what the subject was, he continually asked the question: Why do people do what they do? Lazarsfeld always asked the question directly: Why do people listen to one radio program and not another? Why do they buy one brand of soap and not another? Why do they vote for one candidate and not another? Lazarsfeld worked from the assumption that choosing a product, choosing a radio program, or choosing a political candidate were all active — rather than passive — decisions made in social, political, and historically specific contexts, and that the motives for such choices could be studied by asking respondents to explain their choices.

Theodor Adorno, on the other, hand, was much more pessimistic about what social scientists could learn from the study of the "activity" of radio listeners. Lazarsfeld helped Adorno get a job at the Office of Radio Research in 1937, but he was so struck by Adorno's "foreignness" that he admitted to feeling like a member of the "Mayflower Society." Adorno, for his part, was equally appalled by Americans and by recent European immigrants, such as Lazarsfeld, who he claimed were "more American than the Americans."[13] When Adorno first arrived at the organization's Princeton office, he was also shocked by the corporate and instrumental nature of the research he observed:

I went from room to room and spoke with colleagues, heard words like "Likes and Dislikes Study," "success or failure of a program," of which I could make very little. But this much I did understand: that it was concerned with the collection of data, which were supposed to benefit the planning departments in the field of the mass media, whether in industry itself or in cultural advisory boards and similar bodies.

Adorno, who was put in charge of the "Music Study," found himself in fundamental disagreement with the charter for the Princeton Project, which stipulated that the research be conducted "within the limits of the commercial radio system."[14] Adorno explained that while he did not want to criticize radio simply for the sake of criticizing it, that he did not "strictly obey" the charter. Instead, he was critical of radio music, radio audiences, and the methodology for studying radio audiences; he saw them each as hopelessly ensnared in a tangle of commodification, standardization, and objectification.

Curiously, Adorno still fits the profile of the "audience intellectual."
While working at the Princeton office, he took some delight in conducting "a series of certainly very random and unsystematic interviews." But
he rejected the idea that much could be learned from the "subjective reactions" of radio listeners. He wanted to know to what extent radio audiences were affected by "comprehensive social structures, and even society
as a whole."[15] Ultimately, he spent the bulk of his time at the Office of
Radio Research writing a memo that was 161 pages long, called "Music
in Radio." Lazarsfeld attacked Adorno's memo for being "fetishistic,
neurotic and sloppy." Meanwhile, W. G. Preston Jr., a vaunted NBC
official, condemned Adorno's memorandum:

The paper is so full of factual errors and colored opinion, and its pretense at
scientific procedure is so absurd in view of its numerous arbitrary assertions, that
it is hardly worthy of serious consideration, except possibly as propaganda. In
short, it seems to have an axiom to grind.[16]

Adorno did have an "axiom to grind": more than one, in fact. But his critique of commercial radio was too much for the Princeton Radio Project;
Adorno's "Music in Radio" led to the cancellation of the funding for the
music division of the radio project altogether, and Adorno was fired.[17]
    During his short time at the Princeton Radio Project, Adorno engaged
in his own forms of radio activity. He was critical of virtually every aspect
of commercial radio, from the dramas, to the music, to the advertising,
to the overall commodification of the medium. Adorno was interested in
the criticisms leveled by other radio listeners, and in the reciprocal effect
of listener criticisms on the broadcast industry itself. In this sense, Adorno
had a more holistic picture of the radio industry: he saw the radio programs, products, people (in terms of the audience), and producers as intimately connected. Specifically, he was able to see the dialectical relationship between the activism of the listeners and the broadcast industry itself:
"We must pay special attention to the manner in which the radio companies themselves are 'affected' by the listeners, and how they react to
their listeners' reactions."[18]
    Adorno believed that radio "mutilated" the consciousness of its lis-
teners. But he also believed that this "mutilated consciousness" extended
to the "mutilating power itself": the broadcast industry. He proposed that
one way to assess the consciousness of the broadcasters would be to study
the "internal correspondence" of broadcast companies: "In these letters
people speak frankly about their viewpoints on program-making and thus
their attitudes can be studied." Adorno was right — the internal corre-

spondence of the broadcast industry does reveal a lot about its ideology (see Chapters 4 and 5). Interestingly, however, Adorno wondered if the "anti-highbrow" attitudes of the radio listeners were typical of the broadcasters themselves, arguing that it would be "romantic" to imagine that the "representatives of the ruling strata are more clever than the ruled." In other words, Adorno saw the radio broadcasting system as part of the capitalist system as a whole, and he saw little separation between the network executives and the programs/audiences they produced.[19]

Within this system, however, Adorno contemplated the limited opportunities available to listeners for the articulation of their discontent. He psychoanalyzed the radio listener who got satisfaction from turning off the radio, labeling him "narcissistic," "impotent" and "resentful":

It is utterly probable that this . . . forcing into silence the stream of talk, or the stream of music simply by one slight movement of the hand, is one of the greatest narcissistic realizations of pressure for the impotent and resentful listener.[20]

Adorno, while he had little sympathy with this type of radio listener, realized that such listeners might see themselves as "opponents" of the ruling elements in society. He saw this as a form of petty revenge on the part of the consumer — revenge which was directed at the merchant for making a profit. Adorno also compared the radio listener who turned off his radio to the radio listener who "fiddled" with the dial to find a new station. He called this kind of listener "The 'Bastler,'" and identified the station-switching activity of The Bastler as a gesture of powerlessness.[21]

Adorno, however, did not see all such gestures as ineffectual. While he questioned the power of listeners to "choose" a radio program of their own free will and questioned those who tried to resist radio — by turning if off or changing the station — Adorno saw the capitalistic communications system as an arena which was full of antagonisms. Adorno believed that if these antagonisms could be made visible, then perhaps resistance to the "system as a whole" could be promoted. He made this theory of antagonisms one of his "axioms":

Since in our society the forces of production are highly developed, and, at the same time, the relations of production fetter those productive forces, it is full of antagonisms. These antagonisms are not limited to the economic sphere where they are universally recognized, but dominate also the cultural sphere where they are less easily recognized.[22]

These "less recognized" antagonisms in the "cultural sphere," Adorno argued, had to be exposed. Adorno wondered what would happen if listeners realized how "unfree" they were in the face of this process of standardization: "This process, however, if it were to work openly and undisguised, would promote a resistance which could easily endanger the whole system."[23] This was a strong claim; Adorno envisioned a process of listener awareness that could lead to the destabilization of capitalism as a whole.

Like Lazarsfeld, then, Adorno was a theorist of radio activity. He, too, recognized the dialectic nature of the relationship between radio and listeners. And, as much as Adorno scoffed at the radio reformers, calling them "pedantic," "narrow-minded," and "prudish," he was a keen observer of the limits of the capitalistic system as a whole. He was hopeful that human beings could not be completely controlled, and that individuals still possessed some subjectivity — in spite of the brutality of the "forces of production." He acknowledged that listeners were complicit in the process of their own subjugation but insisted that there was a limit to the alienation that they could be made to suffer:

Human beings, as they conform to the technological forces of production which are imposed on them in the name of progress, are transformed into objects which willingly allow themselves to be manipulated and thus fall behind the actual potential of these productive forces. . . . Because human beings, as subjects, still constitute the limit of reification, mass culture has to renew its hold over them in an endless series of repetitions; the hopeless effort of repetition is the only trace of hope that the repetition may be futile, that human beings cannot be totally controlled.[24]

In other words, Adorno argued, human beings could not be transformed, completely, into objects. His evidence for this fact came from the culture industry itself. If human beings were so easy to control, Adorno argued, then the culture industry would not be forced to repeat its efforts. Adorno saw the "endless series of repetitions" as a hopeful sign — a sign that human beings maintained some agency in the face of objectification.

Lazarsfeld and Adorno exhibited distinct ways of thinking about radio activity. Lazarsfeld started from the premise that radio listeners were active and that they had meaningful choices to make in the commercial and/or political marketplace. Adorno, in contrast, believed that the choices of radio listeners were virtually meaningless when made under the strictures of capitalism. However, both men saw the possibilities for listener resistance. Lazarsfeld studied the listener's resistance to a single advertisement or program, whereas Adorno was interested in the way in which human beings, if they could be made aware of their state of objectification, might come to resist capitalism as a whole.

The Form and Content of Radio Advertising

Radio advertising was different from all previous forms of advertising in that it was the first form of advertising to *disrupt* the entertainment narrative. Magazine and newspaper ads could be ignored — and some consumers even admitted that they *liked* reading print advertisements. In contrast, the only way to avoid a radio advertisement was to turn off the radio. Listeners — glued to the radio, hoping to hear what would happen next in the story or waiting for their favorite program to start — had little choice but to pay attention to the "message from our sponsor." In most cases, radio shows had advertisements which preceded the show, ended the show, and, with increasingly regularity during the 1930s, interrupted the story in the middle.

From the beginning of network radio, corporate sponsors worried that direct advertising would alienate radio listeners. Early examples of indirect advertising included programs and/or singing groups that were named after the product sponsor, such as the Ipana Troubadours (Ipana toothpaste), the Eveready Program (Eveready batteries), the Happiness Boys (Happiness candy), and the Cliquot Club Eskimos, whose six-piece banjo band was described as "sparkling," just like Cliquot Club ginger ale. In one of the more innovative cases, the *Palmolive Radio Hour,* sponsored by the Colgate-Palmolive-Peet company, the two featured singers, Frank Munn and Virginia Rea, went by the show names of Paul Oliver and Olive Palmer. In this way, products were not merely the "sponsors" of a given program, they became synonymous with it. In the minds of radio listeners, the product and the program were fused.

Gingerly, advertising agencies began to experiment with forms of direct advertising. And, as they feared, listeners quickly registered their annoyance. But at the same time, sales of products that used the direct appeal began to increase. As Roland Marchand has argued, radio did not usher in the era of cultural "uplift" for which middle-class radio advocates hoped. Instead, radio became one of the agents of the crass commercialism of the Depression era. And, as advertising agencies began to experiment with this new form of advertising, the academic wing of the culture industry began to lend a hand. Thus, together, radio advertisers and audience intellectuals began to develop a theory of radio psychology to explain how radio was helping to create a new, modern, and electronically motivated listener/consumer.

The word "motivation" was a frequent key word in the discourse of audience intellectuals about the psychology of radio advertising. Scholars and advertisers argued that consumers had to be "motivated" or "activated" in order to purchase, thus challenging the notion that consumers were simply "passive." Cultural theorists have often imagined consumers to be "passive," in the sense that they are the objects rather than the subjects of advertising. In this context, passive means "suffering action from without; that is the object, as distinguished from the subject, of action; acted upon, affected, or swayed by external force."[25] Here, the "external force" is the advertisement, and the goal of the advertiser is to have the advertisement "act upon" the radio listener. In this sense, the word "passive" applies: advertisers *did* hope to become an "external force" that might sway radio listeners to purchase a specific product. They *did* hope that audiences would "obey."

However, audience intellectuals knew that advertising would not work unless the consumer became involved, actively, in the advertisement. They saw purchasing as a process that required the self-conscious "activity" and attention of the consumer. In this sense, consumers were the opposite of "passive," as that word is defined in an alternative way: "Not active, working, or operating; not exerting force or influence upon anything else; quiescent, inactive, inert." Consumers, from the point of view of those who studied them, were not "quiescent," "inactive," or "inert."[26] Rather, consumption was an "active" process that involved the consumer remembering the brand name, going to the store, purchasing the item, and using it. Consumers had to be "motivated" to buy. The only problem was: how to do it?

In order to answer this question, audience intellectuals focused on the ads themselves, on the temporal structure of radio programming, and on the psychological dynamics of the audience — broken down into demographic subgroups. They examined the most effective formal techniques — the kinds of jingles, rhymes, and verbal styles that made consumers remember a particular advertisement. They also studied listeners' resentment of radio ads in order to understand the techniques that led to listeners' rejection of the program and/or product. They discussed the ways in which radio capitalized on the "time habits" of the consumer — the ways in which radio was structured around, and helped to structure, the daily lives of listeners. Finally, they examined the question of audience demographics and radio's effect on listening audiences. Here again, their findings challenge conventional wisdom. While consumers are often portrayed as isolated — even alienated — individuals, audience intellectuals saw consumers as belonging to various demographic groups defined by sex, region, class, and/or age — groups such as men, women, workers, immigrants, Southerners, migrants, housewives, children, etc.

Advertisers studied the attitudes of radio audiences with one question in mind: How could they prevent, or at least minimize, the resentment of radio listeners? They feared that if radio listeners, organized into "audience commodities" seeking "non-commodified group relations" (in the terms of Dallas Smythe), became resentful enough of a particular ad, they might stop listening to the show sponsored by the ad, or, worse still, stop buying the product altogether. This fear, that somehow listener resentment might congeal into a full-scale listener boycott, or "buyers strike," all because of an offensive ad, was relatively unfounded. Listeners rarely directed their anger over advertisements into an organized campaign to stop buying a particular product. But the fear itself is instructive: it helps us to realize that radio ads were structured around the very notion of listener resistance. While ads alone rarely caused a revolt, the annoying nature of radio advertising helped to undermine public confidence in, and acceptance of, radio advertising as a whole. Annoying ads helped to fuel the dialectic between advertising and activism.

In the early part of the twentieth century advertising itself was a nascent form. But as Richard Ohmann has pointed out, print advertising had already developed an idiom for allowing consumers to make meaning out of text and image by the turn of the twentieth century. Ohmann and Judith Williamson argue that print advertising had already adopted the voice of the abstract and impersonal "corporation" which, through stories and pictures, simultaneously addressed both the collective and individual "you."[27] Furthermore, as Roland Marchand, T. J. Jackson Lears, and Stuart Ewen have argued, by the 1920s and 1930s print advertising operated according to a complicated system of signs, deploying a series of symbols that Marchand has labeled "parables" to motivate consumer demand. Radio advertising, on the other hand, given the limitations of the form (thirty seconds to two minutes of oral testimony — spoken or sung), was more stripped down than the print advertising of the same period. The content of the radio text was more direct, less metaphoric, and there was less space, literally, for the invocation of extra-product symbolism. There were four primary styles of radio ad during this period: the "expert" monologue, the testimonial form and/or dialogue between well-known personalities, the dramatic skit, and the musical jingle.

The following analysis of radio ads from this period will show that radio ads anticipated the resistance they generated from listeners and consumer activists. The dialectic between advertising and activism, between the form and the resistance to the form, can be found within the very text of radio commercials. In order to be effective, these ads had to invoke listeners' sense of fear, embarrassment, ill health, and exhaustion from work. Ads also played on consumers' fears of economic instability. Finally, radio advertisements often betrayed the anxiety of the manufacturer that the product being advertised might be harmful to the consumer. Ads depended on negative rhetoric to do their work, and in the process they generated negative responses from radio listeners.

Though separate advertisements describing the product did not become the norm until the late 1920s, the first known spoken "commercial" aired in 1922. It was an ad for a housing development called Hawthorne Court, in Jackson Heights, New York:

Friends, you owe it to yourself and your family to leave the congested city, and enjoy what nature intended you to enjoy. Visit our new apartment homes in Hawthorne Court, Jackson Heights, where you may enjoy community life in a friendly environment.

This commercial employed a technique which became emblematic of the radio age: the use of the opening greeting of "Friends." It is ironic, perhaps, that the first known commercial was an early advertisement for suburbanization, and that the major selling point for Hawthorne Court was "nature" and "community life." But even this early advertisement reflects the conventions of radio advertising. The listener was addressed both as an individual ("you owe it to yourself"), as a member of a family unit ("yourself and your family"), and as a member of a group ("Friends"). Additionally, while consumption is often associated with individual purchases, this ad promised satisfaction for the individual on the basis of the individual's need for community. The logic of advertising was constructed according to the relationship between the individual (family) and the group.

These early advertising techniques, however, were not as self-consciously "anxious" as they would become during the 1930s. As Roland Marchand has argued for print advertisements, radio ads reflected — as well as helped to usher in — anxieties about modernity.[28] Products advertised via radio were mostly small, repeat-use goods, such as soap, toiletries, and breakfast foods. As an early radio economist observed, articles such as "canned foods, flour and cereals, dentifrices and mouth washes, cigarettes, soaps, ginger ale, and similar items, are goods which, though nationally advertised and branded, require constant sales effort to build up and hold any measure of consumer interest, preference, or even acceptance."[29] Radio advertisements had to construct the problem for the listener before they could offer the product as the solution. In the following commercial for Ipana toothpaste, the listener is urged to feel anxious about "flabby" gums, about eating "soft foods," and about having a less-than-lovely smile:

For the sake of your smile, look at your toothbrush tonight. Does it show a faint tinge of pink? That's a warning signal [police whistle]. That's pink toothbrush, and you'd better see your dentist about that. It is a sign that your gums may be flabby and unhealthy, and that you may be in for a more serious mouth disorder. . . . Your gums tend to become soft and unhealthy from lack of exercise. We certainly don't get much exercise from the soft foods we eat these days. When you massage your gums with Ipana . . . you help make them firmer and healthier. Help make your smile more attractive to those you meet. Don't take chances with pink toothbrush. . . . I urge you. Get an economical tube of Ipana toothpaste today.

In this ad, typical of the male voice-over "expert" monologue, the authoritative voice seeks to create anxiety about the modern condition — the condition of being underexercised, flabby, soft, and unhealthy. For every positive value of Ipana toothpaste asserted by the announcer ("especially designed for gum massage," "Help make your smile more attractive"), statements designed to provoke fear were asserted as well: "That's a warning," "You'd better see your dentist," "Don't take chances with pink toothbrush."

An advertisement for a product called Nervine played on the very idea of anxiety itself. This product was a sleeping pill which promised sleepful nights and the end of "nervous tension." In this advertisement, the negative consequences of nervous tension are emphasized, including annoying one's friends and feeling miserable. Again, the voice is that of a male announcer. His voice is deep, and he sounds both confident and condescending. Note the repeated use of the word "mild."

Friends, wakeful nights certainly can make you feel all dragged-out the next day. And that's not very pleasant. Now perhaps you haven't slept the way you should because nervous tension has kept you keyed-up and jittery. Well, when nervous tension ruins your restful nights and spoils your days, try mild Nervine. It has been making good for 60 years. And that's why we say: To sleep well, relax well, remember mild Nervine. It has helped bring restful nights and tension-free days to thousands. Yes folks, if nervous tension sometimes annoys your friends, or makes you miserable, call on mild Nervine. . . . Nervine is a quality mild product.

Caution: Use only as directed. . . . It's N-E-R-V-I-N-E. . . . Yes, to sleep well, relax well, remember mild Nervine.

As with the ad for Ipana toothpaste, this ad has a high ratio of negative to positive statements. Phrases like "dragged out," "not very pleasant," "nervous tension," "keyed-up," "jittery," "ruins your restful nights," and "spoils your days" dominate the text. Even the name of the product, Nervine, evokes the problem rather than the solution — this sleeping pill is not called "Restine" or "Sleep-Ease." And, finally, with the repeated use of the adjective "mild," this ad contains the underlying suggestion that sleeping pills are the opposite of "mild." This point is driven home with the reminder: "Caution: Use only as directed."

These ads draw on what Roland Marchand has called the "Parable of Civilization Redeemed." According to this common trope in print advertisements from the 1920s and 1930s, products as unassuming as toothpaste and chewing gum were imagined to provide the oral and "moral" exercise necessary for healthy gums, and, by extension, a healthy citizenry.[30] But at the same time that these ads promised to reinvigorate the underexercised consumer, they also hinted at the dangers that lurked within the products themselves. As with the repetition of the word "mild" before the brand name Nervine, ads for products ranging from skin creams to dish detergents to cigarettes stressed the "gentle" and "mild" effect of their products. And, in the process of insisting on the mildness of the product, these ads raised the suspicion that such products were, in fact, the opposite of mild — perhaps even dangerous.

In an ad for the skin cream Solitaire (another name which hinted at the problem rather than the solution), a male voice queried: "And is Solitaire kind to your skin?" A woman's voice, with a sing-songy, 1930s lilt, answers: "Adorably kind, because Solitaire has a rich lanolin base that helps prevent skin dryness." Ads for dishwashing detergent frequently insisted that they were "milder to hands" (Vel) and could prevent the "red, chapped" hands that resulted from dishwashing (Super Suds). And cigarette ads, more than any other, insisted that the particular brand in question was mild, not irritating to the throat, and scientifically proven to be safe for the smoker. Camel ads repeated the word "mild" in a jingle: "How mild (mild, mild), how mild (mild mild), mild, mild, mild can a cigarette be?" A Phillip Morris ad claimed it was the only brand that was proven to be "definitely less irritating, definitely milder than any other leading brand." Meanwhile, Raleigh cigarettes claimed, "No other cigarette is safer to smoke."[31] These radio ads, with their insistence on the "mild" properties of their products, while they were meant to comfort, soothe, and reassure, might have raised anxieties about the safety of the products in question.

The negativity of a line like "No other cigarette is safer to smoke" had ironic consequences, not only for listeners but also for other advertisers. NBC, for example, in 1934, found that its many advertisers were getting fed up with "cross-firing" — the attacking of rival products within the text of the advertisement. As *Variety* explained it, "Commercial copy in the negative is being pushed out of the window with NBC feeling that such copy only serves to bring about a sort of guerrilla warfare among the advertisers." As a result, NBC banned all advertising copy that stated the basic idea that "all other products are inferior" and insisted that all advertising copy use the more positive formulation of "our product is the best." While this policy was probably also a response to consumer complaints about negative advertising, negative advertising was not successfully "banned" by NBC. Negative claims in advertising continued with a vengeance throughout the 1930s and 1940s.[32]

Of all the negative consequences of modernity, perhaps none were so exploited on the radio as those connected with housework. The soaps and other home products that were advertised were supposed to relieve the female listener of her daily burdens. However, these ads were surprisingly frank in their repetition of the negative qualities of housework itself. In an ad for Procter and Gamble's White Naphtha soap, a product which sponsored the radio soap opera *The Guiding Light,* the announcer implied that this particular brand of soap might compensate for a lazy and ineffectual husband:

Maybe only last night you were sitting at the supper table having a good time, and then all of a sudden you remembered that when supper was over it was up to you to do that big pile of dishes. It sort of took the fun out of things, didn't it? You know, if you mind dish washing that much I'll just bet you're using a lazy soap. The kind of soap that just lies down and lets you do all the work. When you want to clean up a pile of dishes in a hurry, want to get grease and caked-on food off of plates, pots and pans, you don't need a namby pamby soap, what you need is a go-getting business-like soap. The kind millions of women just like you are using every day. A husky white cake of P and G.

This ad employs a near comic double entendre between the soap and the listener's husband. The commercial begins with a reminder that it is up to the female listener to do that "big pile of dishes." The ad then suggests that she might have a "lazy" soap, a soap that "just lies down and lets you do all the work." The irony of this description is that no matter how "active" a soap might be, the woman involved in the dishwashing will have to do "all the work." And thus the ad implies that the soap might compensate for a lackluster mate. After all, declares the ad, she doesn't want a "namby pamby" soap, but rather a "go-getting business-like" soap. A "husky" cake of soap. These are all descriptive phrases that could apply just as easily to, if not more logically to, a husband. In fact, as the ad continues, the double entendre becomes more suggestive, as the ad refers to the "thick, creamy suds" produced by the soap and the grease that "slides right off the plate."

Ads for cleaning products frequently tried to present the image of an "active" product — a product that would "do" the work for "you," the listener. But these ads did little to hide the fact that the woman of the house was the one who had to do the work. One product, aptly named to take advantage of the aural effects of radio, played on the present tense form of the verb "to do." This soap was the sponsor of the soap opera *The Road of Life*, and it was called "Duz" — an aurally resonant version of the verb "to do," or "does." The ad opened with a musical jingle and then moved into a conversation between a man and a woman. The woman, even though she is the one washing the dishes, is constructed as the "lesser partner" in this dialogue about dishwashing. In addition, her grammatical use of the product name, "Duz," has overtones of the black dialect associated with minstrel performance:

WOMAN'S VOICE: *(Singing)* D-U-Z, D-U-Z, put DUZ in my washing machine, see the clothes come out so clean. When I DUZ my wash I sing, D-U-Z does everything!

MAN'S VOICE: *(Speaking)* Yes, It's the DUZ program, *The Road of Life*. *(Organ music)*

MAN'S VOICE: Everybody's Duzzing, it's the thing to do.

WOMAN'S VOICE: This new kind of soap does everything for you

MAN'S VOICE: In the wash —

WOMAN'S VOICE: And in the dishpan, too.

MAN'S VOICE: Yes, all over the country these days you find Duz doing double duty, it's kept busy in the washtub, and in the dishpan, too.

WOMAN'S VOICE: Right, Duz really does everything. That's because it's a new kind of washday soap with extra qualities that are tailor made for dishes.

MAN'S VOICE: For fast work on greasy pans, for taking care of dishpan hands, it's Duz all the way, you see it's made richer, made finer than any strong granulated soap, and that richer quality really makes a big difference in your dishpan.

WOMAN'S VOICE: Of course we aren't saying that with Duz, you don't even have to hold the dishcloth, but we do say there will be no more hard scouring to get rid of grease on those sticky baking dishes and frying pans.

MAN'S VOICE: And we do say to notice how fast those Duz suds destroy that grease. No soap can beat it for a quick clean up job. Notice how those mountains of Duz suds stand up until the last dish is done.

WOMAN'S VOICE: I want to put in a notice right here about hands.

MAN'S VOICE: OK, give them the good word about hands, partner.

WOMAN'S VOICE: Well, it's this, friends, Duz is extra kind to hands. In fact with Duz care, their looks can actually improve.

MAN'S VOICE: That's a fact. Changing to this wonderful Duz from any of those strong soaps can change rough, scratchy hands, to softer, smoother hands.

WOMAN'S VOICE: Lovelier hands.

MAN'S VOICE: Don't I always say there's never been a soap quite like Duz before? It's a whiz. For fast action on pans, for gentle action on hands, the one and only Duz, does everything. And now Duz invites you to listen to *The Road of Life*.

In other words, Duz "does" your work for you — but not really. At the same time this ad promises freedom from work, the ad itself is filled with reminders of how much work is involved in housework and of the consequences of that work for the houseworker. With the statement, "Of course we aren't saying that with Duz, you don't even have to hold the dishcloth, but we do say there will be no more hard scouring to get rid of grease on those sticky baking dishes and frying pans," the ad acknowledges that the houseworker still has to wash sticky baking dishes and greasy frying pans — with or without Duz soap. Furthermore, the ad acknowledges the consequence of this work: dishpan hands. Though both the man and the woman insist that Duz will improve the look of the woman's hands while she is doing the dishes, it seems they protest too much. Also, the male speaker does not suggest that he will be helping out with the dishes. Though he calls the woman announcer "partner," the ad assures us that the loveliness of *her* hands, not *his*, is at stake.

The problems advertisers sought to address were not entirely fictional.

In a 1950 study of the physical problems associated with housework, a British doctor found that the number one problem cited was "dermatitis" or "dishpan hands." Seventy-nine percent of the housewives studied complained of "tiredness, anxiety and depression." Other maladies included "neuritis, neuroses, varicose veins, low back pain, fallen womb, peptic ulcers, inflamed muscles, vitamin deficiencies, arthritis [and] flat feet." In other words, perhaps the advertisements for dishwashing soap were not wrong to emphasize the negative effects of dishwashing. Chances were that the women listening to the advertisement were indeed suffering from "chapped hands."[33]

But is the function of advertising to present the world as it is — or as it should be? Michael Schudson has argued that advertising is capitalism's way of saying "I love you" to itself.[34] The ads presented here, however, paint a much less rosy view of capitalism — or at least of the modern condition. In the White Naptha soap ad, for example, the tired housewife is reminded of the "pile of dishes" and of the "grease and caked on food" on "plates, pots and pans." In the Duz ad she is reminded of the "hard scouring" and "sticky baking dishes and frying pans." She is also reminded that dishwashing leads to "rough, scratchy hands." Altogether, these ads remind listeners that their world is full of domestic drudgery (White Naptha and Duz), anxiety (Nervine), and alienation (Solitaire), and that it is unhealthy and potentially dangerous (Ipana toothpaste and all cigarette ads).

Did listeners react to the negativity presented in radio ads? Many ads were structured to anticipate just such a reaction. In an ad for the sponsor of the Fred Allen show, a laxative called Sal Hepatica, the ad announcer explains to Fred when he introduces the commercial that "we're not even going to take much time for Sal Hepatica." This simple statement betrays the anxiety advertisers felt over appearing to spend too much time on the "word from our sponsor." Of course, the announcer went on to say quite a few words about the laxative with a peculiar name:

Friends, one of the products that makes it possible for us to present Fred Allen . . . is Sal Hepatica, the mineral salt laxative. Now whenever you need that kind of medicine we suggest that you take Sal Hepatica. It will cleanse your body of poisonous waste speedily, gently, thoroughly. And that's not all it does. When you have waste in your body you also have an acid condition throughout your system, and Sal Hepatica is the laxative that also combats the acidity building up your alkaline reserves so necessary for your health. In other words, Sal Hepatica can correct both troubles. So keep Sal Hepatica in your medicine cabinet. Don't suffer from a half sick condition, sick headache, upset stomach . . . Take Sal Hepatica and get a head start on buoyant, alert, normal health in just no-time.

Sal Hepatica was a laxative made by Bristol Myers. First introduced in the 1890s, its sales shot up between 1903 and 1905. Hepatica is the name of a plant — a three-lobed flower that was native to England — which was thought to look like the liver. The "Sal" in Sal Hepatica probably was short for "salt" or "saline." Bristol Myer's chemist J. Leroy Webber called Sal Hepatica the "poor man's spa." Intentionally, or accidentally, the name of the laxative also sounded like a man's name — and a funny sounding one at that.

Ads for laxatives, deodorants, toothpaste, bad breath medicine, and other products of a potentially offensive nature were a constant target of attack by radio listeners throughout the 1930s. The wasteful nature of these products — they were products designed to be used quickly and then thrown away, or to clean bodily waste, or to clean the body of foods that were quickly turned into waste, or medicines designed to move waste more quickly through the body — had an eerie resonance with one of the most common critiques of advertising: that it was a wasteful enterprise. Critics charged that advertising was "non-productive," and therefore wasteful, a drain on the social surplus, while defenders insisted that a little waste was necessary for the attainment of choice and freedom.[35] Perhaps, as Roland Marchand has argued, the very condition of constipation was a "symbolic manifestation" of the waste produced by the exigencies of modern capitalism. Marchand argues that "plugged intestines seemed both a literal and a 'symbolic manifestation' of 'the poisons of waste which too civilized people accumulate within themselves.'"[36] Is it possible that the radio airwaves, so filled with talk of waste, dirt, poor health, pink toothbrushes, body odor, restless nights, and sore throats, helped radio listeners — ever so subconsciously — to see capitalism as an essentially wasteful and, possibly, even a harmful system?

The Resentment of Radio Advertising

Advertisers asked themselves this very question. Advertisers knew, as did Adorno, that negativity and repetition were the keys to successful selling. On the other hand, an annoying radio commercial that listeners heard over and over again could backfire — causing listeners to resent either the program that was being interrupted or the product itself. According to audience intellectuals, radio was the superior medium for "capturing" the attention of its audience since it was difficult for the listener to turn off, or turn down, the radio commercial that was interrupting the program without sacrificing some of the programming itself. As one expert argued, "The broadcast media . . . show a much greater capacity than the print media to capture a person's attention. Indeed, it may take even physical effort to avoid such exposure."[37]

Advertisers understood that with print advertising readers had to make little effort to avoid reading the ad, whereas with broadcast advertising listeners had to physically (or mentally) exert themselves in order to avoid an ad.

Radio broadcasters have argued that radio has an advantage in that it is so easy to listen. The radio audience must make an effort to *avoid* hearing the advertising messages. Listeners must either adjust the program selector or start some competing activity to escape what the announcer is saying. Contrary to popular impressions, one does not "turn off" his mind.[38]

There was one way to turn off radio commercials from a distance. The first remote control for the radio was invented in the 1930s, ironically, it turns out, by an advertiser who wanted to give listeners the ability to tune out the commercials of competing sponsors. But because radio was a sound medium, it was hard for the listener to know when to turn the radio volume back up. A careless use of the radio remote and a housewife could miss the next few minutes of her favorite soap.[39]

Listeners also resented the fact that commercials interrupted the narrative flow of their favorite programs. Advertisers had code names for the different placements of commercials within the show: the commercial that aired right before the start of the show was called the "cowcatcher"; a commercial for another product of the same sponsor was called a "hitchhiker"; and a commercial for an entirely different sponsor was called a "spot" announcement. In the mid-1930s sponsors were just starting to use the "middle" commercial — the one that aired in the middle of the drama (which was generally only fifteen minutes long to begin with). The middle commercial, Paul Lazarsfeld noted, produced considerable resentment: "The 'middle commercial' offers a special problem. It interrupts the program and is, therefore, a frequent object of resentment. At the same time, it is one of the surest ways to reach the listeners with a sales message. Thus, it might eventually become a symbol in the struggle between balancing commercial advantages and maintaining the good will of the audience."[40] The middle commercial was part of the paradox of radio advertising: it worked to sell goods, but it also threatened goodwill.

Advertisers were split about the role that irritation played in the process of making a successful sale. While most acknowledged that irritating commercials were remembered by the listener, they did not agree on whether or not irritating listeners was the best way to increase sales:

While irritation advertising can sell goods, it cannot sell good-will for the sponsor, and good-will is a valuable asset. So make your commercials either extremely well liked or extremely disliked, but remember: when you put repetitious, irritating blurbs on the air, you may be taking chances.[41]

Advertisers were afraid that listeners might be so irritated by some commercials that they would be motivated to do the wrong thing: not to purchase, but to protest.

Sometimes broadcasters themselves expressed resentment of radio commercials. NBC executive John Royal wondered in 1937 if NBC "might get many more millions of listeners if these programs were improved from the standpoint of commercials?" NBC executive Niles Trammell concurred, complaining about the length of Procter and Gamble commercials, which he claimed had "probably the longest commercials of any client on the air." He added: "I personally resent them because I don't like long commercials." A Mr. Witmar, one of the advertising representatives at NBC, also agreed that Procter and Gamble should be "prevailed upon to cut down on their commercials." In this internal memo exchange, it becomes clear that Theodor Adorno was right: broadcasters' views were not far removed from those of the radio audience. Plenty of listeners resented long commercials, and so, it turns out, did Niles Trammell and his colleagues at NBC.[42]

Besides tinkering with the length and the placement of commercials, sponsors had other ways of using entertainment programming to "capture" the listener. Shows like *Pot O' Gold* and *Captain Cash* gave away money to listeners called at random during the program or when listeners themselves called the station in response to a magic word. This practice "in effect pay[ed] the audience to listen."[43]

Records are spun for consecutive hours a day, not with a view to entertainment but to bribing listeners to keep their ears pricked for the "commercials" with which these programs abound. . . . In these programs the content and interest of what is broadcast are deliberately subordinated to the purpose of inducing listeners, by a monetary appeal, to subject themselves over long periods of time to sales appeals.[44]

Though the FCC frowned on this kind of programming, in some ways it was a logical extension of the economic system on which radio was founded. Listeners were exposed to commercials, and for their time they were rewarded with "free" entertainment. As Sut Jhally has argued, in the world of advertising-sponsored media, participants are paid a kind of "wage" for their "work" — the work of paying attention to advertising.[45] The "wage," Jhally argues, is the entertainment itself.

But what if listeners started to feel dissatisfied with the "wage" they were being offered for the "work" of paying attention? The urge to protest, advertisers feared, might be stimulated more by radio than by other media, in part because of radio's capacity to activate the listener's imagination. Advertisers feared that radio might stimulate the listener in a way that would diminish the goodwill that a sponsor had established. Goodwill, a word used frequently in advertising manuals, was defined as, "the expression of approval for a product which comes in the form of sales sooner or later."[46] Advertisers worried that negative reactions to radio advertising would destroy this intangible — but precious — commodity:

Radio, appealing only to the ear, has always left a great deal to the imagination. The listener is free to construct mental images in the privacy of his home. Suggestive words and sounds can easily produce a bad impression. . . . The consumer has it in his power to boycott not only the show which the advertiser sponsors but, if he chooses, to boycott the advertised products as well.[47]

A boycott brought on by an annoying advertisement was the advertiser's ultimate nightmare. Ads were supposed to motivate the consumer to act, but what if they irritated listeners so much that they stopped listening, or, worse yet, stopped buying the products that sponsored the radio programs?

These fears were not completely unfounded. While listeners were unlikely to launch a full-scale boycott simply because of an annoying ad, in advertising studies conducted by the audience intellectuals listeners did talk about what they might do when they were really annoyed by an ad. In one of Lazarsfeld's studies, one listener reported that an irritating ad made her dislike the product, a cleaning supply called "Bab-O": "I dislike the way they repeated the word, Bab-O. They kept hammering on one word over and over until it drove me almost crazy. They seemed to be talking down to us — as though they were trying to impress a child. It makes me antagonistic toward the product."[48]

In a similar study, another woman listener connected her feelings about the product to her feelings about the advertisement: "As a result of hearing this ad, I'm quite sure that only a mistake in shopping or famine would make me buy this product — or any other [sausage] product. Honestly, it's just disgusting."[49] With the end of World War II — and the

TABLE 2. Responses of 1,100 St. Louis Residents to Different Forms of Advertising, 1950

Advertising form	Percentage of respondents who remembered the product:	
	After one month	After two months
Two voices, conversational	34%	37%
Rhyming, musical jingle	50%	61%
Straight, non-rhyming announcement	49%	51%

SOURCE: Hattwick, *How to Use Psychology for Better Advertising,* 254.

end of wartime rationing — another listener explained her willingness to boycott a particular product whose ad annoyed her: "Just wait! Now that I can ask for special brands again, I'm not going to buy the products whose commercials annoy me. Times have changed."[50] Such threats of boycotts in response to annoying advertisements were rarely carried out, but it was a refrain that advertisers heard repeatedly in their surveys of consumer attitudes about advertising.

Unfortunately for advertisers, the thing that made radio listeners dislike an advertisement was often the very thing that made them remember it. Advertisers learned from studies of listener memories that repetition, and sometimes even revulsion, were key to brand identification. In one study it was discovered that musical jingles — often the most annoying form of radio ad — were also the most effective form. In this study of radio commercials, listeners were tested on their ability to remember the product advertised after one or two months, with the structure of the ad as the variable for different programs. Table 2 shows the percentages of those in the study who were able to recall the advertised products, according to the advertising form used, for various products after one month and after two months. As the table shows, listeners remembered the rhyming jingles for the longest period of time. Advertisers agreed that rhythm and rhyme were effective radio techniques. Posing, for a moment, as literary critics, advertisers sought to find the best meter for selling; was it trochaic, iambic, dactylic, or anapaestic?[51]

Jingles, advertisers argued, were also among the best ways to create a sense of group identification with a certain product. As the audience intellectual Herman Hettinger argued, rhythmic movements were connected to "bodily activity," and that rhythm was based in a need for "some organizing principle in effecting concerted group action."[52] Ads with rhythm and meter, according to this logic, could induce the same physical reaction — foot tapping, chanting, or finger drumming, for example — in a mass of listeners. Such bodily engagement with the advertisement increased the likelihood that the commercial would be remembered. Thus, advertising jingles were key to the creation of a group consciousness, or what Cantril and Allport called a "consciousness of crowd": "The radio, more than any other medium of communication, is capable of forming a crowd mind among individuals who are separated from one another."[53]

In rare cases, a radio jingle would break free of its advertising context to become a cult classic. This happened in the case of the "Chiquita Banana" jingle, which quickly became a popular tune. The lyrics of the song were meant to teach consumers how to eat and care for bananas — a relatively novel fruit in America in the late 1940s, when Chiquita made her debut:

I'm Chiquita Banana
and I've come to say
bananas have to ripen
in a certain way.

When they are flecked with brown
and have a golden hue
bananas are the best
and are the best for you.

You can put them in a salad
You can put them in a pie
Any way you want to eat them
It's impossible to beat them.

But bananas like the climate
of the very very tropical equator
So you should never put bananas
in the refrigerator.

With the success of this song, Chiquita became an animated figure, even starring in her own cartoon feature. The Chiquita jingle was so successful that the demand for bananas imported by United Fruit was "20 percent ahead of supply" in 1950.[54]

In advertising textbooks of the time, the Chiquita campaign was considered the exception which proved the rule about annoying commercials. The Chiquita banana song became one of those rare singing commercials that entered the annals of American folklore:

Radio advertisers who interrupt at the station break often find it difficult to create a favorable listener attitude. One notable success is the "Chiquita Banana" song. . . . It was used with great success along with spot announcements. Entertainers picked it up quickly, and a popular song was written around it. More recently, a series of animated motion-picture advertisements was developed, based on the same music and character. Hundreds of motion-picture theaters, previously closed to all commercial films, opened their doors to the "Chiquita Banana."[55]

Though Chiquita was quickly transformed from a song character into a cartoon character, her initial success was strictly via the airwaves. Three separate women provided her voice: Patti Clayton was the original banana, Elsa Miranda sang the Spanish version, and Monica Lewis became the voice of Chiquita in 1949.

The story of Chiquita Banana exposed the dilemma advertisers faced when they set out to "capture" radio listeners. They wanted radio listeners to become active participants in their advertisements: through singing, humming, or chanting the advertising jingle. But if listeners hummed, sung, or chanted the song too many times, there was always the danger that they would grow sick of it. So sick, perhaps, that they might confuse their irritation at the jingle with the product it was meant to advertise. The Chiquita song was so popular that it "educated and expanded" the banana market in the United States. Not all jingles were this effective.

Thus, to create successful advertisements radio broadcasters tried to create popular shows with high rates of "brand identification." Advertisers wanted listeners to think "Chase and Sanborn Coffee" when they heard the radio ventriloquist program *Charlie McCarthy* or "Lux Soap and Flakes" when they heard *Lux Radio Theatre*. The radio program itself was part of the advertisement: the product and the program were meant to be fused in the listener's mind. And thus advertisers tried to create shows that were not only popular but that also had high rates of brand identification. Table 3 lists popular radio programs, their sponsors, and the percentage of listeners who recognized the sponsor's product as related to the radio show. All of the shows had high rates of brand identification.[56] *Lux Radio Theatre,* which had the highest percentage of product recognition, presented film scripts, novels, and plays over the air; the name of the product was part of the name of the program: "Lux Radio Theatre." Walter Winchell, the newscaster who was sponsored by Jergen's Lotion, created a fictional newspaper over the air called "Jergen's Journal."[57] The commercial for Cheerioats, which sponsored *The Lone Ranger* show, was accompanied by the sound of a horse galloping, a horse whinnying, and

TABLE 3. Audience Recognition of Products by the Programs That They Sponsored, 1950

Program	Product	Percentage of listeners who recognized brand
Lux Radio Theatre	Lux soap and flakes	87.9%
Take It or Leave It	Eversharp pen and pencils	81.6
Fibber McGee and Molly	Johnson's floor wax	80.9
Bop Hope	Pepsodent products	76.7
Your Hit Parade	Lucky Strike cigarettes	76.6
Walter Winchell	Jergens Lotion	75.1
Truth or Consequences	Duz soap	70.7
Lone Ranger	Cheerioats	70.3
Music Hall	Kraft cheese	69.2
Sunday Evening Hour	Ford Motor Company	68.8
Jack Benny Show	Lucky Strike	67.5
Supper Club	Chesterfield tobacco	66.8
Screen Guild Players	Lady Esther products	65.6
Charlie McCarthy Show	Chase and Sanborn coffee	65.1

SOURCE: Hattwick, *How to Use Psychology for Better Advertising*, 230.

a clip-clop voice saying "Cheerioats" repeatedly, which was followed by the first strains of the Lone Ranger's theme song.[58] In each case, the product was integrated into the program, or the program was integrated into the commercial plug. Thus, as Paul Lazarsfeld argued, the effectiveness of a commercial could be increased by trying to increase the "audience's liking for the radio program itself."[59]

The third piece in the puzzle of brand identification was made up of the "people" that were being targeted by the product and the program. Radio differed in an important way from the mass media that preceded it, such as movies, newspapers, and magazines. While consumer access to these other forms of media was limited by available money and time, in theory, someone could subscribe to more than one magazine or newspaper, or see more than one movie in a single day. Radio was the first cultural form that limited the access of the listener to a single program during a single time slot, and thus radio networks had to compete with each other for audiences, who could only tune into one radio program at a time. As radio evolved into an advertising medium, advertisers discovered that if one network produced a show that attracted an upper-class audience, a successful strategy might be to create a program that attracted a lower-class audience. While networks competed openly for the same kind of audience, they learned, over time, to split up the dial among themselves according to time of day, kind of programming, and demographic subgroups.

But how did advertisers know who was listening to what, and when? In 1929 the Cooperative Analysis of Broadcasting (CAB) was established, featuring the work of an opinion pollster named Archibald Crossley. Crossley's primary method of creating radio ratings was the "telephone recall" method, which involved telephoning listeners and asking them to recall what they had listened to on the previous day. The CAB was a nonprofit cooperative run by broadcasters and advertisers. In the 1940s Crossley's main competitor, C. E. Hooper, edged CAB out of the market by using the "telephone coincidental" method. Under this system, researchers called radio listeners and asked them what program they were listening to at the time of the telephone call. Both of these methods came under attack because they relied almost exclusively on the telephone — a luxury for more than half of the American public. By the 1940s almost twice as many homes had a radio than had a telephone. As a result, another organization, called the Broadcast Measurement Bureau (BMB), joined the ratings fray from 1945 to 1950. The BMB, which was a joint effort sponsored by broadcasters, advertisers, and ad agencies, used mail ballots to determine audience response.[60]

The real goal of audience measurement, however, was to learn the number of "psychological impressions" that had been made by a particular program or commercial. "Impression" was one of the keywords that defined the discourse of audience intellectuals in the 1930s and 1940s. "Impression" possessed a double meaning, conveying both solidity (to make an impression, an indent, or a mold) but also vagueness (to make an impression is to be brief or fleeting, to fake, or to fool). The language of "impression" betrayed the insecurity that audience intellectuals felt about their mission. How were they supposed to make an "impression" on, or "mold the mind" of, an "unseen audience"? How were they supposed to find these moldable minds? And how did they know when the "impression" was made? In response to these concerns, C. E. Hooper and A. C. Nielsen created competing ratings services, which focused on personal interviews, listener diaries, telephone surveys, and grocery store surveys in an attempt to describe the relationship between listening to a program and buying the products that sponsored that program.

Under the new system of radio ratings, the audience became quite literally a commodity in the transaction between broadcasters and advertisers. One advertising textbook referred to the ratings process as "Audience Accumulation and Duplication," thus comparing radio audiences to physical entities that could be added up and reproduced. In another advertising textbook, A. C. Nielsen used an industrial tone when talking about the "quality of the radio audience":

Just as the factory manager analyzes the quality of each purchase, so the radio manager would measure the quality of each radio purchase. . . . To measure the quality of a radio audience, we need audience data . . . dividing listeners according to income class (upper, middle, and lower); city size, time zone, brands used by listeners (meaning type of products they are likely to use).[61]

Audience raters like Nielsen were constantly trying to develop new methods and machines for measuring audiences. After World War II the "Instantaneous Audience Measurement Service" was introduced. It was a device placed in listeners homes that emitted a "high radio frequency," which then reported on when the radio set was in use and what station the radio was tuned to, information which was then combined with the income level of the listening family and their location. A high-tech device called a "Radox" could transmit similar kinds of information via a telephone line and teletype.[62]

As audience intellectuals devised new methods of counting and rating the audience commodity, they also categorized the audience, breaking it down into the following basic groups: "Men, Women, Children, Young adults, Middle age or older, Middle and lower income brackets, Upper income brackets, Urban, Rural and farm." Each of these categories needed to be evaluated according specific criteria, such as the "psychology, living, and listening habits" of the group, the types of programs that appealed to the group, the best time of day to reach the group, and the most effective commercials for the group.[63]

Audience intellectuals stressed the importance of keeping the "masses" of the "middle and lower income brackets" in mind when creating radio programs. As Herman Hettinger argued, advertisers were often drawn from the "upper income brackets" and as a result they probably saw much of American radio as "trite, uninteresting and childish." The tastes and preferences of the advertisers, insisted Hettinger, were "not a valid criterion for judging the listener appeal and the advertising value of most radio programs."[64] To reinforce his point, Hettinger gave the example of a mid-sized radio market in which a local fuel company put on a corny, sentimental sketch opposite a program featuring a famous comedian. The sponsor of the famous comedian was surprised to learn that the target

TABLE 4. Economic Stratification of the Radio Audience, 1940

Income group	Approximate equivalent annual income	% of total
"A"	$5,000 and over	6.7
"B"	$3,000–4,999	13.3
"C"	$2,000–2,999	26.7
"D"	Under $2,000	53.3

SOURCE: Beville, "The ABCDs of Radio Audiences," 197.

audience preferred the hackneyed, local offering.[65] Hettinger explained the problem using class terms: "The comedian's humor was typically 'Broadway,' and to many people it had no appeal. . . . Consequently the local dramatic sketch had a virtual monopoly of the listeners to whom the comedian's wisecracks were uninteresting."[66]

At the Princeton-based Office of Radio Research, in 1939 Lazarsfeld oversaw a detailed study of the economic stratification of the radio audience. H. M. Beville, research director for NBC, conducted the study. He divided the radio audience into four income/educational categories, which he labeled "A," "B," "C," and "D." "A" represented the most educated, wealthiest group, and "D" represented the least educated, lowest income group (see Table 4). What is most striking about the results is that the large number of radio listeners were found to be the "D" group. Beville argued that since it was shown that the largest market for any show was in the lowest income categories, an advertiser going after the largest market possible should create programs that appealed to the largest groups, that is, audiences "C" and "D." The study data also demonstrated that even for programming that was directed at the "A" and "B" groups, such as symphony shows, members of the "C" and "D" groups still made up the majority of the audience for these shows (see Table 5). Indeed, the "C" and "D" audiences combined made up more than 60 percent of the total audience for all radio shows in the survey. In the case of shows like *Amos 'n' Andy* (a black-face comedy), *Major Bowes* (a local participation show), and the *National Barn Dance* (a hillbilly/country variety show), these two audiences combined made up 80–90 percent of the total audience. Boake Carter, who was one of the three most popular newscasters of the 1930s, also drew the majority of his listeners (72.5 percent) from the "C" and "D" classes. This meant that a

TABLE 5. Composition of Total Program Audiences by Income Group, 1940
(percent)

	Income group				
	"A"	"B"	"C"	"D"	Total
(Normal Distribution)	6.7%	13.3%	26.7%	53.3%	100%
Philadelphia Orchestra	14.2	16.6	26.0	43.2	100
General Motor Symphony	11.9	20.3	29.9	37.9	100
Maxwell House Show Boat	8.3	17.8	32.4	41.4	100
Boake Carter	8.5	19.0	33.4	39.1	100
A & P Gypsies	7.9	19.1	32.1	40.9	100
March of Time	7.6	19.8	34.6	38.0	100
Amos 'n' Andy	4.7	13.5	30.8	51.1	100
Major Bowes	4.3	10.8	30.1	54.8	100
National Barn Dance	2.8	7.7	29.5	60.0	100

SOURCE: Belville, "The ABCDs of Radio Audiences," 206.

"mass" audience *was* a "class" audience, or, to put it another way, a *classed* audience.

Ironically, perhaps, audience intellectuals found that listeners in the lower income strata were less resentful of radio advertising than were listeners from the "A" and "B" groups. Table 6 shows that even among radio listeners with a college education 57 percent still "liked or didn't mind" radio advertising. But the percentages for those who only had a grammar school education were much higher. Lazarsfeld argued that less-educated listeners liked radio better because it was geared to their tastes, lifestyles, and time-habits. At the same time, he argued, the "more educated" minority had a "greater sophistication of taste" and "more initiative in choosing what is to their liking." Thus, the more educated listeners, who were more "articulate" and "intellectually more mobile," were "more likely to be critical of radio."[67]

On the other hand, Lazarsfeld's studies also revealed that working-class listeners possessed a keen understanding of the economics of radio advertising: they knew that if they did not buy the products advertised on their favorite shows, they might not have their favorite shows to listen to anymore. As one machinist from Worcester, Massachusetts, pointed out, someone had to pay: "Someone has to pay so that we can get the good programs. We wouldn't get the programs if it weren't paid for by sponsors, you can rest assured of that." A retired police sergeant from Belleville,

TABLE 6. Audience Tastes in Programming and Advertising by Education
Level, 1946
(percent)

	Level of education completed:		
	College	High school	Grammar school
Those who like or don't mind radio advertising	57%	65%	72%
Those who prefer radio with ads	54%	62%	71%
No suggestion for improving it	41%	59%	70%
Never feel like criticizing	23%	31%	49%

SOURCE: Lazarsfeld, *The People Look at Radio,* 68.

New Jersey, noted that even if commercials annoyed him, they were part of the price he had to pay: "The commercials are a nuisance. They interrupt the programs and they talk too much. But I guess we have to stand it as we get the service for nothing."[68] One listener even admitted that he tried to buy from the sponsors of his favorite shows: "I am a radio fan who tries to pay for his entertainment by always patronizing the firms who pay for it. I know that radio's life depends upon delivering the goods, and I look at it from that angle."[69] These respondents understood that the listener had to "pay" for the programming — by enduring the commercials and/or by buying the products advertised.

When audience intellectuals asked radio listeners if they would be willing to pay directly for radio — and thus eliminate advertising — the answer was generally "no." In 1935, in a study cited by Cantril and Allport, more than two-fifths of radio listeners claimed that radio annoyed them at least some of the time, but only one-quarter of them said they would be willing to pay a tax of two dollars per year to be able to receive the same programs without advertising (see Table 7). Radio annoyed three-quarters of the population "usually" or "sometimes." But this same 75 percent of respondents was unwilling to pay even two dollars a year (about 20 percent of a worker's weekly salary) for the privilege of listening to the same programs without advertising. A similar study done by Lazarsfeld in 1946 found that only 20 percent of radio listeners would be willing to pay a tax of five dollars per year. This data made advertisers feel safe: radio may have been annoying, but it was not annoying enough to induce listeners to overthrow the system.

Interestingly, however, the less educated listeners in Lazarsfeld's study

TABLE 7. Survey Respondents' Answers to Questions about
Whether They Would be Willing to Pay Directly for Radio
to Avoid Advertisements, 1935

Does radio advertising annoy you?

Always	7%
Usually	16%
Sometimes	59%
Never	18%

*Would you be willing to pay a small tax (2$ per year) to have the same
programs without advertising?*

Yes	24%
No	76%

SOURCE: Cantril and Allport, *The Psychology of Radio,* 103.

were also more open to the idea of government-owned radio. American radio network officials feared the "BBC"-ification of American radio and lived in terror that a successful consumer movement might install government ownership of radio. And thus emerged another paradox: though the more educated listeners in Lazarsfeld's survey were more critical of radio, the less educated listeners were more open to government ownership:

The people in the lower stratum, the ones who have never gone beyond grade school, are two and three times as inclined to favor public ownership [meaning government] as are those in the highest stratum, who have gone to college.[70]

Perhaps working-class listeners saw government ownership as an alternative to paying for radio out of their own pockets. The advertising structure of radio was acceptable to these listeners only because it made radio, one of their favorite forms of entertainment, seem relatively "free."

Conclusion

Radio advertisements constituted the fulcrum in the dialectic between advertising and activism. On one side of the dialectic were audience intellectuals frantically searching for ways to compel consumption. It was their job to create the ads and study listeners' reactions. On the other side were the radio listeners. It was their job to "act" in some way in response to the advertisements: to buy things, to criticize, and sometimes to boycott. In this chapter, I have tried to shed light on the world of the audience intellectuals, who comprised one pole of the dialectic. In the following chapter, I will explore the other pole: the world of the "consumer intellectuals," whose resentment of radio advertising sometimes evolved into a call for collective action.

CHAPTER TWO

"Poisons, Potions, and Profits"

Radio Activists and the Origins of the Consumer Movement

In 1934 Paul Lazarsfeld and his colleagues at the Office of Radio Research conducted a study of consumer habits for the Consumer Advisory Board of the consumer testing agency Consumers' Research. After the study was completed, one of Lazarsfeld's coworkers suggested that they had a unique opportunity to capitalize on the hostility to advertising that was gaining ground in the consumer movement. He suggested that their agency could be the "focal point of criticism against advertising" and that "all indications are that there will be, before long, a real campaign against advertising." "In fact," he continued, "such a campaign is already under way." Lazarsfeld's colleague proposed that they position themselves as "expert witnesses" so that they would be ready to testify when the case against advertising "goes to trial, so to speak," and there is "a demand for evidence." Their evidence, he continued, was "nonpartisan" and could be used "for both sides." This was the case, of course, because in 1934 Lazarsfeld and his colleagues would conduct studies for anyone who could pay, from Lux Soap and McFadden Publishing, to General Foods, Swift and Armour, and even Consumers' Research.[1]

By 1934, the case against advertising had already gone to trial. But the trial was not yet over. The consumer movement of the Depression era was a progressive and sometimes radical coalition of educators, writers, workers, housewives, and technicians who had begun to question certain facets of capitalism from the perspective of the consumer. The movement was both inspired by, and attempted to reform, the practices of radio advertising. The movement failed, however, to transform the commercial nature of American radio. As Susan Smulyan and Robert McChesney have documented, the most serious popular threats to commercial radio had been quashed by 1935. But legislative and structural losses on the part of consumer activists did not silence the voices of those who continued to argue that commercial radio was controlled by business interests, damaging to American democracy, and hard on the ears.

As a result, when we look at the many consumerist tracts against radio, we need to see more than failure. We need to see that the critique of radio, for writers as well as readers, was foundational to the ideology of the consumer movement. Advertising often provoked listeners to think of themselves more self-consciously as consumers. In the process, while radio advertising was designed to make consumers buy, it sometimes made them balk. And, when they did, they often became involved in progressive coalitions to change more than what they heard over the air. Moreover, when consumer intellectuals published their diatribes against radio, they formulated a negative critique of radio advertising, on the one hand, and a positive notion of what it meant to be a consumer, on the other.

In this chapter I begin by examining the relationship between the consumer movement and advertising during the Depression decade. Next, I examine three radio activists and their involvement in the consumer movement: James Rorty — a recovering ad-man and poet/radical; Ruth Brindze, whose *Not To Be Broadcast* (1937) was one of the most widely circulated critiques of radio during the 1930s; and finally Peter Morell, who wrote *Poisons, Potions, and Profits,* and whose disgust with radio turned him from a labor playwright into a consumer agitator. These three author/activists offered different critiques of 1930s radio, and they modeled different styles of consumer activism. Rorty was the model of the left-wing intellectual who was attracted to a wide variety of radical movements — many of which he critiqued as severely as he did capitalism. Brindze was typical of the grassroots consumer activist — she was a leader of several consumer organizations and a chronicler of the movement, declaring in 1935 that "there has never been a consumer movement quite like the one now on the march."[2] Morell was a left-leaning cultural producer who turned to the consumer movement as a way to give artists more democratic access to radio as a dramatic medium.

Advertising and the Consumer Movement

Colston Warne, one of the founders of the consumer movement, argued that advertising had been responsible for its "birth" as well as its "growth." What he meant by this was not that advertisers themselves had created the movement, but rather that progressive coalitions organized to fight advertising had been among the first to identify themselves as consumer activists. In the 1920s mass advertising was still relatively new, but its effects were widespread and many resented the practices of deception deployed by what Stephen Fox has called the "mirrormakers." And, as Charles McGovern has argued, advertising and consumer advocates, together, helped to "invent" the modern consumer.[3]

Colston Warne may not have been the most charismatic leader of the consumer movement, but he was one of the most reliable. As one historian has argued, from the 1930s to the 1970s Colston Estey Warne "was the most influential consumer leader in the country." He was born in 1900 in central New York, studied at Cornell University, and was influenced early in his career by the writings of Thorstein Veblen. He wrote his doctoral dissertation at the University of Chicago on the subject of the international cooperative movement. Warne spent his early years as a professor at the University of Denver and the University of Pittsburgh, though he left the University of Pittsburgh when he felt that his academic freedom was in jeopardy. Finally, after 1930, Warne settled at Amherst College, where he continued to teach economics for forty years. He was affiliated with a variety of radical movements throughout the Depression era, including the Communist Party and the CIO, for whom he conducted a training institute in 1933.[4]

In the 1930s Warne became one of the leaders of a consumer movement that had been launched by Stuart Chase and F. J. Schlink in the 1920s. Chase, an economist who had been fired from the Federal Trade Commission for his "liberal" politics, and Schlink, a mechanical engineer who had worked for the U.S. Bureau of Standards, published a controversial book in 1927 called *Your Money's Worth: A Study in the Waste of the Consumer's Dollar,* which advocated the formation of a federally sponsored product testing agency. Such an agency, they argued, would make the need for advertising as a source of consumer information obsolete. With the success of *Your Money's Worth,* Chase and Schlink set up a consumer testing agency of their own in White Plains, New York, and called it Consumers' Research, Inc. Schlink, along with fellow activist Arthur Kallet, published another popular exposé of advertising and manufacturing in 1933, called *100,000,000 Guinea Pigs: Dangers in Everyday Foods, Drugs, and Cosmetics.*[5] The book argued that consumers were like laboratory "guinea pigs": the unwitting specimens upon whom corporations experimented with harmful products. In this same period, consumer testers embraced consumption as an "active" process. As Charles McGovern has argued: "By adopting an experimental attitude, consumers would ultimately train themselves to demand more from industry and to learn more easily when they were satisfied."[6]

As the coauthor of *Your Money's Worth,* Stuart Chase was among the first of the consumer activists to take a stand against radio advertising. He argued that radio advertising was akin to medical quackery, that it "did not pay," and that listeners did not like commercials. Early radio listeners referred to advertisements, he noted, as "punishment." He insisted that broadcasting was not a sales medium and that radio listeners would not support the continuation of radio advertising: "The public will no more stand for direct advertising, in the long run, than it will stand for a guest trying to sell insurance over his host's dinner table." Chase was wrong, of course, as the listening public did begin to "stand" for direct advertising, even as they continued to see it as a form of aural abuse.[7]

The movement that Chase, Schlink and Kallet started in the late 1920s began to fracture in the mid-1930s. A strike of employees at Consumers' Research in 1935 led to the formation of a rival testing bureau, Consumers Union, which published its findings in a bulletin called *Consumer Reports.* As Larry Glickman has shown, the strike revealed that the consumer movement was divided ideologically into two camps: one camp (represented by Schlink and J. B. Matthews) emphasized "expertise" and "individualism," whereas the other (represented by Chase, Kallet, Warne, and Rorty) emphasized "collective action" and "a social conception of consumption and the labor that made the products." By the end of the 1930s the rival testing bureaus had a combined readership of 140,000, which included the members of more than forty-two consumer organizations across thirty states. These consumer organizations represented diverse constituencies: women's groups (the National Federation of Women's Clubs), pro-labor consumer groups that used consumer pressure to improve working conditions (the National Consumers League), consumer cooperatives (the Consumer Farmer-Milk Cooperative), and home economics educators (American Home Economics Association). Some of the groups would be short-lived, others would last for thirty or forty years, and a few, like the American Home Economics Association, Consumers' Research, and the Consumers Union, remain active today.[8]

Despite the ideological differences among consumer leaders, some of the first "movements" of consumer activists were focused on advertising — on criticizing it, on coming up with alternatives to it (in the form of consumer testing bureaus), and on fighting for federal legislation that would regulate it. Consumer organizations provided an alternative source of consumer education, enlightening their members about false/misleading advertising or involving them in legislative campaigns. In a sense, the publications of Consumers' Research and Consumers Union *competed* with advertising. These publications exposed bad products, but they also promoted good ones. A good review in *Consumer Reports* was often the best "advertising" a product could hope for. Moreover, the consumer movement could boast of two legislative victories during the Depression: (1) the Copeland Act, passed in 1938, which gave the Federal Drug Administration (FDA) "new powers over the sale and manufacture of drugs"; and (2) the Wheeler-Lea amendments to the Federal Trade Commission Act, also implemented in 1938, which made "deceptive acts of commerce" (false advertising) illegal. Wheeler-Lea also gave the FTC the power to seek injunctions — the most famous of which was brought against Fleishmann's Yeast: the FTC forced the company to cease claiming that its yeast "cured crooked teeth, bad skin, constipation, and halitosis."[9]

These legislative victories were minor, however, compared to the strength that business and advertising leaders *imagined* that the consumer movement possessed. In 1940 *Advertising Age* declared that the consumer movement "has now indubitably moved into the position of the number one problem of American business."[10] The consumer movement was perceived as threatening for three reasons: (1) consumer activists linked their critique of advertising to a critique of capitalism as a whole; (2) they frequently threatened collective action; and (3) they represented an emerging, white-collar social formation that was sympathetic to labor.[11] Business leaders were right on the first point — the consumerist critique of advertising was, at times, an attack on capitalism — and business leaders fought back by writing their own faux "consumerist" tracts, like H. J. Kenner's *The Fight for Truth in Advertising*.[12] As far as the second threat, collective action, this was rarely achieved by the consumer movement. According to one historian, the movement was made up of "an unorganized mass of individuals — teachers, office workers, labor union members, [and] liberal publicists," who "read the proliferating consumer literature and sympathized with the movement's goals."[13] On the other hand, consumer activists were often *represented* as a powerful collective; the advertising trade magazine *Tide* noted in 1935 that the revolutionary figure leading the consumer movement was not "Marx's proletariat" but rather "an army of embattled consumers and housewives."[14] And, as Glickman has argued, this representation "vastly overstated" the "cohesiveness" of the consumer movement.[15]

As for the third threat, business leaders were right to fear the tentative alliance that seemed to be forming between "Marx's proletariat" and white-collar professionals. Not only did some consumer activists threaten to use the tactics of organized labor — such as the boycott, many consumer activists embraced labor unions. Educators were at the forefront of the movement: a Gallup poll in 1939 showed that 83 percent of teachers had read a consumerist book and 87 percent called for stricter laws to control advertising. Business leaders did not want to alienate an emerging, professional middle class, of which teachers were an important part. As historian Stephen Fox has argued, "Even if advertising did not sell much to this sector, it could not keep offending these articulate, politically active citizens."[16]

Meanwhile, as radio increased in cultural and economic importance, radio advertising became one of the chief targets of consumer activists. Radio advertising and consumer activism each helped to provoke, define, and explain the other throughout the Depression decade. *Variety,* for example, noted that the consumer movement attacked advertising in general, and radio advertising in particular: "The increasing belligerence of the 'consumer groups is putting radio on the defensive.'" At a convention of consumer activists at Stephens College in 1940, which was "angeled," or bankrolled, by Alfred H. Sloan, activists proposed that advertisers eliminate the emotional appeal in advertisements. *Variety* argued that listeners would "turn a deaf ear" if legislation were passed forcing advertisers to "explain merely that Zippies breakfast food consisted of corn in flaked form, rice that has been blown up, or wheat that is shredded." Sponsor dollars would drop if they could not mention the "muscle building powers of Zippies, the sinus curing capacity of Aroma ciggies, and the mile-devouring qualities of Put-Put gas."[17] *Variety* claimed that the Stephens College participants derived their ideas from the likes of "Stuart Chase," the "book-writing economist."

Writers like Stuart played a crucial part in the dialectic between radio advertising and consumer activism during the 1930s. Three consumerist writers, in particular — James Rorty, Ruth Brindze, and Peter Morell —

explained the relationship between radio, capitalism, and class to their con-
sumer-activist audiences. Rorty argued that advertising, and especially
radio advertising, was inextricably linked to capitalism. Brindze, from her
perspective as a journalist/activist, saw radio advertising as an institution
that prevented workers from having access to radio air-time. And Morell,
as a pro–civil rights, pro-labor playwright, imagined that only a powerful
consumer movement made up of white-collar and industrial workers could
cure what ailed the airwaves. Rorty was more of an economic critic, Brindze
focused on radio and politics, while Morell focused on the relationship
between radio and culture. Each of these authors, in his or her own way,
saw the possibilities for a cross-class movement of consumer/workers
whose collective power could overthrow the most corrosive and undemo-
cratic features of a sponsor-controlled radio system. The fact that their
visions were never realized is not as interesting as the visions themselves:
their negative critiques of radio were inextricably bound up with their positive vision of what it meant to be a consumer. In the end, their writings
explain the ways in which advertising — and especially radio advertising —
helped to shape the consumer movement as a whole.

James Rorty and the Economics of Radio Advertising

> Do you ask for bread? I give you
> Not bread, but the wine of power;
> The tread of strong men marching,
> The inevitable hour.
>
> James Rorty,
> "Ballad of the Breadlines," 1932

Like so many twentieth-century ad-men, James Rorty was a frustrated
poet. Born in Middletown, New York, in 1890, Rorty attended college at
Tufts University. After graduating he moved to New York City in 1913,
"determined to embark on a literary career." When this plan failed, Rorty's
brother secured him a job at the H. K. McCann advertising agency. Rorty
claims he was nearly fired for resisting the whims of a client; he escaped
this fate by joining the army in 1917.[18] After World War I Rorty roomed
in the same boarding house as Thorstein Veblen. According to historian
Daniel Pope, it was in these shared quarters that Rorty "regaled Veblen
with macabre tales of the machinations of Madison Avenue." The theoretical influence of Veblen on Rorty's career, claims Pope, would last a life-

time. In 1920, newly married to social worker Maria Lambin, Rorty turned to the advertising trade in San Francisco. But soon his marriage crumbled, he became ill, and in 1924 he returned to Manhattan, now smitten with Winifred Rauschenbush, the daughter of social-gospel minister Walter Rauschenbush.[19]

Rorty married Winifred and went back to the advertising grind in New York City. This time, Rorty found the business harder to stomach: "I returned to my advertising vomit, prodding my fair white soul up and down Madison Avenue and offering it for sale to the highest bidder." Meanwhile Rorty's politics were creeping increasingly leftward. In 1926 he became one of the founding editors of the *New Masses,* along with Mike Gold, Joseph Freeman, and Egmont Arens.[20] In December 1930, with the Depression in full force, Rorty was fired from the BBDO advertising agency. He was elated: "I'm a human being again, and seldom have I felt so cheerful." Rorty spent the early 1930s fighting on the cultural front — he joined the New York chapter of the John Reed Club, protested Hoover's policy toward poverty, and became secretary of the group promoting the Communist Party's presidential ticket, the League of Professional Groups for Foster and Ford. According to Pope, it was during this time that Rorty coauthored a pamphlet called "Culture and the Crisis," which urged "'brainworkers' to ally with 'muscle workers' in supporting the Party slate." In the early 1930s Rorty imagined a movement that would unite intellectuals and laborers.[21]

Rorty wrote two important critiques of advertising in 1934. The most comprehensive, *Our Master's Voice: Advertising,* was part autobiography, part mass-media critique, and part economic philosophy. Though Rorty devoted only one chapter of *Our Master's Voice* to radio, in the same year he authored a short pamphlet called *Order on the Air!,* which was more oriented toward consumer activism and radio reform and was a reaction against what Rorty called the "drunk and disorderly" state of radio advertising.[22] In these critiques Rorty showed how advertising, and especially radio advertising, was linked to capitalism as an economic system. Rorty proved that they were connected; in criticizing the one (radio advertising), he criticized the other (capitalism).

As a veteran of the advertising industry, Rorty had a unique insight into its inner workings. His economic critique was directed, ironically, at people like himself — the proliferating number of professionals associated with the advertising industry. In this group he included ad-men, printers, illustrators, scriptwriters, announcers, magazine editors — everyone, in short, who produced advertising or entertainment for the mass media.

Rorty argued that the ad-man was not entirely responsible for the degradation of his craft; rather, he was carrying out the orders of capitalism: "Behind him is the whole pressure of the capitalist organism, which must sell or perish."[23] Capitalism, Rorty argued, needed its own class of intellectuals, and the ad-man answered the call:

He is, on the average, much more intelligent than the average business man, much more sophisticated, even much more socially minded. . . . [Advertising men] are, in a sense, the intellectuals . . . of our American commercial culture.

Some ad-men, he argued, became morons; some became "gray faced cynics"; some became so depressed they "jump[ed] out of high windows." And some became "extreme political and social radicals, either secretly while they [are] in the business, or openly, after they have left it." Rorty placed himself in this last category. Advertising, without meaning to, had turned Rorty into a Red.[24]

Rorty admitted as much in an unpublished manuscript called "On Being Fired from a Job," which narrated the frustration and elation he felt when he was fired from BBDO. Rorty was constantly trying to reconcile his radical and poetic tendencies with the fact that he had earned his living in the 1920s working for the "church" of capitalism:

What is a radical? What kind of radical am I? I am not quite sure. In fact it is only by the most strenuous self-analysis that I am able to extract this tentative definition: I am a student; a radical student, because what *is,* is always more interesting than what seems, and makes better poetry. For the observation of what is, there are few better watch-towers than this excruciating modern contrivance, the advertising agency. I have been in and out of the advertising business for nearly fifteen years. If I am a radical, whose fault is it? Advertising has made me what I am today.[25]

Here, Rorty says plainly that advertising made him into a radical. No doubt, after he wrote *Our Master's Voice* with the time available to him on the unemployment line, the advertising industry regretted having made him thus. As Charles McGovern has argued, advertisers saw "Comrade Rorty" as a "malcontent, a failed ad man, an 'artiste' who fancied himself too good for the profession, and an outside agitator. But what advertisers couldn't dismiss was that he had been one of them."[26]

Rorty also saw that advertising, while it served industry, was becoming an industry unto itself. He understood that advertising was becoming more than a simple function of the "superstructure" — advertising was becoming an essential part of the capitalist mode of production:

Advertising on the grand scale ha[s] become an industry no less essential than coal or steel. It ha[s] become a profession endorsed, sanctified and subsidized by dozens of Greek-porticoed "Schools of Business Administration" in which a new priesthood of "business economists" translate the techniques of mass prevarication into suitable academic euphemisms. . . . The ad-man ha[s] become the first lieutenant of the new Caesars of America's . . . imperium — *not merely on the economic front but also on the cultural front.* [emphasis in original]

In other words, Rorty argued, advertising men were beginning to play a key role in the cultural and economic life of the nation.[27]

But Rorty's economic critique of radio was also directed at the listener. He sneered at the naiveté of radio listeners who thought their entertainment was "free." He argued that the radio listener "pays" and "pays heavily by lending his ears . . . to the . . . deceptive sales talk of radio advertisers." Moreover, he argued, the listener pays by "submitting to the countless varieties of . . . propaganda which are the business-as-usual of commercial broadcasting." Finally, he argued, the listener "pays for his receiving set, for keeping it in repair, and for the current it uses."[28] Rorty reported that radio set owners spent $300 million a year on purchasing and repairing their radio sets, whereas broadcasters spent no more that $80 million to produce radio programs. In other words, listeners invested six times more than broadcasters in the business of radio.[29] With this critique, Rorty exposed the myth that radio was "free"; he showed how capitalism had become a fundamental part of radio listening.

Readers got the message. Many reviewers noted that *Our Master's Voice* was written as a critique of capitalism, above all:

Written by a former ad-man the book is a vigorous indictment of modern American advertising methods. Mr. Rorty argues that our whole acquisitive economy is bound up with advertising, newspaper, periodical press and radio, and that so long as competitive capitalism remains, advertising cannot be materially reformed.[30]

Rorty's former advertising boss interpreted *Our Master's Voice* in a similar manner. Roy Durstine, the "D" in BBDO, saw *Our Master's Voice* as an attack on "our present conditions" and "our competitive economic system."[31]

But if advertising could not be reformed without transforming capitalism, why did Rorty write *Order on the Air!* — a distinctly reformist text that concluded with a series of activist recommendations? Lawrence Glickman has argued that Rorty, as a founding member of the consumer movement, favored an organized, activist movement over the technical, bureaucratic model favored by rival members. And thus Rorty called for such radio reforms as the "elimination of advertising sales talk" on the radio, the "freeing" of radio from its corporate bondage, and the "effective utilization" of radio by educators, writers, critics, artists, physicians, scientists, and health workers. He also wanted "minority" groups — such as women, African Americans, and labor groups — to be able to use radio for "political, economic and social education, propaganda, and agitation." Rorty, though he was skeptical of the possibilities for radio reform, still wanted radio to be a medium available to progressive activists and educators. Curmudgeon that he was, and anti-Communist that he became, James Rorty was a consumer activist committed to the principles of collective action.[32]

By the time Rorty wrote his radio critiques he was already starting to break with the Communist Party. In the late 1920s he had been ousted from the Communist group that founded the *New Masses,* and in 1932 "his anger with the Communist party flare[d] up again." Later in life, he would refer to his former organization, "The League of Professional Groups," as "The League of Professional Gropers." Like so many left-leaning intellectuals of this period, he was to become increasingly anti-communist; in 1954 he argued that anti-communism would be more successful if the movement could purge itself of the demagoguery of Senator McCarthy. Toward the end of his life his hatred for Communism had evolved into a paranoia:

By the 1960s, Rorty was convinced that the Communist Party had planted its agents as handymen on his Connecticut farm, had joined forces against him with Morris Fishbein of the American Medical Association, and had induced fellow-traveling bookstore clerks to hide his writings from public display.

Although Rorty became an anti-communist, as Pope argues, he remained an anti-capitalist. His experiences as an ad-man throughout the second decade of the century and into the 1920s gave him a unique insight into the emergence of consumer capitalism and its auxiliary institutions — especially radio.[33]

After writing his radio critiques, Rorty continued to work on behalf of the consumer movement. He edited *The Consumers Defender* for two years, from 1935 to 1936. He began working for the magazine after a man named Jack Lever challenged him to edit the publication for free. Lever was the head of an organization called Cooperative Distributors, which was one of the many cooperative experiments launched by consumer activists in the 1930s. Rorty vividly recalled their first meeting:

I first met Jack Lever when . . . I visited his neat little office . . . and replied with an indignant "no" to his suggestion that I edit . . . "The Consumers Defender" at a salary of nothing a month. Jack was shocked and hurt. "We're fellow idealists aren't we," he remonstrated. Weakly, I said yes to his proposition and dummied up a modest periodical. In four months "The Consumers Defender" quadrupled its circulation. CD's business boomed, until for a while there seemed to be a real chance that it might become a co-op rival to Sears Roebuck and Montgomery Ward.

Though the experience brought Rorty closer to the consumer movement, it alienated him further from the Communists. He later claimed that Colston Warne, a "champion" of "fellow travelers," had taken control of the board and fired Jack Lever, which ultimately led to the bankruptcy of the co-op.[34]

Though Rorty conducted a lifelong battle against the Communist movement, he also waged a lifelong war against the excesses of capitalism. As a writer, propagandist, and researcher, Rorty devoted much of the remainder of his life to consumerist, health-related, and ecological reforms. Once labeled "the last of the muckrakers," Rorty continued to write progressive tracts, such as *American Medicine Mobilizes* (1939), *Brother Jim Crow* (1943), *Tomorrow's Food: The Coming Revolution in Nutrition* (1947), and *We Open the Gates: Labor's Fight for Equality* (1958). As Daniel Pope has argued, Rorty's turn to medicine, nutrition, and ecology allowed him to establish a position outside of the mainstream of American culture — he remained the consummate anti-corporate critic.[35]

Meanwhile, Rorty's criticisms of radio advertising in 1934 had not fallen on deaf ears. His call for the establishment of a government bureau to regulate radio was realized by Roosevelt's creation of the Federal Communications Commission. On the whole, however, his critique of radio advertising, while it resonated with a larger movement for radio reform, did not win the day. Advertising secured complete control of the radio industry, and by 1935 even the most fervent anti-advertising warriors admitted defeat.[36]

Ruth Brindze: Radio and Political Freedom

Accepting defeat, however, was another matter. Radio advertising continued to annoy, anger, and provoke consumer activists. In 1937 Ruth Brindze expanded Rorty's critique with an attack of her own: *Not To Be Broadcast: The Truth About Radio*. Brindze was the archetype of the grassroots consumer activist. She was in her thirties, well educated, from a middle-class home, and chair of the Consumers Council of Westchester County, New York. She was politically active, a prodigious writer, and concerned about everything consumerist — from the dangers of radio censorship to the best way to distinguish silk from rayon. While the most notorious figures associated with the consumer movement were men — like Schlink, Kallet, and Chase — the majority of its grassroots activists were women. These women, by participating in the consumer movement, turned their private consumption into political action.

Brindze was born in Harlem in 1903, "when goats were still grazing in the streets."[37] "Entranced by books," she learned to read at a young age and thus began a love affair with the printed page. Brindze reflected on her childhood in an autobiography she wrote for young readers in 1963:

In addition to reading, playing ball and swimming, I enjoyed writing and compositions about things experienced and imagined. During my high school days some books I read on the romantic aspects of newspaper work made me decide to be a reporter, and in preparation for a newspaper career I spent my last two years of college at the Columbia University School of Journalism. However, I worked on newspapers for only a few years and then began to write magazine articles and books.[38]

After graduating from Columbia, Brindze started her writing career as a ghostwriter for celebrity autobiographies. Later, as a resident of New Rochelle in Westchester County, she wrote for the *New Rochelle Standard Star* and the *Larchmont Times*. By the early 1930s she was a regular contributor to *The Nation*. She was also appointed by Roosevelt to lead the Westchester County Consumers Council. And, in 1935, at the age of thirty-two, she published her first book — a contribution to the literature of the consumer movement called *How To Spend Money: Everybody's Practical Guide to Buying*.[39]

Her first effort at consumer propaganda combined radical political critique with practical advice. She advised readers on how to buy such varied goods as fabric, men's suits, hosiery, mattresses, canned fish, and ice cream. While Brindze advocated collective action for the consumer, she also stressed the importance of individual action: "Until consumers are sufficiently organized to force Uncle Sam . . . to establish consumer standards and to enforce them, the individual consumer can serve himself and the cause by intelligent buying." Brindze self-consciously patterned her book after *Your Money's Worth* and *100,000,000 Guinea Pigs*. Without these "pioneers," argued Brindze, "it is doubtful if the consumer would have received even the meager attention he now commands." She also argued that once consumers informed themselves about how to get the best deals, their "word-of-mouth" advertising could be "more potent than a nation-wide hook-up of the mightiest broadcasting station in the land." In other words, the rabble — if organized — could function as an alternative to radio.[40]

With *How to Spend Money,* which was praised by *The Nation* for being "practical and sensible," Brindze launched the next phase of her career as a consumer advocate.[41] In October 1935 *The Nation* announced that Brindze would be writing a consumer column for the weekly, explaining that consumer news was frequently excluded from daily newspapers, which were dependent on advertising for their revenues:

Beginning next week, therefore, *The Nation* will publish a department to appear bi-weekly under the direction of Ruth Brindze, author of "How to Spend Money," which summarizes significant reports of the Federal Trade Commission, the Bureau of Standards, the Consumers' Advisory Board, the Department of Agriculture, the Food and Drug Administration, and the American Medical Association.[42]

Brindze's subsequent columns kept readers informed about a wide variety of consumer issues: she reported on the ban of an obesity drug, Marmola; on the difference between a "sealskin," made of real seal, and a "Hudson sealskin," made of muskrat; on threats to the power of the Federal Trade Commission; on the rising price of milk; on the corruption of radio advertising; and on the competition between radio broadcasting and the newspaper press.[43]

While researching a series of *Nation* articles on radio, Brindze began to write *Not To Be Broadcast,* which was published in 1937. Like Rorty, Brindze questioned the economic structure of radio advertising and the fact that Americans had surrendered radio to "the money rulers of America." But Brindze took her criticism of radio censorship further than Rorty had, putting the issues of free speech and politics at the heart of her critique. *Not To Be Broadcast* functioned as a virtual encyclopedia of radio censorship during the Depression.[44]

Brindze was especially critical of the role that pro-business radio agencies and radio monopolies played in preventing certain political viewpoints — especially those of labor — from reaching the airwaves. She cited one incident in which the Federal Radio Commission targeted the socialist radio station WEVD (named after Eugene V. Debs) for broadcast license review. WEVD operators refused to show that their "continued operation would serve public interest" on the grounds that there should be "at least one [radio] channel . . . open to the uses of the workers.[45] In the end, WEVD was allowed to continue broadcasting — albeit on a less desirable channel. Meanwhile, the Radio Commission denied the application of WCFL — the AFL's radio station in Chicago — to expand its broadcast schedule beyond 6:00 p.m. In order to secure a clear channel for evening broadcasting, WCFL had to take its case to Congress. After months of lobbying and compromise, the station was finally allowed to broadcast during the evening hours.[46]

Brindze was also critical of the difficulties workers faced in getting their viewpoints broadcast during labor disputes. She cited the case of a group of General Electric workers in Schenectady, New York, who were deciding on whether to remain a company union or join the CIO. The Radio Workers' Union asked permission to argue the case for joining the CIO over radio station WGY — a station owned by GE and managed by the National Broadcasting Company. "The request was denied on the grounds that the controversy was only of 'local interest.'"[47] In another case, striking elevator workers in New York City in 1936 were allowed to use WEVD to get their message out — whereas their employer used the largest commercial broadcast stations in Manhattan, WABC and WJZ, to make its case. These types of incidents, Brindze noted, were not limited to the censorship of labor activists. Radio censorship was also used to thwart consumer activists. She recounted an incident in which the Utility Consumers League was prevented from broadcasting a speech attacking telephone rates over radio station WNEW. Worse still, the editor who initially accepted the program was fired.[48]

Brindze reserved some of her harshest criticisms for corporate "goodwill" programming. Her prime target was Henry Ford, whose radio programs she excoriated in a chapter titled "His Master's Voice." According to Brindze, the weekly music program sponsored by Ford and hosted by William J. Cameron performed a subtle kind of propagandizing on the "peepul." The program, she admitted, was very popular: "The praise of the music has been lavish and the enthusiasm for Mr. Cameron's Sunday night sermons inspires two thousand fans to write him every day."[49] However, what made this program so insidious, according to Brindze, was that even though the show was broadcast without commercial breaks, Cameron made frequent favorable references to Ford, "the Ford methods, or to the superlative advantages enjoyed by Ford workers." The ultimate goal of these programs, Brindze argued, was to mold the social and economic viewpoint of the audience "to the Ford pattern."[50]

With this critique, Brindze explained the relationship between radio, capitalism, and the working class. She showed how those with the least access to capital — labor unions and consumer activists — also had the least access to radio as a means of communication. Moreover, with her example of the Ford music program, she showed how the commodity form had infiltrated the pleasure of listening. Not only was radio being used to sell goods, it was also being used to make consumers. And, as Brindze argued, these consumers, like the Model T's and Model A's that Ford had to sell, were being assembled according to the Ford pattern. Radio was not just making music: it was turning people into consumers.

Brindze hoped that her book would "arouse" these very same people to revolt against radio censorship. She believed that listener resistance to radio propaganda would provide the best defense against a capital-controlled radio system:

How is this subversive material to be controlled? The answer, and an entirely unsatisfactory one, is only by the final censorship of the radio audience itself. Only by turning the dial, only by refusing to listen to these fake patriots, can their rising power be checked.

On the one hand, Brindze patronized her potential audience of worker/listeners, calling them the "peepul" and criticizing them for buying into the Ford music hour, but in another sense, she was a populist. She knew that the reform of radio lay in collective action — in the collective rejection of the economics of radio advertising by "average" listeners.[51]

Not to Be Broadcast was widely read, widely reviewed, and widely praised. The most flattering assessment of the book appeared in *Literary Digest*. In her photograph, which accompanied the review, Brindze appeared girlish and thin, with short, dark hair and wide, brown eyes. But her sweet appearance belied the harsh tone of her attack on radio. *Literary Digest* speculated that her book would provoke "hot discussion" on the topic of "freedom of the air":

The former *Nation* columnist, an avowed Leftist and consumer-defender . . . gathered together all the facts she could find, hammered them into a sharp accusation against the [radio] chains, [and] hoped to duplicate the popularity of "100,000,000 Guinea Pigs."

Brindze was praised for her practical suggestions for reform, which included "arous[ing] the listening public," setting up a chain of government-owned stations, requiring stations to disclose their financial backers, providing free air time for minority groups, and limiting chain ownership to prevent monopoly.[52]

After the publication of *Not To Be Broadcast,* Brindze began to write for a younger audience. In 1938 she wrote a children's book on consumer spending called *Johnny Get Your Money's Worth (And Jane, Too!).* Brindze recalled how she made the transition to writing for children:

James Henle, then president of Vanguard Press, encouraged me to write [my first children's book]. We were discussing a manuscript on consumer buying I had recently completed when I remarked that someone should write a book telling children how to avoid the tricks of the market place. Jim suggested I tackle the job.[53]

Though it was aimed at children, *Johnny Get Your Money's Worth* shared certain continuities with *Not to Be Broadcast.* Indeed, the book included a humorous section on children's radio, which warned children to beware of offers that came over the air. In 1938 Brindze began writing a monthly column for a youth-focused educational magazine, *Scholastic.* In "Getting Your Money's Worth," Brindze presented to her high school readers advice on such topics as how to choose a fountain pen, how to choose cosmetics, how to lodge a complaint with the Better Business Bureau, and the importance of the Federal Trade Commission.[54]

Brindze was fast becoming one of the most well-known consumer writers of the decade. In 1939 she was hailed by the *Journal of Home Economics* as "one of the sanest and most successful writers of consumer guides."[55] In that same year she received high praise for *Johnny Get Your Money's Worth.* Helen Woodward, a reformed advertising copy writer (à la James Rorty), described *Johnny Get Your Money's Worth* as a necessary piece of "household equipment," assuring readers that even though it was written for children there was "plenty in it for grown-ups."[56] Another reviewer noted that Brindze treated her young audience with respect: "Ruth Brindze writes with authority. She also writes with enthusiasm and with a sincere belief that boys and girls are intelligent enough, once they understand the need, to learn to buy wisely and thoughtfully, and thus not only profit themselves, but help to promote honest selling and reliable advertising."[57]

Johnny Get Your Money's Worth was the beginning of Brindze's prolific career as a children's book author. Between 1938 and 1975 she wrote seventeen books for children, including the award-winning *Gulf Stream* (1945). Her children's books were less explicitly political than her earlier works had been — she wrote about the ocean, the origin of gold, Native American totem poles, and boating. Brindze's turn to children's literature may have been part of a political trend. According to Alan Wald, children's literature was a literary genre adopted by a number of left-wing writers during the McCarthy era. On the other hand, Brindze never completely abandoned her consumerist bent. Brindze continued to write consumer-oriented books throughout the war, including *Daily Bread and Other Foods, Stretching Your Dollar in War-Time,* and *You Can Help Your Country Win the War.* In 1959 she suggested to her publisher, Vanguard Press, that they consider reprinting *100,000,000 Guinea Pigs.*[58] A decade later, in 1968, Brindze wrote a book about the stock market in which she counseled readers on how to influence large corporations by attending shareholders meetings.[59]

Though she devoted much of her writing to children, Brindze made a conscious choice never to have children of her own. Her sister-in-law remembers that the Depression was a terrible time to consider bringing children into the world. Brindze was married — she married a lawyer named Albert Fribourg in 1926, five years after meeting him at a game of bridge. The couple was crazy about boating — they even spent their honeymoon in a canoe. While married to Albert Fribourg, however, she remained Ruth Brindze. Friends and family teased her for refusing to take her husband's name. They called her a "Lucy Stoner" — a reference to the Lucy Stone League — a feminist group whose members swore never to change their last names. Moreover, though her first name was Ruth, she was known to her closest friends as "Jim." No one remembers how she got the nickname, but her sister-in-law speculates that she was from a generation of feminists who sometimes "acted too much like men."[60]

At the same time, Brindze and her husband had a close and loving marriage. In 1939 Brindze dedicated her first sailing book to Albert: "A good captain and the perfect shipmate — above and below deck."[61] In the late 1930s she and her husband moved to Mount Vernon, New York, where they lived for the rest of their lives. Ruth Brindze died in 1984, of a heart attack, while listening to Mozart. Albert, devastated by her death, died four months later.[62] Albert's grief may account, in part, for the fact that Ruth Brindze is so little remembered today. Although she was, by its own admission, one of Vanguard Press's "most important authors," and her many books were positively reviewed in major newspapers throughout her life, Albert refused to hold a funeral after her death — let alone announce her death to the newspapers. Thus, in 1984 there was not so much as an obituary to commemorate the life of this remarkable woman.

At the beginning of her career, Brindze made radio one of the villains in a melodrama about the pitfalls of consumer capitalism. She was active in the consumer movement before she wrote *Not to Be Broadcast* — but

Not to Be Broadcast was her most radical book: it represented her most complete statement of consumer dissatisfaction with the relationship between politics and radio, and between culture and capitalism. And while she painted a negative portrait of radio advertising, she developed a positive meaning of what it meant to be a consumer activist.

Peter Morell and the Culture of Radio Advertising

While Brindze was writing *Not to Be Broadcast* in Westchester County, another melodrama about culture and capitalism was being produced in Harlem. On 26 June 1936 the Negro Unit of the Federal Theater Project presented *Turpentine* — a play which narrated the struggle of a group of black workers in the turpentine swamps of central Florida. Peter Morell, a soon-to-be-consumer advocate, was one of the play's authors.

According to Hallie Flanagan, the Federal Theater Project's brash director, the writing of *Turpentine* "lacked fluency," but "the production possessed breathtaking fervor." The *New York Times* also praised the production:

The authors — J. A. Smith and Peter Morell — have taken as their people the workers in a turpentine camp in Central Florida. It is a story of subjection of the black to the white, and a plea for equality. The workers are starving, underpaid, harshly treated: unionization is the only solution and so they seize it. As played at the Lafayette much of "Turpentine" is exciting as melodrama and just as much is moving as a social document.[63]

Turpentine attracted an enthusiastic working-class audience: "Judging from the warm reception given *Turpentine,* plays of protest against exploitation and oppression anywhere are welcome to Harlem's exploited, oppressed and police-ridden people."[64]

The coauthor of *Turpentine,* J. Augustus Smith, was also the star of the play — playing the character "Forty-Four" — and using the stage name "Gus Smith." Smith was among a team of three black directors chosen to succeed John Houseman as the head of the Negro Unit. As for Peter Morell, John Houseman described him as Smith's "white collaborator." Another historian wrote that in spite of the fact that Morell had "little dramatic background," he displayed "a desire to reveal what [went] on in the Florida pines." Because of his involvement with Harlem's Lafayette Theater, Morell has frequently been mistaken for a black playwright.[65]

Though indeed white, Morell did have some experience in black theatre. He worked on the short-lived black musical *Africana* in 1933 and wrote a radio play about a group of Harlem actors stranded in the South in 1936. The story of his radio play appeared in a book Morell wrote in 1937 — a consumer activist diatribe against radio called *Poisons, Potions, and Profits: The Antidote to Radio Advertising*. In the book, Morell described the racism that led to the cancellation of his radio play:

Through our agent, Miss Freda Fishbein, we submitted to CBS a continuity which concerned a group of Harlem actors stranded in the deep South and their experiences there. Several of the officials appeared to be enthusiastic about the idea and eventually we were referred to a Miss Singleton. After some consideration she informed us that the radio audience did not like the Harlem type of Negro on the air, and that they preferred the old Southern type of Negro. We disagreed, of course, and pointed out that it was unfair to confine portrayal of the Negro to the radio audience as a servile buffoon, clown, or in an otherwise menial, degrading role. Miss Singleton quite suddenly became very busy and dropped the discussion.[66]

Thus was Morell's radio play killed by CBS.

It may have been this very experience that drove him to write *Poisons, Potions, and Profits*. Morell began his tract by thanking Consumers Union — the more radical of the consumer-testing agencies — for permission to use their archives. He also thanked the anti-advertising activist, S. Harry Evans, who at the time was Secretary of the National Committee on Education by Radio, "for his many courtesies." In the early 1930s, Evans had been one of the most effective lobbyists on behalf of progressive radio reform.[67]

At first glance, the connection between Morell's two projects seems remote; *Turpentine* told the story of African American struggle against oppressive working conditions, whereas *Poisons, Potions, and Profits* told the story of consumer struggle against misleading advertising claims. But the projects shared a fundamental logic. *Turpentine* asserted that the revolt of black workers was a direct product of the oppression of a racially dominated capitalist system. In a similar way, *Poisons, Potions, and Profits* asserted that a revolt against radio was a direct product of the false, annoying, and sometimes dangerous advertising claims. If capitalism could provoke a revolt of workers, could it not also provoke a revolt of consumers? Morell hoped that it would.

Morell was a humorous writer — even his acknowledgments were witty. He explained that his choice of the title "Poisons, Potions, and Profits" did not mean that all of the products he criticized were poisonous: "Some are worthless, some are injurious, some are sold through exaggerated advertising claims, and some are unnecessarily expensive." Morell also explained that the ephemeral nature of radio had made it difficult for him to obtain transcripts of radio advertisements. He had had to resort to a Dictaphone to transcribe the commercials under scrutiny because the radio networks "emphatically refused the author's request" for scripts.[68]

The book that resulted from Morell's labors was typical of the literature of the consumer movement. Like the authors of *100,000,000 Guinea Pigs*, Morell enumerated the claims of various consumer goods and then debunked them. He attacked the beauty industry, the diet industry, as well as ads for Fleishmann's Yeast, toothpaste, and over-the-counter medicines. But what made Morell's approach unique was that he focused exclusively on products that were advertised on the radio — small, incidental items, such as drugs, tobacco, and cosmetics. These products were cheap to produce, and marketers believed that they were best suited to the repetitive sales approach which radio advertising had perfected. In chapters titled "Beauty at Any Price," "The Slenderizing Way to Death," and "Dental Nostrums," Morell proceeded to deconstruct the claims of the advertisements for the leading sponsors of commercial radio. But Morell focused on more than just inadequate products; he also focused on the ads themselves, often reproducing their text in full. His goal was to make the reader wary — not only of the products, but also of the methods by which the products were being sold.

More than Rorty or Brindze, Morell was interested in the cultural effects of radio. This was especially evident in a chapter called "Peddling Human Misery for Profit," in which Morell attacked the radio program *Good Will Court*. On this show, downtrodden individuals told their sob stories to the show's fatherly host, A. L. Alexander, and an anonymous "Judge." In the opening minutes, host Alexander would explain that the show was meant to instruct listeners in how to avoid misfortune:

One of the sad conditions of life is that experience is not transmissible. No man will learn from the misfortunes of another. . . . It is true, nevertheless, that much of the satisfaction realized in presenting this hour lies in the fact that if there exists even one person on the brink of doing something which he would have had good reason to regret, to avoid a danger because of some situation here.[69]

In his book, Morell offered up the transcripts of three *Good Will Court* cases. In case number 10755 a woman who had returned a handbag full of jewels complained that she had been given only a paltry reward of $5. Host

Alexander and the Judge concluded there was nothing she could do to force a larger reward. In case number 10772 a man complained that his sister owed him money because he had taken care of her baby for seven months during the hours she was at work. The *Good Will Court* counseled the man to sue his sister for the money she owed him. In case number 10775 a woman complained that her unemployed, adult son had become a burden on her. The son complained that his mother had given him an inferiority complex. The Judge scolded them both, and, in the end, they reconciled.

These transcripts provide a rare glimpse into a radio program that has since been forgotten. They also serve as convincing evidence for Morell's argument that radio advertising was exploitative. As Morell noted, Chase and Sanborn Coffee — the show's sponsor — was the real victor in the *Good Will Court* (the show's announcer claimed that "with every pound of *Chase and Sanborn Coffee* that you buy you help the great work of this Court"); Morell pointed out that the problems of the "poor, neurotic and overworked woman and her unemployed son" had not really been solved by the *Good Will Court*. The "sufferer was left with his troubles," while "human misery" created a profit for the radio network and Chase and Sanborn Coffee.

What was to be done? Morell, like Rorty and Brindze, offered a final chapter that was full of solutions. He urged legislation that would require medicine labels to distinguish between pain relievers and actual cures.[70] He also recommended a Canadian method of drug regulation which prohibited "*any* advertisement" of medicines designed to treat serious ailments — such as cancer or diabetes.[71] Morell also pointed out that such legislative efforts would be wasted unless the government made greater efforts to enforce food and drug laws. He urged the government to make industries bear the cost of food and drug regulation. Finally, Morell urged the activation of a "consumer front" to "mobilize popular support for adequate consumer protection."[72]

In the end, Morell offered a coherent vision for a consumer movement that would be made up of organized labor and consumer activists. He argued that "organized labor can and should play a dominant role in the fight for real protection for consumers." He pointed out that the consumer and the worker were, in fact, the same person:

It is often forgot by the small minority of organized consumers as well as by organized labor that the trade unions are today the largest and most effective association of consumers. . . . Closer cooperation between the workers who have recognized their plight as consumers, and between consumers who have recognized their existence as workers, will prove to be the most effective means of getting results.

In order for such a coalition to take place, Morell argued, the "young clerk" in an insurance office and the "division manager" in a department store needed to see that "their problems of wages, working hours, and adjustment of grievances" were not that different from those of "linotype operator[s]" or "automobile worker[s]." Workers were consumers and consumers were workers, Morell argued, and they needed to recognize their commonalties in order to mobilize for change.[73]

The conclusion of *Poisons, Potions, and Profits* reflected the respect for workers Morell had demonstrated in his play *Turpentine*. As a dramatist, Morell was interested in the reform of radio not only because he feared its political and economic power: he also wanted the opportunity to produce culture with a leftist and anti-racist slant for commercial radio. Morell was a cultural producer who wanted a less commercial fate for the powerful and dramatic medium of radio.

Poisons, Potions, and Profits was well received by publications sympathetic to the consumer movement. Reviewers acknowledged the role that Consumers Union played in Morell's book, and praised him for bringing the problems of radio reform and the consumer movement together in one volume:

A little alcohol, a little water, some coloring matter, a large advertising campaign, and you have it — a new, miraculous remedy. This is the thesis of *Poisons, Potions, Profits,* a study of radio advertising which Mr. Morell has based on reports from Consumers Union. Consumer movements are not new to this country. . . . Among them is Consumers Union, which, though it has nothing to sell, devotes itself to advice on what to buy and what not to buy.

Forum went on to praise Morell for refusing to seem "suicidal" in his presentation of depressing facts. Rather, *Forum* explained, Morell offered a "hopeful, persuasive plan for making this country a safe place to shop in."[74]

Ruth Brindze, when she had an opportunity to review Morell's book for *The Nation,* was not as kind. She complained that *Poisons, Potions, and Profits* was an unoriginal contribution to the literature of the consumer movement:

Unfortunately, the products Mr. Morell names are also advertised in our best newspapers and magazines, and therefore have been exposed by almost every other guinea-pig writer. Mr. Morell brings some of this material up to date by drawing freely from the records of the Consumers Union, but practically he has added little to what has been said before. The subtitle of his book, "The Anti-dote to Radio Advertising" seems over optimistic. More than a new food-and-drug law is needed if the radio is really to be operated in the public interest.[75]

Brindze was right — Morell did present information that had been offered by previous writers. But she missed his larger point altogether: that radio advertising offered less information than other forms of advertising, and was therefore more dangerous. She also missed the fact that Morell called for much more than new food-and-drug laws: Morell called for a full-scale, organized, cross-class consumer movement powerful enough to change drug laws — as well as the commercial structure of radio.

Morell's book drew the ire of the pro-business lobby. The Depression era saw the publication of a great deal of alarmist literature about the consumer movement, but perhaps none was so hyperbolic as the pamphlet entitled "Who's a Guinea Pig," produced by the American Druggist Association in 1938. The pamphlet characterized the consumer movement as the "Trojan horse" of modern-day advertising — a force that would destroy advertising (and by extension, the drug industry) from within. It claimed that consumerist "debunking literature" threatened the respectability of "nationally advertised products" which provided "the foundation of modern American business." These debunking books were dangerous, according to the pamphlet, because they "shook" the faith of consumers, including their "FAITH in products, FAITH in methods," and "FAITH in manufacturer's honor." Among the worst of this debunking literature, according to "Who's a Guinea Pig," was Morell's *Poisons, Potions, and Profits.*[76]

Morell eventually became the victim of a right-wing backlash; after writing *Poisons, Potions, and Profits,* Morell had a hard time finding work as an author or a playwright. A fire in his Manhattan apartment destroyed all of his manuscripts in 1948, and his wife, Margaret Horgan, destroyed all remaining documents in the 1950s when the FBI began to investigate her husband's left-wing activities. Their only child, Valdi Morell, remembers that her father was blacklisted for writing *Poisons, Potions, and Profits.* McCarthyism, she claims, helped to ruin her father's career. This is a hard claim to substantiate; Morell and Horgan were secretive about their lives. Horgan, from a wealthy family that settled in Butte, Montana, came east to New York to be educated and to work as a model in the 1920s. In Greenwich Village she met her future husband — a man with a mysterious past and excellent taste in clothes. Morell, born Peter Mindell, was Jewish — he had been born in England, where his family lived after emigrating from Russia, before they came to America. Peter Mindell had taken his great-grandmother's maiden name, Morell, as his pen name, which he made into his legal name when his daughter, Valdi, was born in 1948. Valdi Morell speculates that it was partly because of ethnic prejudice that her father changed his name to Morell.

Valdi Morell also recalled that "by the time I came along, life had already dealt [my parents] quite a blow." But she also remembered her parents' luxurious apartment near Washington Square: it had fourteen rooms and parquet floors inlaid with games — like shuffleboard and hopscotch. In that apartment her parents hosted lively cocktail parties which were attended by artists, playwrights, intellectuals, and actors. Gradually, however, the family's fortune dwindled. Her father dealt in antiques for a few years, and, later, the family moved to a farm in Amagansett, Long Island, where her mother worked as a secretary for the Diebold Corporation. Finally, after years of Peter Morell's drinking and unemployment, the family lost the farm on Long Island, too. Peter Morell died a forgotten man in 1963, after years of alcohol abuse and bankruptcy. He was sixty-eight.[77]

Still, Morell left behind an important legacy. *Turpentine* and *Poisons, Potions, and Profits* demonstrate the relationship between cultural producers and consumer activists. In order to make radio more accessible to artists like himself, Morell transformed himself from an equal rights playwright into a consumer advocate. In so doing, he began to imagine a consumer movement that could bring industrial and white-collar workers into a radical alliance.

Conclusion

The writings of James Rorty, Ruth Brindze, and Peter Morell did not produce the radio reforms they had hoped for. Nonetheless, they should not be read as the death knell of a fading reform movement. The movement to decommercialize radio would continue beyond the postwar era. In its 1946 publication, called the "Blue Book," the FCC would attack commercial radio, condemning its "advertising excesses," such as "the number of commercials presented in a given hour; the piling up of commercials; the time between commercials; the middle commercial . . . and the intermixture of program and advertising."[78] New consumerist battles would be launched over the addition of FM channels. Pacifica Radio would redefine radical radio for the postwar era. And using consumerist tactics, civil rights activists would effectively bring down WLBT, the most powerful — and the most racist — television station in the South. Thus, it is important to see the work of the 1930s radio activists in historical perspective: every generation fights anew for democratization of the airwaves — sometimes fighting against commercialization, other times using consumer power to demand that advertisers respond to audiences.[79]

For Rorty, Brindze and Morell, voicing their criticisms was also a trans-formative act. In the process of writing their radio critiques, these authors evolved as consumer activists. In Morell's case, writing about radio made it possible for him to *become* a consumer activist. In the end, the lives of Rorty, Brindze, and Morell offer evidence for Colston Warne's thesis that advertising was responsible for the birth and the growth of the consumer movement. Marketers sought to "activate" consumers to buy, but their tactics sometimes backfired: sometimes they created consumer activists. The radio advertising industry of the 1930s helped to spark a movement of intellectuals, journalists, and cultural producers who sought, in turn, to change the economic structure of the medium. Their efforts failed, but the consumer movement persisted. These radio activists believed that change was possible. And, although they did not always see the changes they fought for come to fruition in their lifetimes, their writings and life stories remain an inspiration. As the African American character Sue says at the victorious conclusion of *Turpentine,* people just have to "keep fightin' an' organizin'" if they are going to "keep livin'." These are pow-erful words from a forgotten playwright — and they provide a powerful lesson from an overlooked movement that had its origin in the 1930s and survives among us still.

PART TWO

Consumers on the March

CIO Boycotts, Active Listeners, and Consumer Time

CHAPTER THREE

The Consumer Revolt of "Mr. Average Man"

Boake Carter and the CIO Boycott of Philco Radio

In 1936 the *Major Bowes' Amateur Hour* was one of the most popular shows on the radio. Each week, Bowes, who had a "mellifluous voice," invited the audience to decide which of the "sweet voices from the rank and file" might become a big name. Much like *American Idol* or *The Gong Show*, the *Major Bowes' Amateur Hour* gave about fifteen amateurs (from a pool of six hundred applicants per week) a chance to perform a musical number. Major Bowes, who originated the use of a "gong" to end a subpar performance, would give an "inept" contestant about thirty seconds, while the more tolerable acts were allowed to finish. Listeners voted for their favorite each week by telephone and by postcard. The show featured such "hard luck" contestants as Alexander Roy, a "tenor and glass blower from Pittsburgh," who walked most of the way to New York accompanied by his thirteen-year-old son. But the show also launched such stars as Frank Sinatra. The success of the *Major Bowes' Amateur Hour* turned audience-participation shows into a national craze.[1]

Not everyone, however, was thrilled with the program — or, more specifically, with its Sunday night time slot. In early March 1936 the Reverend G. Reid Smith, pastor of the First Street Methodist Church in Macon, Georgia, launched a boycott of Major Bowes's sponsor, Chase and Sanborn Coffee. Pastor Smith, and one hundred of his parish members, angry that the *Amateur Hour* conflicted with Sunday night church services, vowed they would continue their boycott until the show's time slot was changed. Major Bowes responded to the threat with good humor, inviting Pastor Smith to "install a radio and let the congregation listen in." But his suggestion "fell on deaf ears." Later that month the boycott was joined by a convention of Presbyterian ministers in Ontario, Canada, who wrote Chase and Sanborn asking that the coffee company change the program from the Sunday night hour, "which has always been regarded as a church hour."[2]

At the time of the threatened boycott, the *Major Bowes' Amateur Hour* was selling more coffee than any other program on the air. Thus, Chase and Sanborn was not particularly intimidated by the threats of a few parishioners and church leaders in Georgia and Ontario. Although it caught the attention of *Variety,* this threat was typical in that boycotts were frequently threatened during the 1930s and 1940s but they rarely achieved their goals. Certainly, sponsors were vulnerable to organized attacks at the point of purchase, but it would have required a lot more than a few religious leaders to make a dent in the selling power of the *Major Bowes' Amateur Hour.* Church leaders would just have to adjust the hours of their scheduled services or suffer the consequences; such was the power of a single radio program in 1936.

The Church was involved in still another threatened boycott in 1936. Certain clergy affiliated with the Catholic Church had organized effective boycotts of "improper" films during the mid-1930s, and in 1936 one of the leaders of this movement, a congressman from Massachusetts, William P. Connery, threatened to extend the boycott to radio. He charged that radio was becoming as "indecent" as the movies and that listeners needed to organize:

It is not at all improbable that the American people may find it necessary . . . to take similar action by refusing to purchase the products of those concerns who use the radio facilities of such radio stations as permit the broadcasting of indecent or otherwise unfit radio programs.

Connery also asked Congress to investigate the FCC because of "allegedly indecent programs permitted." Connery did not succeed in launching this boycott, but the threat prompted a flurry of memos at NBC. NBC executive Frank Russell asked NBC vice-president John Royal, "What is there to this?"[3]

In a few telling cases, listeners did manage to launch successful boycotts. These could have a significant impact on the targeted radio programs. One such case was that of Alexander Woollcott, who hosted the popular talk show *The Town Crier,* sponsored by Cream of Wheat. When

Woollcott attacked Hitler and Mussolini for their actions in Western Europe, Italian- and German-Americans in the Chicago area organized boycotts of Cream of Wheat, which in turn led Cream of Wheat to dump Woollcott's show. Woollcott was so bitter after this experience that when NBC approached him to host another show he informed them that "no amount of money would tempt me." He explained that he would only be attracted by "some new notion of how broadcasting might be made more pleasing to the broadcaster."[4]

In another documented case of a successful sponsor boycott, a left-leaning news commentator, Johannes Steel, whose Boston-area radio show was sponsored by the Parker Watch Company, was forced off the air when the watch company was boycotted by a right-leaning movement that called itself "America First." Steel, who spoke at a rally to protest his canceled sponsorship, complained about the power of political conservatives: "Your radio stations give you little else but canned goods and have been terrorized by Coughlinite fascist influences into what amounts to a conspiracy of silence on vital issues."[5] "Coughlinite" referred to the right-wing, populist, anti-Semitic, proto-fascist, and Catholic radio commentator Father Coughlin.[6] Ironically, however, it was not just the "Coughlinite Fascist" that made Steel vulnerable to cancellation; it was also the power of the sponsor boycott in the radio age.

During the late 1930s and the early 1940s the two most powerful boycotts of a product sponsor were conducted by organized labor. Though boycotting is a tactic that has been linked in the last forty years to consumer activism (the California grape boycott, for example) and global political pressure (the boycott of companies doing business with South Africa), it has it roots in the Land League and the labor movements of the nineteenth century. In fact, it was in Ireland in the 1880s that this political and economic tactic was given its name. The "boycott" was named for the English army captain Charles Cunningham Boycott, whose repressive land management policies led to the formation of Land Leagues in Ireland. Ironically, the rent strikes conducted by the Land Leagues, and the Land Leagues' ostracizing of Captain Boycott and his family, ended up glorifying the name of the man they sought to punish.[7] In the United States the term "boycott" was used to describe protests organized by labor, and it was not used widely to denote consumer protests until the 1960s. Rather, consumer boycotts were often referred to as "buyers' strikes." Thus, since the nineteenth century, the consumer power of workers has been an important weapon — in the form of the boycott — for the resolution of labor disputes.[8]

As Lawrence Glickman has argued, the American labor movement in the 1880s was based on the principle of "labor consumerism" — the idea that workers should fight for a "living wage" to be used for the consumption of basic necessities and more time for leisure — "eight hours for what we will."[9] It is not surprising, then, that organized labor would use both the tactic of striking — the withdrawal of labor — in conjunction with the tactic of boycotting — the withdrawal of consumption.[10] Harry Laidler, an early-twentieth-century boycott historian has argued that the boycott emerged as a popular union tactic when laborers discovered that the strike was not effective on its own to prevent employers from hiring "scabs." Workers realized they could "use their power as consumers, in their struggles for improved conditions . . . and thus cut off, as far as possible, not only [the employers'] labor force, but [the employers'] market as well."[11]

During the late nineteenth century, the boycott became such a common tactic of the labor movement that a definition of the boycott appeared in a report of the New York Bureau of Statistics of Labor in 1886. Between 1885 and 1892 there were 1,352 boycotts reported to the Bureau of Labor, in industries ranging from food, building, clothing, transportation, printing, furniture, and lumber. Unions engaged in these boycotts for many reasons: to protest a company's use of non-union labor, to reduce hours, and to increase wages. The boycotts that were most successful were those that targeted "primary necessities of the laboring class," products that entered "into daily consumption and [were] of such a character [as] to be made the subject of ordinary conversation." The most effective boycotts were those that union leaders could make a part of the everyday lives of their communities. Meat, beer, cigars, and newspapers were all frequently — and effectively — boycotted.[12] Thus, the labor union, more than any other American organization, has understood the role the boycott can play in pressuring corporations at the point of consumption.

Regardless of who organized the boycott, however, in the radio age sponsors were perceived as vulnerable because it was their name — and their name alone — that was attached to a controversial radio program. And because so many companies used radio to build that intangible commodity known as "good will," even a controversy that had little impact on sales was still considered to be bad for business. Consumers and listeners had relatively little power to change commercial radio throughout the radio age. But when listeners banded together to write letters or to organize a boycott, sponsors took notice. They could not afford not to.

Each of the next three chapters looks at a particular form of radio programming and a specific kind of "radio activity" provoked by that pro-gramming. In this chapter I examine the sponsor controversies that were provoked by radio newscasting — and the commentary of one news-caster, Boake Carter, in particular. Radio news broadcasting was in its infancy in the mid-1930s, and, as war broke out in Europe, the radio became one of the most important sources of news and information. In 1937 even James Rorty wrote a positive assessment of the role that radio commentators played as Europe prepared for war. He was especially impressed that "commercialism" had taken a back seat during coverage of the European crisis in the fall of 1938: "Program after program was post-poned or interrupted by flash bulletins and special broadcasts."[13] Rorty, who only four years earlier had been the scourge of the broadcast indus-try for writing *Our Master's Voice,* received advance praise for his article on radio news broadcasting from the head of the Press Division at NBC.[14]

Not all war-related broadcasts pushed commercialism to the back-ground. One of the most popular commentators of the late 1930s, Boake Carter, was also one of the most successful salesmen of his sponsor's prod-uct: Philco Radios. Carter always managed to plug his sponsor, whether he was talking about yachting (his favorite hobby), or why women and men were not equal (one of his favorite topics), or of war-torn Europe. Without missing a beat, Carter could make the newest Philco radio model seem as dramatic, and important, as the war itself. In this excerpt from a Carter broadcast, the real "actor" of the paragraph does not emerge until Philco radio enters the picture.

Thus when the shadows of two mailed fists etch their dark outlines across war-torn, fire-ridden Madrid today, there stretched another dark shadow across the whole of Europe.

So today too we find many a new Philco tuned to the far-flung capital cities of Europe to keep many an American home informed of these critical events of history in the making on the anvil of time. For it is indeed a simply easy thing to follow the world the Philco way now, especially when you have a Philco high efficiency aerial attached to your set.[15]

The short but dapper Brit-turned-American had a clipped style and a crisp delivery. Dismissed by radio historian and former NBC executive Eric Barnouw as "barely a newscaster," Carter blended his news commentary seamlessly with his own opinions and his sponsor's advertisements.

Carter was one of the first newscasters of the radio age to have his own sponsor; before him, news programs were generally "sustaining" programs, aired without commercial sponsorship or interruption. But Carter and Philco demonstrated that news and commerce could work well together, and soon the airwaves were filled with such sponsored newscasters as H. V. Kaltenborn, Lowell Thomas, and Walter Lippman. Carter's sponsor was an unusually appropriate one, in the sense that Carter was a radio commentator and Philco made a range of inexpensive tabletop radios. Philco profited, in the beginning, from Carter's pugnacious style and growing popularity. As one Philco historian has noted, from 1928 to 1937 "Philco transformed itself from a nearly defunct producer of storage batteries and radio power supplies into the nation's leading manufacturer of radio receivers." Philco's strategy, which allowed the company to outsell its competition by more than double in 1934, was to sell a higher volume of smaller, less expensive radios to working-class consumers. Philco also spent more than its competitors on advertising — including its sponsorship of Carter's news program.[16]

Though Carter and Philco profited together from the sale and promotion of radio sets, they also shared some of the same hardships. In 1937 the CIO-led union that had organized the Philco manufacturing plants in 1933 grew weary of Carter's constant attacks on John L. Lewis and the Congress of Industrial Organization. James Carey, the leader of the United Electrical and Radio Workers, led one of the most successful boycotts against a sponsor and a commentator. In a bold move, he helped to organize a CIO-member boycott of Philco radios — the very product made by his union members. Carey's goal was to get his employer to stop sponsoring a commentator who was wreaking material and cultural damage on the union — and on organized workers everywhere. The CIO-led boycott hurt Philco sales, and, ultimately, led to Carter's downfall.

The Boake Carter story allows us a unique lens onto the intersection of production and consumption within the context of advertising-sponsored mass culture. The workers who made Philco radios had a keen sense of how their labor was connected to the sale of their product. When they believed that Carter was threatening those sales, their solidarity, and their identity as working-class consumers, they organized a boycott of their own product. Carter, for his part, never fully recovered from the blow.

The Rise of Boake Carter

Boake Carter hated to be photographed standing up. Most photographs of Carter show him from the shoulders up: behind the microphone, dressed in a three-piece suit (with a handkerchief), high cheekbones, a short, full bristle mustache, hair high off the forehead, two vertical creases between his eyebrows, and a cleft chin. Carter was born in Baku, South Russia, in 1898. His father was a British oilman who traveled the world, leaving his wife and daughter behind in London. Boake Carter, whose given name was Harold, worked with his father in the oil fields of South America and Oklahoma. Later, father and son moved to Philadelphia, where Carter's father had taken a job as the director of an oil-refining company. But in Philadelphia Carter's father died, leaving Carter nothing. Carter remained in Philadelphia and found a job working for a local newspaper.[17]

At the *Philadelphia Daily News* Carter was considered a fair writer but a sloppy journalist. He got his first break in radio when Leon Levy, the program director for WCAU — the flagship station for the young CBS network — decided to broadcast a rugby game and Carter was the only man he knew in Philadelphia who had ever seen one. But Carter's first stint as a commentator was short-lived: listeners could not understand his accent. He got his second break as the narrator for Hearst–Metrotone newsreels — a narrating practice known as "globe trotting." After a successful stint as a globe-trotter, Carter began narrating regular news broadcasts on WCAU. He soon attracted the sponsorship of a local chain of car mechanics, Pep Boys. WCAU thought that "Harold" was too common a name for a radio personality and so Carter chose to be known as "Boake" — a family name on his mother's side.

The man who became Carter's agent, Leon Levy, was a Philadelphia dentist and one of the owners of WCAU. More importantly, Levy was the brother-in-law of William S. Paley, the president of CBS. Levy had faith in Carter, believing that if Carter could get some exposure, "the family and CBS would acquire a national asset." But Carter, unlike the pioneering radio newscasters of the era, such as Walter Winchell and Lowell Thomas, was not already a nationally known news authority.[18] Carter finally garnered national attention with his coverage of the Lindbergh kidnapping case. He broadcast details of the kidnapping from the Stacy Trent Hotel in Trenton, New Jersey. His newscasts regarding the case were full of exaggeration and speculation, harping on what Carter saw as the likely culprits: bootleggers and gangsters. In fact, Carter's broadcasts were so loosely based in fact that CBS pulled him from the air. But the people who had been listening to Carter's broadcasts, and to his "incongruous valedictory 'Cheerio'," given after every grim story, demanded his return. Carter had become a radio personality, and in 1933 Philco signed a five-year deal as his exclusive sponsor.[19]

Carter quickly became identified with his sponsor. He was a popular radio commentator, and his sponsor manufactured affordable radios. And though he had a distinct voice, he was soon to acquire a recognizable face. In addition to plugging Philco radios, Carter became a spokesperson for a host of other products, including Gillette razor blades, Nash automobiles, Pullman railroad cars, and Underwood typewriters. His face became an icon associated with these products in magazine ads, and he was frequently profiled in the mainstream magazine press.

Carter had a pugnacious style. His newscasts were a mix of fact, opinion, fancy, and purple prose. Though he was British by birth and made frequent references to his past, he was a naturalized American citizen and always used the pronoun "we" when referring to "Americans." His newscasts veered wildly in topic, from the failings of Roosevelt's New Deal, to the heroism of single mothers, to seeing-eye dogs, from the activities of "vigilante" union thugs, to the duties of wives, to the joys of sailing. As one of his contemporaries observed, he had "no consistent political philosophy. . . . He thinks that low wages increase the market for manufactured goods, and opposes protective tariffs, tax-exempt securities, industrial unions, reckless driving, cowardice at sea, and meddling in the Orient."[20]

On the other hand, while Carter frequently denied having any political affiliations, he did admit to being influenced by his friend and fellow radio demagogue, Father Coughlin. And while Carter playfully referred to Roosevelt as "the Boss" and occasionally backed a White House mandate, he continually attacked Roosevelt and the New Deal, in his broadcasts and in his newspaper column. Roosevelt tried to ignore "Croak" Carter (a nickname given to Carter by the Secretary of the Interior). At the peak of Carter's career, Roosevelt quipped: "If the President . . . were to undertake to answer Boake Carter, he would have no time to act as the Executive head of the Government."[21] Indeed, Carter seemed intent on pecking away at the "big men" of his era. In addition to Roosevelt, Carter targeted the head of the Congress of Industrial Organization, John L. Lewis. While Carter always claimed to uphold the principles of the "working man," he had great contempt for what he called the "tyranny" of the CIO and the "dictatorship" of Lewis. Carter varied his treatment of Lewis — sometimes condemning him, at other times praising him — but he never wavered in his hostility to the CIO.

Meanwhile, in the late 1930s Carter was on his way to becoming one of the most popular radio commentators of the era. In April 1937 he began writing a syndicated newspaper column entitled "But —." The title reflected Carter's philosophy that argument was everything: "Meat is in argument. . . . If I can provide an argument, so much the better."[22] After its first month, Carter's column was being published in fifty-two news-papers, including the *Boston Daily Globe, Chicago Times, Philadelphia Evening Ledger,* and the *New York Daily Mirror.*[23] His newspaper reader-ship was estimated to be 7 million, while his radio audience was estimated at between 10 million and 16 million listeners.[24] He also published a hand-ful of popular books in the mid-1930s, including his defense of free speech, *I Talk as I Like,* and a compilation of listener letters, *Johnny Q. Public Speaks.*[25]

Carter dedicated *Johnny Q. Public Speaks* to his listeners, "whose book this really is and who therefore [are] due the credit for making it possi-ble." Ironically, however, the ordinary, working-class listeners who made Carter and Philco so profitable also helped to put an end to Carter's career. As one contemporary observer noted, Carter had become increas-ingly identified with his sponsor, and Philco had become increasingly identified with working-class consumers: "Philco was the first large Eastern manufacturer to concentrate on cheap but good small sets. . . . The firm sold millions of these sets during the depression while com-petitors were still vainly trying to peddle their expensive cabinet mod-els."[26] Thus, in 1936, when Carter broadcast the first of his virulent attacks on members of the CIO, he began to feel the effects of a listener backlash. It started small at first, when his home station, WCAU, began receiving a few letters of complaint.

By the summer and fall of 1937, however, the CIO had launched a full-scale boycott of Carter's program and Philco products. The working-class listeners whom Philco targeted with their affordable radios were the same listeners who were offended by Carter's broadcasts. Carter's attacks on labor drew the ire of working people all over the country, but especially those in Philadelphia — the very workers who made Philco radios. These workers had a powerful union — led by the young CIO upstart James Carey. In late 1937 Philco noticed a drop-off in radio sales, which forced Carter and John L. Lewis to come to an agreement, in which Lewis prom-ised that the CIO would end its boycott. But CIO members would not comply.[27]

Ultimately, for Philco workers, the boycott had its desired effect. With the boycott still in progress, it was rumored that Philco wanted to drop their commentator. Indeed, in February 1938 Philco refused to renew Carter's contract. At that point, Carter's contract was picked up by General Foods. Colby M. Chester, chairman of the board of General

Foods, actively opposed the New Deal. He had been president of the National Association of Manufacturers, one of the most pro-capital, anti-labor organizations in the country. Ideologically, he and Carter were a good match.

But other stockholders in the company were concerned about the bottom line. What if Carter provoked cereal consumers in the same way he provoked radio consumers? Marjorie Post and her husband, Joseph E. Davies, who was the U.S. ambassador to the Soviet Union, were among those concerned that Carter's broadcast style would hurt sales of General Food cereals. They were assured by CBS that Carter would be kept under control. Meanwhile, the CIO was still after Carter. They sent a letter to Colby Chester, president of General Foods, in December 1937, warning him not to take on the sponsorship of Carter's program. When Chester refused to reply, the CIO council voted to boycott Carter's new sponsor. In a February meeting of the CIO one member proposed that the CIO rescind the boycott. The proposal was overwhelmingly rejected, and even CIO leaders were surprised at the membership's determination. The boycott was getting personal.[28]

Despite his troubles with the CIO, 1938 marked the pinnacle of Carter's career. Under Philco's sponsorship, Carter's show could be heard on over sixty stations three nights a week. With General Foods as his sponsor, Carter could be heard on over eighty-five stations five nights a week. In June 1938 the *Radio Guide* named Carter the most popular radio commentator in the country. His newspaper column "But — " was syndicated in sixty newspapers and was second only to Walter Winchell and Dorothy Thompson in number of readers.[29] Carter had become such an icon that a board-game manufacturer created the game, "Boake Carter, Star Reporter." (Players, reporting for the city of Urbania, used metal airplanes and telephone pieces to "bring in as much 'news' as possible").[30]

But by August 1938 Carter had lost his job at WCAU, his sponsorship with General Foods, and his former advocates at CBS now barred him permanently from the network. Historian David Culbert has argued that Carter's constant attacks on Roosevelt's foreign policy led key industry leaders and government officials to pressure CBS and General Foods to fire Carter. Carter himself charged that "the New Deal — through the state, treasury and navy departments — is trying to 'run me off the air and probably out of the country.'"[31] After Carter lost Philco as his sponsor, he became increasingly unstable. His attacks became increasingly filled with what Culbert has called "innuendo, invective, distortion, and misinformation."[32]

The last years of Carter's life are relatively undocumented. He continued to broadcast, sporadically, finding occasional sponsors, such as United Airlines and Chef-Boy-Ar-Dee. He joined a religious group called the Anglo Saxon Federation of America and converted to a sect of Judaism called "Biblical Hebrewism." This group believed that Anglo Saxons were members of the lost tribe of Israel. He divorced his wife, married again, started keeping a kosher kitchen, and changed his name to Ephraim Boake Carter. Observers claimed that Carter distanced himself from the Anglo Saxon Federation when he found out that it was an anti-Semitic organization. These last years of his life are disturbingly chronicled in a book called *Thirty-Three Candles,* which was written by an ardent member of the sect named David Horowitz.[33] It is clear from the photos of Carter in the book — standing up, on the beach, barefoot, and without a shirt — that Carter had lost a sense of himself as a public persona. Carter died on 18 November 1944, of a heart attack, at the age of 46. He was remembered by Alfred de Grazia, an American soldier writing to his fiancée, as one of the "great men" who had been lost that year.[34]

But "Croak" Carter did not go down without a fight. After he was forced off the radio by CBS in 1938, he went on a speaking tour throughout the United States, drawing large crowds in cities like Portland, Oregon, and Oshkosh, Wisconsin. At a lecture in Oshkosh, Carter told a crowd of nearly one thousand listeners, "Thanks to Mr. Roosevelt . . . I am enjoying a vacation after eight years of being a slave to the radio."[35] Carter believed that it was "the 'Great White Father in Washington'" who had forced him off the air. Carter claimed that the White House had threatened to use the power of the FCC, which could renew or reject station licenses every six months, to scare CBS into firing him.[36]

Historian David Culbert argues that members of the government were investigating Carter's origins with an eye to deporting him. In 1937 Congresswoman Virginia E. Jenckes wanted Carter thrown out of the country because of some cracks he had made about chopping down all the cherry trees in Washington. At the same time, as Carter's attacks on the Roosevelt administration grew sharper, the Special Intelligence Unit of the Treasury "began its own inquiry into the newscaster's origins." Bristling at the insult, Carter defended the legality of his American citizenship, denied that he had any political ties to his place of birth (Russia), and denounced the government for suspecting that he was not a loyal citizen: "The cardinal sin that I commit is that I should be so despicable as to criticize out loud in public forum. It just is 'not done,' which to the British is the same thing as betraying tradition. That is the sin I committed in becoming an American citizen! But it is a sin I shall ever be thankful that I had sense enough to commit."[37] Carter muzzled his commentary during the spring of 1938. However, though he curtailed his attacks on the State Department, he did accuse the administration of "destroying radio commentators' freedom of speech."[38] In the summer of 1938 he resumed his attacks on administration policy. Finally, in August 1938, CBS replaced Carter with commentator Joe Penner.

It is clear that the government played a role in Carter's firing in 1938. But in the 1940s it was organized labor that would claim the credit for "neutralizing" Boake Carter. At a meeting of labor leaders in 1943, a member of the AFL complained that the broadcasts of conservative radio commentators had led to the passage of the Connally-Smith anti-strike bill. He pledged that labor would fight back, arguing that "freedom of the air does not include the right of commentators to become special pleaders for special causes." He warned radio commentators that they, too, could meet the same fate as Boake Carter: "Commentators will either stick to objective news facts or face the open opposition of organized labor. We neutralized Boake Carter and we shall fight to the bitter end those who figure the privilege of the air is synonymous with the right to blow off their political arguments."[39]

Did organized labor neutralize Boake Carter? This is still a difficult question to answer, but it is clear that the CIO boycott played a role in Philco's decision to drop Carter in early 1938. And even though General Foods increased the number of nights per week that Carter aired his broadcasts when they picked up his contract, Carter was never as comfortable selling cereal as he had been plugging Philco radios. As his contemporary A. J. Liebling noted, when Carter was with Philco he mixed news and radio sales with a "maddening casualness," but when Carter was working for General Foods, his "most difficult feat" was "the establishment of a daily liaison between floods, earthquakes, politics and breakfast food."[40] The social and economic factors which made Philco and Boake Carter successful during the 1930s were the very forces that helped to bring an end to Carter's career in 1938. Carter may have been an effective salesman for Philco products, but he was brought down by the very men and women who made Philco radios and who objected to his anti-labor commentaries.

Carter, Philco, and the CIO

Philco was the brand name of the Philadelphia Storage Battery Company, which got its start in 1906 manufacturing storage batteries for electric automobiles, trucks, and mine locomotives.[41] In the 1920s Philco began producing batteries and electric light-socket adapters that were used to power radio receivers.[42] In 1927 the largest producer of radios, Radio Corporation of America, began to manufacture radios that could be plugged directly into the wall.[43] As a result, Philco's batteries and "socket-power" units were no longer in demand, so the company began to manufacture radio sets. According to one of the company's founders, Philco recognized that most Americans still could not afford to buy a radio: "Radio was for the millions, not the thousands. . . . So why not produce radios on a production line basis, just like automobiles?"[44]

In 1929 Philco sold 400,000 radios and became the number two radio manufacturer in the country. According to Philco's promotion manager, in order to stay competitive the company introduced a "small, compact, comparatively inexpensive radio."[45] Known as the "Baby Grand," and priced at $69.50, this affordable table-top radio helped to make Philco the leading producer of radios by 1930, with $34 million in sales. Philco, known as a "depression baby," began to prosper even as the rest of the nation was beginning to suffer.[46] Philco's financial success can also be attributed to the company's "bait-and-switch" tactics, in which they would advertise the cheaper table-top models but try to push their larger, cabinet-sized, and more expensive models in their showrooms. By 1931, competitors were offering "midget" radios to undermine Philco's sales, but Philco responded by increasing its advertising budget and sponsoring such programs as the Army-Navy football game and Leopold Stokowski, who conducted the famous Philadelphia Orchestra.[47]

Philco operated on the principle that more people would buy radios if there were more quality shows on the air. Philco's ads thus promoted the company's radio sets, while the entertainment prodded listeners to invest in more expensive sets. As Philco's president James M. Skinner explained, "The more the public appreciates good music and good programs, the bigger and better radios they will buy and the more money there is to be made in the radio set business." Implementing this philosophy, Philco signed a five-year contract with Boake Carter in 1933; by 1934, Philco radios were outselling its nearest competitor, RCA, by more than double.[48] Philco targeted its brand, as well as its radio programming, to a poor, working-class listening audience. One of the company's surveys, undertaken by the Princeton Radio Project headed by Paul Lazarsfeld, found that the Boake Carter news program was most popular among the "C" and "D" classed audiences — meaning those who had an income of $3,000 a year or less.[49]

Competition between Philco and RCA, whose manufacturing facilities were located just across the Delaware River from one another, remained fierce. In the summer of 1936, RCA demanded that Philco pay royalties on the RCA patents Philco used to manufacture its radios; Philco countersued, charging RCA with monopolistic practices. At that point, Carter entered the fray, attacking RCA and defending Philco over the airwaves.[50] Finally, to placate those who charged that Carter had a biased interest in the suit, Philco took out a full-page ad in *Time* magazine, denying that Carter was motivated by company loyalty:

Observations unhampered, untrammeled, uncensored. Whether or not they agree with the listener or the sponsor. Five times a week Boake Carter expresses his opinions on any subject his news-sense deems important. No matter how controversial the topic . . . no matter whose toes may be trod upon . . . he is at liberty to voice his personal opinions and reactions . . . Philco's year round expression of its belief that freedom of speech means freedom of the air as well as of the press.[51]

The ad was an impressive statement in defense of free speech; however, given Carter's close identification with his sponsor, as Culbert has noted, "Few were convinced, least of all RCA."[52]

Philco continued to dominate the radio market for another year. In the summer of 1937, the company announced a new line of radios which featured an angled display panel that made tuning the radio easier. In order to promote the new feature, Philco then launched a series of ads that showed a group of young women crouched in front of the radio, with the slogan "No Squat, No Squint, No Stoop." The slogan caught on and was parodied in movie titles and political cartoons of the era.[53] But despite the success of the ad, in 1937 Philco's sales leveled off and the company was hit by strikes and boycotts organized by its own workers. Although Philco was one of the most profitable radio manufacturers of the Depression era, it was also the crucible for the United Electrical, Radio, and Machine Workers Union, which in turn became one of the most radical and effective unions within the Congress of Industrial Organization. Ironically, while the company marketed its radios on the showroom floor to poor and working-class listeners, it struggled to contain the organized force of its own working-class radio technicians on the shop floor.

In 1932 a group of young Philco workers formed the "Philrod Fishing Club." While club members ostensibly involved themselves with plans to buy a fishing boat, in truth they were raising money to fund a union organizing drive at the Philco plant. According to historian Ronald L.

Filippelli, this preemptive organization allowed the young union leaders to "successfully resist the pressure for a company union."[54] Even more impressively, the Philrod Fishing Club succeeded in organizing a union which signed a contract with Philco after only a three-day strike in 1933. The contract included an eight-hour day, a forty-hour work week, time-and-a-half for overtime, seniority, a grievance procedure, and raises of up to 30 cents per hour. These working conditions were "without equal" in the industry at the time. Why did Philco sign such a favorable labor agreement at the peak of the Depression? According to Filippelli and Mark McColloch, Philco may have capitulated in order to avoid a boycott of its radios that had been threatened by the AFL. Filippelli and McColloch conclude that "the concessions probably resulted from a combination of factors, including ignorance on the part of the company as to the lasting significance of their concessions and a desire to resolve trouble with the unions so as to capitalize on the business upturn in 1933."[55]

James Carey, age twenty-three, one of the Philrod Fishing Club upstarts, was soon to become one of the youngest and most influential union leaders in the country. Carey was a Philadelphia native, a Democrat, and a Catholic. He had been one of the delegates of the fledgling electrical workers union who had crowded into a car one day and driven to Washington to persuade the director of the National Recovery Administration to approve their application to run a "union-shop"—which meant that anyone hired by Philco would automatically become a member of the union after two weeks of employment. Two years later, dissatisfied with the direction of the AFL, Carey and fellow Philco worker Julius Emspak formed the United Electrical and Radio Workers and asked John L. Lewis to accept them as part of the CIO. When the UE became an official CIO union in 1936, Carey was elected its president and Emspak its secretary-treasurer.

Carey, according to Filippelli and McColloch, "was a man who enjoyed the warm glow of the spotlight." Early on, he was schooled in radical social thought:

His first exposure to organized labor came as a teenager when he participated in a strike of movie projectionists in a New Jersey theater where Carey worked part-time as a projectionist's helper. He attended night school at Drexel and the University of Pennsylvania, but his true education in trade unionism came largely from two sources, an upbringing in an atmosphere of liberal Catholic social thought . . . and advice from a socialist, and strongly anti-communist, hosiery worker in Philadelphia who gave him counsel during his days as a young labor leader at Philco.

From a small office in New York City, which they furnished with $99 from the UE treasury, Carey and Emspak began to lead the UE. They organized a successful strike at the Camden location of RCA in the summer of 1936, a short strike of Philco workers in 1937, and a longer and more protracted strike at Philco in 1938.[56]

Carey may have coveted the spotlight, but as Elizabeth Fones-Wolf has pointed out, he was also one of the few labor leaders of his era who understood what the media spotlight could do for the union movement. Throughout the 1930s he continued to imagine the radical potential of radio for the purposes of labor organizing. Under his leadership, the UE "explored the possibility of buying a station in Philadelphia" and tried to convince the CIO "to establish a chain of labor stations." Carey, as a man who had manufactured radios and organized radio workers, was in a unique position to think about the power of radio for reaching ordinary workers. Moreover, it is likely that the growing threat posed by Boake Carter's anti-CIO radio commentaries — sponsored by Carey's former employer — heightened Carey's awareness of radio's potential.[57]

As president of the UE, Carey received many letters complaining about Boake Carter in the fall of 1936. On the West Coast the longshoremen were on strike, and Carter was launching daily attacks on the maritime unions, complaining that the union leaders charged high dues to pay for their "fat salaries." Eleanor Fowler, the Labor Secretary for the Women's International League for Peace and Freedom, wrote Carey to complain that Carter's broadcasts were "practically an incitement to violence against the Maritime Unions of the Pacific Coast." In his response, Carey assured Fowler that he had "registered a complaint with the Philco Corporation . . . and advised them that I am receiving a considerable number of complaints in regards to the Boake Carter broadcasts." He also told her that he was trying to arrange a meeting with Carter in person.[58]

Carey did try to meet with Boake Carter on several occasions. In November 1936 he wrote Carter a carefully worded letter explaining that he had enjoyed some of Carter's recent broadcasts and that he appreciated Carter's salesmanship of Philco radios. Then he politely warned Carter that because of the controversial nature of his remarks about the maritime unions, a boycott of Philco radios was under consideration: "I have been advised that these unions have adopted resolutions calling for a boycott of the products you advertise." Carey insisted that he would object to such a boycott, but asked Carter to reconsider his views about the salaries of union leaders. Carey offered his own salary of $50 a week as an example of a modest union leader's salary and made the insightful point that "where a union leader receives a high return for his services, he is accused of being selfish, and where he works for comparatively little, he is considered a Communist."[59]

Carey's letter did not have much of an effect on Carter. Carter reinvigorated his attack on the CIO in April 1937, kicking off with the accusation that John L. Lewis was a dictator. After condemning the role of the CIO in sit-down strikes, and lecturing workers for breaking their "agreements," Carter charged Lewis with "cracking down" on the Senate, Ford, the AFL, the Supreme Court, and the workers. His column ended: "Dictator, 1937 model, United States style: John L. Lewis." But how could a mere labor leader become a dictator? For Carter it was as much a question of style as it was a question of absolute power. Carter called Lewis an "amazing man" who had "raised the miners from abject poverty and serfdom to better conditions," but who had, as Carter explained it, "the iron hand of a dictator."[60] A few days later Carter warned that revolution was coming to America and that sit-down strikes amounted to the revolutionary seizure of property.[61] Finally, at the end of April, after a face-to-face meeting with the charismatic labor leader, Carter softened his line on Lewis, proclaiming admiration for the labor leader's humble origins and his "sincere . . . sympathy for the underprivileged." But, he continued, the CIO was "out of control": "If everybody in the CIO were like John L. Lewis, it would be a darned fine movement. But it has got out of control. Lewis told me so himself."[62]

Throughout the spring and summer of 1937 Carter continued his attack on the CIO. He increased the volume of his torpor when, after the Little Steel strike began in May, he repeatedly sided with the steel companies and with steelworkers who crossed the picket lines. He portrayed the CIO workers as vandals, revolutionaries, and thugs. He claimed that the CIO promoted "not better relations between men and management," but rather, "bitterness, dissatisfaction, perpetual strife and social turmoil." He claimed that the CIO was made up of "have-nots" who wanted all the things possessed by the "haves" but who did not think that they should have to work for them. He claimed that the CIO was a racket, not a union.[63] He turned the idea of worker's power and solidarity on its head, suggesting that the union organizers were the real "tyrants" and the ones to blame for the strike.

By mid-July Carter was explaining "Why Lewis Will Lose," accusing American workers of being spoiled ("terribly so"), and recounting the story of a group of children who had opened a fire hydrant in Jersey City and declared a "sit down strike," thus blocking traffic. Their behavior could be excused, Carter reported, because they were simply modeling themselves after their elders: "When grownups go around armed with clubs, lead pipes and baseball bats, when they gang up and inanely destroy factory windows, smash machinery, smear paint on private homes, turn over automobiles, how can we expect to breed respect for law and order or instill a little consideration for other people in the oncoming generation?"[64]

Meanwhile, Carey and the Philco workers had heard enough. Tired of "turning the other ear," in late July 1937, UE Local No. 101 of the Philco plant wrote a series of letters to the editor of the *Philadelphia Evening Ledger,* a newspaper in which Carter's column appeared, as well as to Leon Levy, the station manager of Carter's home station, WCAU, and to Boake Carter himself. In each letter, they explained that their 5,200 members had "voted unanimously to condemn [Carter's] anti-labor radio comments uttered under the sponsorship of the Philco company."[65] The letters declared that Carter's remarks would not "impede the march of American unionism," but that the union movement could not have "respect or friendship" for the *Ledger,* for WCAU, or for Carter if the newscaster's remarks continued. Without directly threatening a boycott, the UE Local demonstrated a keen awareness of the market, suggesting that they were the wrong group of workers — and consumers — to anger: "We feel that the good-will of the laboring people, which you must admit constitutes your biggest potential sales field, is being alienated by . . . continued statements of falsehood about the union movement." They were especially angry that Carter, who had championed "Johnny Q. Public" in his earlier broadcasts and books, was now betraying his working-class listeners (and Philco workers) with his anti-CIO broadcasts.[66]

When addressing Carter directly the members of Local No. 101 showed their understanding of the relationship between production and consumption, demonstrating the connection between their production of Philco radios, Philco's sponsorship of an anti-labor commentator, and the potential effect of this upon sales of Philco radios to a working-class audience. They said they had a "special interest" in Carter's statements because his "expressed opinions have a direct bearing on our job." Carter's false statements, they complained, and "vicious slanders," are "placing Philco products in ill repute with the millions of consumers in the American Federation of Labor and the Committee for Industrial Organization." They demanded that Carter "cease lying" about the CIO on the radio and in print. They concluded by co-opting Philco's own advertising slogan for their own political humor: "We hope that you will neither have to stoop, squat, nor squint to see the logic of this letter; and that you will change your policy before you talk hundreds of us — and yourself — out of jobs."[67]

James Carey also informed the president of Philco, James M. Skinner, that Carter's broadcasts were unacceptable to UE workers — especially those who were manufacturing Philco radios. Carey explained that his concern was material; he tried to alert Skinner to "the growing hostility to the company" as a result of Carter's "recent groundless, red-baiting diatribes against the Committee for Industrial Organization." Carter's attacks could no longer be ignored, Carey explained, because when he and his members "turned the other ear," they "heard only a mounting protest from the millions of consumers who compose the membership both of the American Federation of Labor and the Committee for Industrial Organization." Carey appealed to Skinner's sense of business acumen, explaining that "Carter's nightly preaching against the CIO has been detrimental to our efforts to organize the rest of the radio industry" and that it was in Philco's interest to see the rest of the radio industry organized, thereby eliminating "the unfair competition of low-wage concerns." Carey insisted that he had no desire to see Philco plagued by "stoppages, unauthorized strikes and bad feeling." But he concluded by telling Skinner that he so feared for diminished sales at Philco that he wanted Skinner either to replace Carter, or offer "year-round" guarantees for Philco jobs.[68]

Skinner replied quickly, trying to reassure Carey that Boake Carter's remarks would not lead to a loss of sales at Philco or to the elimination of Philco jobs. Carter, Skinner said, was "Philco's #1 salesman." Skinner insisted that Carter's sympathies were "generally speaking . . . liberal, pro–New Deal and pro-labor." Skinner suggested to Carey that he try and get a personal audience with Carter in order "to get his ear and give him the facts to correct any misinformation he now has." If Carey succeeded in converting Carter "to [his] cause," Skinner continued, then the CIO would receive the kind of "unbiased publicity which could not be bought for money." Skinner maintained that he could not tell Carter what to do, but that he could arrange a meeting. "It is always proper for us to see he gets first hand information on any subject, especially one as vital as the CIO labor movement." He concluded by explaining that Carter was in the hospital with pleurisy, but should soon be available to meet.[69]

Meanwhile, the *Labor Record,* the "official organ" of the CIO got into the fray, publishing a one-page editorial which "lambaste[d] Boake Carter for his anti-labor views." The *Labor Record* took aim at the owners of

WCAU, Ike and Leon Levy, and called for a boycott of Philco products so long as Carter was attacking the CIO. Carter, the paper charged, was guilty of many sins, including "raising red scares, lauding vigilantism, encouraging strike breaking, fawning upon the Tom Girdlers, uttering pious and patriotic platitudes and generally ranting monotonously like a man in a padded cell who thinks they are coming to take his last yacht away from him."[70] Carter did have aristocratic tastes in leisure — he owned a 58-foot sailboat and belonged to the Delaware Yacht Club. He also liked to hunt, paint, and play tennis.[71] And, as the *Labor Record* proclaimed, Carter probably did not expect "Johnny Q. Public" to talk back. "But he is talking back all the time and it won't be long before Boake the Bloke finds it out."[72]

Carter used his column to respond to the *Labor Record*, complaining on 11 August that he did not believe in "constructive" criticism because "all criticism will be hateful to someone." "Small men," declared Carter, "confuse criticism of ideas with criticism of people." He then suggested that leaders recently thrust into a position of power were often thus confused, including leaders of movements based on "mass hysteria," such as "CIOism."[73] These were fighting words, but perhaps it was the CIO's open threat of a Philco boycott that compelled Boake Carter to agree to a second in-person meeting with his arch rival, John L. Lewis. On 17 August Lewis and Carter had lunch, and the encounter seemed to have an impact on Carter — at least for a few weeks.

On 21 August he devoted his entire column to an eloquent tribute to Lewis's character and potential for success. He described Lewis as "a thick-set man, with fast graying hair that tumbles in disarray over his forehead" and "eyebrows, bushy and thick," which were the "barometers of his emotions." He described his eyes as gray, sometimes cold, and always tired. While some, according to Carter, called Lewis "sinister," Carter insisted that he was the opposite — an idealist:

He hates shammers, soft-soapers, the sly patrony of the aristocrat for those not blue-blooded born, the sycophants, and the superficial; but he likes those who are honest in their convictions and are unafraid to take an honest oath unto themselves; those who are not doublecrossers and those in whom spirituality is not dead, for he himself, strangely enough, is deeply spiritual.

Carter apologized for having previously called Lewis a dictator, admitting that Lewis was "a more firm believer in the American system of democratic government than the people who accuse him of wanting to be a dictator." The tone of Carter's tribute was tragic; he suggested that despite his lofty ideals Lewis would be brought down by the immaturity of his young followers (whom Carter referred to as the "young cockatoos" of the labor movement). He lamented the fact that Lewis would never achieve his dream, but celebrated Lewis for having the courage to try: "Were it not for these types the world long ago would have atrophied to nothingness."[74]

With this high praise Carter put John L. Lewis in his pantheon of "big men," seeing him as a tragic hero: well-intentioned, but misguided. For a short while after their meeting, Carter's columns returned to such subjects as Roosevelt's misguided speeches, the poor service on railroad cars, Russian communism, and the problems with the National Labor Relations Board; he did not mention the CIO by name again until the first week of September — during which time a convention of the UE was being held in Philadelphia. On 8 September Carter seemed to applaud Lewis for believing that American labor should "get a better share of the industrial profits," "secure the right to organize," and even get a "Labor Party." But in the same breath he criticized Lewis for delivering a "'call to arms' speech, rather than one which, had it outlined the real aims and objects in the back of his mind and his reasons for so entertaining them," Carter opined, might "win him more friends where he needs them the most."[75] Carter fancied himself an expert in public relations: he saw Lewis taking the CIO in a dangerous direction.

While Carter continued to wrestle with the CIO, trouble was brewing between the broadcast technicians and the Levy brothers at WCAU. The broadcast industry as a whole was experiencing a wave of unionization drives at individual stations, and the broadcast technicians at WCAU were threatening to affiliate with the CIO. As Dennis Mazzacco has argued, during the 1930s the broadcast technicians "attempted to force a largely monopolistic and anti-democratic corporate broadcasting system to grant them a more visible role in the workplace decision making."[76] According to the lead organizer for the technicians, Willard Bliss, WCAU employees wanted a pay-scale which equaled that of CBS technicians in New York, a provision allowing them to honor other broadcast union picket lines, overtime pay in cash (as opposed to compensatory time), and a one-year (as opposed to a two-year) contract. Leon Levy agreed to a 7.5 percent raise, but balked at the other provisions, remarking that he "couldn't understand what . . . had happened in his 'one big happy family'" at WCAU. In mid-October WCAU employees began picketing the station, carrying signs that read "WCAU unfair to organized labor," and by 21 October Levy had obtained an injunction against the picketing.[77]

In essence, by the end of 1937, labor problems were starting to affect the bottom line for WCAU, for Carter, and for Philco Radio. In November 1937 it was rumored that Philco was about to drop Boake Carter as a commentator — or at least get him out of the country. His contract was up for renewal in February 1938 and industry insiders were spreading the rumor that Philco was trying to send Carter on a paid "jaunt" through Europe "until some of the antagonism Carter has aroused among labor and liberal organizations has blown over."[78] Philco managers denied the rumor, but they could not deny that their sales had fallen during the time that CIO leaders were calling for a boycott of Philco radios. Philco historian John Wolkonowicz found that "mounting labor problems and a general business recession caused Philco to register a small loss in 1937."[79] Thus, amid flagging sales and rumors of Carter's departure, Philco prepared for the December celebration of the ten-millionth Philco radio to come off the factory line. In addition, Philco chose this moment to launch their new Model 38–116XX with an ad campaign that was heralded as "the biggest ad budget ever used to promote the sale of a single model."[80]

In a last-ditch effort to appease the CIO, Boake Carter and Leon Levy met with union activists in December 1937. The CIO reported that Carter had agreed to end his attacks on their organization. According to Carter, however, he had simply pledged never to mention the CIO again — for good or for ill:

I reminded those Johnnies of Big Bill Thompson, the former mayor of Chicago. . . . I told them how Big Bill had complained so much of the treatment he got in the newspapers that the Chicago editors decided to stop mentioning him. "I shall never mention labor again," I told those Johnnies. They begged me to reconsider, but I stood firm. I haven't mentioned labor in a broadcast since.[81]

Carter's balderdash was impressive, but it was too late. By the time Carter's contract came up for renewal in 1938, it was public knowledge that he was through at Philco and that General Foods, led by the conservative Colby M. Chester, was going to pick up his contract. The new sponsorship did not deter the CIO, however. In early February the CIO voted to continue their boycott — even if that meant boycotting Carter's new sponsor, General Foods. When Joe Knes, editor of the CIO organ *The People's Press,* proposed to the CIO Council that the boycott be rescinded, delegates from the Newspaper Guild, the UE, and William Leader, president of the CIO council, all voted to continue the boycott against Boake Carter, who they dubbed the "gabber."[82]

The CIO delegates were motivated to continue the boycott in part because General Foods president Colby M. Chester had refused to reply to their 9 December 1937 letter protesting the company's sponsorship of Carter. CIO members were also angry that Leon Levy refused to put in writing his agreement that Carter "would cease slamming the industrial unionists." At the same time, however, in an attempt to placate the CIO, WCAU was trying to promote one of its more liberal commentators, Alan Scott, whose broadcasts had recently helped to win "three-cents-a-day hospital insurance for Philly residents." WCAU boasted that Scott "was free to speak his mind without censorship on any subject."[83]

In the radio age, no one broadcast free of "censorship on any subject." But the Boake Carter case represented a key moment in the struggle to define what "freedom" would mean on American radio in the 1930s and 1940s. While Carter represented himself as a victim of government conspiracy and the closed-mindedness of the union "Johnnies," labor used the Boake Carter case to make its voice heard over the air. Thus, when Carter defined freedom of the air as the freedom to attack the CIO and the New Deal, the CIO defined freedom as the right to use labor's consumer power to hurt the profits and the stature of one of the most powerful broadcasters and one of the most powerful companies in America.

The CIO boycott of Carter did not result in the immediate end of Carter's fame and influence. But it was certainly the beginning of the end. CIO organizers proved that labor could make its impact felt at the point of consumption; the boycott, the drop in sales, the negative attention Carter drew to Philco, and to WCAU, was finally enough to offset what Philco had gained from his popular broadcasts. Carter, for his part, had been broadcasting and writing on the subject of the "freedom of the air" for several years leading up to his firing from Philco. Carter defined this freedom as the freedom to speak without censorship from sponsors, from the government, or from "Mr. Average Man." At the same time, labor defined "freedom of the air" as the right to respond to conservative commentators like Carter. In the late 1930s and 1940s, the CIO began to see radio as a key pressure point in the struggle to build the union movement.

"In a time of war the first casualty is truth." This is the quote for which Carter is most famous. But what were the parameters of "free speech" over the airwaves? In January 1936, during an interview with Postmaster General James A. Farley, Boake Carter began to construct his definition of "freedom of the air." Betraying with every question his own views on the subject, Carter started by asking Farley what he thought of the system of American broadcasting — "and by that I mean our American system of cooperative enterprise as against the European system of strict governmental monopoly control." After identifying the government as one potential threat to the freedom of the air, Carter next posed a question which he might as well have asked his sponsor, Philco: "Do you think a reputable and accredited news commentator . . . should be allowed to be the sole judge of what he shall say and how he shall say it regardless of any policies which private companies might try to dictate to him?" For Carter, the answer was clearly, "Yes." But Carter did not seem to recognize the contradiction implicit in his question. On the one hand, he favored the "system of cooperative enterprise," but at the same time, he was loathe for any of those "cooperative enterprises" to tell him what to do.[84]

One year later, the *Saturday Evening Post* allowed Carter to express his views on radio news. Under the pen name "Richard Sheridan Ames," Carter explained that when a newscast was sponsored by a company that the newscaster was transformed into an advertiser — a representative of the product sponsor: "He is primarily an advertiser, no matter how much he may emphasize public service, and it would be illogical to ask him to put something on the air that would make enemies rather than friends for his product." However, at the same time that Carter acknowledged the selling function of the sponsored broadcast, he called on sponsors to be "fearless." It was easy, he argued, to offend sponsors and listeners, but those offenses did not amount to much when it came to sales. He ended with a warning to sponsors: "Don't sponsor news unless you know what news is and are not too cash conscious to present it fearlessly."[85]

But what commercial sponsor was not cash conscious? Certainly not Philco, nor General Foods. And, while Carter declared that he wanted to be beholden to no one, to "no financial or business interest, no political or social outfit," he was equally conscious of the extent to which he was beholden to his sponsor, and, by extension, to his sponsor's target audience: working-class radio listeners. In his 1937 defense of freedom of speech, *I Talk as I Like,* Carter blamed the typical radio listener, or "Mr. Average Man," for the curtailment of that freedom. The public, he explained, was the "greatest censor in any democracy." When Mr. Average Man took his pen in hand, writing in "wrathy indignation" that he would "not think of buying that firm's products" when viewpoints were expressed by a newscaster contradicting his own, then who could blame the sponsor for coming to the newscaster and saying, "Lay off this or that topic"? The listener, insisted Carter, and not the sponsor, was to blame: "I blame primarily Mr. Average Man. . . . If Mr. Average Man did not shower commercial sponsors in American radio with the intolerance of threats to destroy their business just because he may disagree with a view-point expressed . . . there would be a far more sound, intelligent and keen reporting and discussion of radio news and radio news editing." Carter explained that there were not enough pages in a book "to list the headaches . . . I have battled in the last eight years" from dealing with the intolerance of "Mr. Average Man."[86]

Carter pleaded with sponsors to ignore the angry letters they received from listeners. It was impossible to please everyone, he argued, and listener memories were short:

People love to write and say: "Dear Sir: I wouldn't buy your dishwasher, if it were the last on earth, while you have that loud-mouthed, know-it-all Bill Brown, talking on your program." It gives them a sense of power and a feeling that "Well-I-put-that-bunch-in-their-place-they'll-fix-that-guy's-feet." But unless it is an organized boycott, such sporadic denunciations do not mean the loss of sales, even though sales managers fondly believe they do — at times.

But sponsors knew, and Philco learned the hard way, that angry letters could lead to an organized boycott, and that listener boycotts could affect sales. While listeners had a relatively limited sphere of influence when it came to broadcasting, their letters were carefully considered by radio advertisers. In the age of the sponsor, when the reputation of the sponsor was fused with the content of the program, listeners wielded more power when they made the crucial decision to act: to talk, organize, or boycott as they liked.[87]

When it came to radio, of course, labor advocates were rarely permitted to talk as they liked. As Elizabeth Fones-Wolf has argued, in the late 1930s, "just as union interest in radio was expanding, labor found its access to the air sharply curtailed." The National Association of Broadcasters, who adopted a number of "voluntary" codes throughout the 1930s to stave off government regulation, "adopted a new voluntary code of ethics" in 1939. The code prohibited stations from broadcasting "controversial issues" — which included labor. It also prevented organizations from using radio to invite listeners to become a member of a given organization. And, finally, in a direct blow to labor, member stations of the NAB were prohibited from selling commercial airtime to unions.[88]

The CIO fought these restrictions, explaining to its members that the NAB codes were voluntary and therefore could not be enforced. In 1944 the CIO's Political Action Committee produced a radio handbook designed to teach union locals about their radio rights and the possibilities for using radio to expand the labor movement. Phillip Murray, then leader of the CIO, explained: "It is up to our labor leaders as well as all those interested in 'freedom of the air' to acquaint themselves with their rights to radio time." Radio, Murray insisted, was intended to serve "the best interests of the people." He pointed out that there were fifty-four million people "working in factories and farms in the United States. Naturally they are interested in their own problems." But unionized workers, he explained, had not taken advantage of their "right" to use radio: "Labor has a voice. The people have a right to hear it."

The CIO proposed that working people act as radio monitors. Labor had a right, the CIO explained, to reply to nationwide network programs. Specifically, if a commentator attacked labor, "or the fundamental principles for which labor stands," station managers had to allow labor to reply to such a commentator. "A station which broadcasts one point of view and refuses to broadcast opposing points of view is in a peculiarly vulnerable position." Protests, insisted the CIO, "should be promptly filed and widely published." The CIO Radio Handbook explained that radio stations took "telephone calls, telegrams and letters" very seriously, and that "letters have a tremendous influence on those responsible for continuing a program or dropping it." In other words, the CIO counseled union members to use their voice in a manner in which the radio industry could not ignore. The handbook constantly prodded its readers to consider their rights: "Remember, the air waves belong to the people."[89]

Conclusion

The airwaves did belong to the people, but it was only in rare instances that the people expressed their sense of ownership through the tactic of the boycott. After Philco fired Boake Carter in 1938, another popular commentator came under attack. H. V. Kaltenborn, who had been a widely syndicated newspaper columnist before he became a radio commentator, gained notoriety on the airwaves in 1938 when he provided round-the-clock coverage of the Czechoslovakian crisis. But after his first week on the air as the spokesman for Gold Medal Flour, the sponsor General Mills started to receive angry letters from a bakers' association "composed of Germans or German descendants who did not like the anti-Nazi position taken by Kaltenborn."[90] In addition, the public relations director for General Mills, Henry Adam Bellows, received an angry letter from a Catholic priest who argued that Gold Medal Flour was "tainted" by Kaltenborn's attacks on Spain's dictator, Francisco Franco:

You are not manufacturing lawn mowers or automobiles which go into the garage when the day's usefulness is over. You are manufacturing articles which go into the intimacy of Catholic homes where little children cluster around the breakfast tables. Articles admitted into these sacred surroundings, Mr. Bellows, must come there free from even the slightest taint of suspicion on the thing about which we have been discussing.

The priest hoped that a solution could be found to "obviate" the "loss of Good Will" which would "inevitably follow" if Kaltenborn was not removed or muzzled. General Mills caved in to the pressure. Historian David Clark speculates that the Catholic members of the board at General Mills "forced the decision" to fire Kaltenborn.[91]

General Mills claimed that their decision to fire Kaltenborn was a decision to get out of the business of "violent political emotions" during the war. To everyone's surprise, however, Pure Oil decided to take up that business, picking up Kaltenborn's contract and giving him a raise. Kaltenborn's detractors from his days with General Mills, however, felt energized by his firing, and assumed that their boycott had been effective. According to David Clark, many of those who had written General Mills also wrote angry letters to Pure Oil complaining about Kaltenborn's anti-Nazi and anti-Franco commentaries. At the same time, Kaltenborn was attracting new enemies with his complaints about "slow production rates" upon entering the war. As Elizabeth Fones-Wolf has shown, in 1942 Midwestern union supporters began a boycott of Pure Oil in order to protest Kaltenborn's anti-union stance:

By late spring 1942, Pure Oil dealers were already feeling the impact of the boycott. The local Pure Oil agent in Duluth, Minnesota, asked the company to discontinue the program immediately, and in 1943 the West Virginia agent complained that "business is too damn hard to get at this time to pay somebody to drive business away from you." F. H. Marling, the company's advertising director, advised Kaltenborn that "if this sentiment from our field sales organizations spreads, we will be up against serious trouble."

Pure Oil kept Kaltenborn on the air — despite their dropping oil sales in the Midwest. In a case of conservative ideology triumphing over the bottom line, Pure Oil president Henry May Dawes was confident that Pure Oil stockholders would be willing to take a loss in profits in order to keep

Kaltenborn on the air. Kaltenborn, Dawes explained, "appealed power-fully to all of my personal feelings and instincts."[92]

As the story of Kaltenborn and Pure Oil suggests, the case of Boake Carter versus the CIO was indeed unique. In no other instance in the radio age was a radio commentator brought down by organized labor. But even as an extreme case, the Boake Carter story can teach us lessons about the unintended consequences of radio advertising. In this case, the radio commentator, combined with the radio sponsor, provoked Philco workers to reject not only the commentator but the product he sponsored. It is a fitting, if bizarre irony that in order to attack Carter the Philco workers were forced to boycott their very own product. On the other hand, perhaps it was the ultimate expression of the ownership they felt over their labor: these CIO workers did not want their company to be lining the pockets of the man who would have them sacrifice their union, their job security, and their hard-won working conditions for his personal idea of "democracy." These activists, in this rare and dramatic incident, were not just active. They were radio-active.

CHAPTER FOUR

Washboard Weepers

Women Writers, Women Listeners,
and the Debate over Soap Operas

In 1937 the soap opera author Jane Crusinberry created a rough-and-tumble labor leader character, Rufus Kane, as a romantic rival for one of the main characters on her soap opera, *The Story of Mary Marlin*. NBC executive Sidney Strotz warned Crusinberry that she could not make Kane too similar to a certain real-life labor leader — John L. Lewis of the CIO:

I want to point out to you the danger of you using any situation in the development of your story that might be parallel to any controversy arising because of John L. Lewis's CIO in which any action in your script might be the same situation or the same action occurring in actual life.

Strotz reminded her that such a plot twist could bring government criticism down upon "the National Broadcasting Company, Procter and Gamble, Compton Advertising, or yourself." Moreover, Strotz insisted that Crusinberry send him a synopsis for the story and "keep in mind the dangers as outlined above."[1] NBC executives, perhaps wanting to spare themselves the grief that Philco had experienced when Boake Carter attacked the CIO, were wary of any references to labor and/or labor controversies in their radio programming. In addition to enforcing their own "code" which prohibited any explicit mention of labor issues, NBC policed the content of its shows for endorsements of — or attacks on — labor unions and/or the current system of government.

Soap operas, though dismissed as "washboard weepers" by dozens of male radio critics, were the most financially profitable radio programs of the radio age. They made huge profits for their sponsors, and, in effect, subsidized much of the rest of the programming that was heard on the radio. And though the appearance of a labor leader as a major character on a daytime drama was relatively rare, soap operas were a potent site for conflicts over work: the work of the soap opera writer, the work of the characters depicted in the stories, and, importantly, the work of the soap opera listeners. During the radio age, the punny resonance between the terms "broad" (as slang for "women") and "broadcasting" was more than an uncouth linguistic coincidence. When the broadcast industry targeted its "broadest" audience, the audience it had in mind was aged 25– 34, married with children, unemployed (outside of the home), and female. With the assumption that women did most of the shopping for the postwar family, and that they were within earshot of their home radios during the day, the broadcast industry created a schedule of daytime entertainment — dominated by soap operas — designed to keep women entertained and to keep them shopping.

As a result, the daytime radio programming was structured around women's work. Music shows, household "hint" shows, news, and soap operas — many sponsored by Procter and Gamble, the largest single sponsor of daytime programming — offered housewives an entertainment reward for their hard work. The housewife listened to the radio while she worked in the home and, broadcasters hoped, bought the products advertised on the radio when she left the house to shop. Throughout the 1930s and the 1940s, women's work in the home was inextricably linked to her role as an advertising target. The broadcast industry acknowledged her double duty: her work in the home as well as her work as a consumer.[2]

In a classic cartoon by H. T. Webster an aging gentleman tells his daughter, "When I was a little boy *nobody* owned a radio. There weren't any." Sweetly, with her elbows leaning on the arm of the chair and her chin in her hand, his daughter queries, "But Daddy, how did they sell soap?" Radio did sell soap, and no form of programming sold more soap than the genre that became known as the "soap opera." In fact, one of the biggest controversies over soap operas during the radio age centered on the problem of what to call them. While most radio professionals referred to them as "daytime dramas" or "daytime serials," those who sought to discredit them referred to them as "strip shows" (from the comic strips), "love dramas," "soap operas," "soapers," "cliffhangers," and "washboard weepers." These nicknames contained within them a reference to the radio serials' primary sponsors (soap companies like Proctor and Gamble) as well as a reference to the emotional character of the serial listener ("opera" and "weeper"). The term "washboard weeper" suggested another valence as well: the fact that women listened while they lamented the laundry.

The meaning of the soap opera for its fans has been a much-studied question since the birth of the genre. Paul Lazarsfeld organized one of the earliest studies of the soap opera; his second wife, Herta Herzog, conducted one in 1944.[3] Rudolph Arnheim, who wrote the compelling treatment of the art of sound (*Radio*, 1936), also conducted a study of soap operas for Lazarsfeld, and Lloyd Warner and William Henry studied the listeners of the soap opera *Big Sister* which was published in *Genetic Psychology Monographs*.[4] Since then, an entire field of soap opera studies has emerged, and, as Charlotte Brunsdon has argued, the rise of soap opera studies mirrored the rise of second-wave feminism in the 1970s: "The critical writing about soap opera . . . has been mainly by feminist critics, and so teaching and learning about soap opera also involves thinking about ideas of femininity, feminine pleasure, and feminism."[5]

Radio soaps had plenty of detractors throughout the 1930s and 1940s, including a group of Westchester, New York, housewives who started a series of "I'm Not Listening" campaigns aimed at the genre. Soap operas were singled out because they dominated daytime radio programming and because their target audience, women, was thought to be a highly "suggestible" population. Critics claimed soap operas represented the worst of the broadcast industry's "assembly-line" culture, and that they possessed little educational uplift value. But defenders of soap operas claimed that they offered a comforting distraction from the lonely drudgery of housework. Some defenders even went so far as to argue that soap operas had some redeeming social and cultural value — teaching women how to cope with family problems and/or providing them with an emotional scapegoat for the problems they could not solve.

Meanwhile, as soap operas relieved the boredom of housework, the public controversy around soap operas helped to expose the "hidden" labor performed by women in the capitalist economy: housework and shopping. While Marxist theorists have long debated whether or not this work can be understood as "productive labor," it has been increasingly common to think about consumption as an activity that is closer to work than leisure.[6] Women listened to soap operas while they did their housework, and they bought the products which sponsored their favorite dramas. Hence, the debate over soap operas became a debate over women's work in the home, women's work as consumers, and women's leisure.

Though women were often figured as passive in this debate over the value of the soap opera, that is not how broadcasters and advertisers saw the women who made up their audience. They knew that the secret to the success of an advertising campaign was not a woman's passive reception of the message, but, rather, her active engagement with it. Broadcast professionals believed that consumers needed to be actively engaged in an entertainment program in order for the commercial to do its job. Soap opera sponsors often used premium offers or box-top "sweepstakes" to gauge the size of their listening audience, and to involve the women in a project that linked their favorite radio program with the sponsor's product.

In fact, for a single genre, the soap opera generated an unusual amount of "radio-activity." From the mid-1930s until the mid-1950s about 50 percent of American women were active listeners — attentively listening, writing letters to sponsors, sending in box-tops for premium giveaways, and buying the products advertised. A smaller group of club women actively *opposed* soap operas — organizing meetings to discuss the genre, and, in at least one case, organizing a full-fledged boycott. Doctors, psychologists, radio columnists, sociologists, and audience intellectuals, who were mostly, though not exclusively, male, wrote countless articles, studies, surveys, and editorials — most of which condemned the genre. Finally, there was the radio "activity" of those who produced soap operas: letters, memos, articles, and interviews by network executives, advertising copywriters, and the soap opera authors themselves.

The Debate over Soap Operas

In 1946 there were more than forty, fifteen-minute soaps on the radio, drawing a combined audience of twenty million women and provoking one observer to remark that soap operas were "the most ubiquitous form of mass entertainment ever devised." [7] In 1940 the two networks that produced soap operas, NBC and CBS, made "fully one-third" of all their income from the sale of advertising time on soap operas. [8] In 1945 radio soaps earned $30 million, a sum that represented 66 percent of the total daytime earnings for NBC and CBS and "22 percent of their total revenue." [9] Soap operas were also cheap to produce. The genre was invented in Chicago, where producers did not have to pay New York or Hollywood talent rates, and where actors could be hired for "$2 to $10 an episode." Even after soap opera actors were organized by the American Federation of Radio Artists, raising their salaries to $25.41 a day, annual talent costs for the entire industry were still only $4 million a year — 13 percent of the total income brought in by advertising.

Nonetheless, soap operas were loathed by an articulate and respected minority. Newspaper critics, psychologists, certain active clubwomen, and select radio insiders complained about the effect of the soap opera on the psyche of the average housewife. From the late 1930s until the late 1940s, soap operas occupied the center of a debate over what was the proper form of entertainment for the American housewife, as well as over the commercial nature of radio production. On the one hand, these critics offered a useful critique of the commodity nature of mass culture; on the other, they betrayed a fear of the consuming power of women — and their influence over the form and content of daytime programming.

One of the opening salvos in the war on soap operas came from the six hundred Westchester County clubwomen who attended a forum on "love dramas" in New Rochelle, New York, in November 1939. The women voted unanimously "to urge radio chains to broadcast fewer love dramas," which they described as an "insult to intelligent women." The forum lasted two days and was sponsored by a coalition of forty different Westchester women's groups. Leading the forum was the home econo-mist Ida Bailey Allen; she told the Westchester women that less than 1 hour out of a total of 378 broadcast hours per week was spent on pro-grams about the home. Allen, herself a radio pioneer, hosted a radio show called *The National Radio Home-Maker's Club* in 1934, and she was the author of several popular cookbooks.[10]

The Westchester clubwomen continued their protest of soap operas into the new year. In January 1940 their "urge" to radio stations to reduce the number of serials became an official boycott. They formed a network of "I'm Not Listening" committees, which they hoped would spread across the country. The campaign was hatched at a meeting of the New Rochelle Woman's Club, headed by Mrs. Everett L. Barnard: "We object to the serial romances that are flooding the air in the morning and after-noon. . . . We hope to influence the program sponsors and the broad-casting companies into providing better balanced programs."[11] The boy-cott continued into the spring, when a handful of New York radio executives attended another forum organized by the tenacious club-women. A. L. Simon, publicity director of WHN, told the Westchester women that they rejected serial dramas, in part, because of their relative privilege: "To women not so culturally fortunate as you club ladies, radio is a boon." Meanwhile, Mrs. Everett L. Barnard reported that the "I'm Not Listening" campaign had spread to thirty-nine states.[12]

The *New York Times* paid close attention to the campaign, and so did radio network executives. NBC president Niles Trammell discussed the growing clamor against the soap operas with his advertising colleagues and his coworkers at NBC. John McMillin of the Compton Advertising Agency wrote Trammell with his strategy for how to answer the growing criticism. First, McMillin complained about the attacks: "Daytime radio programs are constantly attacked in the pages of *Variety,* in radio columns, by women's clubs, and by semi-intellectuals in the more literate magazines." Then, he proposed that the network should rebut the attacks with its own version of the "story" of daytime radio — a story which would emphasize the unique qualities of serial dramas. He argued that daytime dramas constituted a new form of culture that radio had invented, and that the serials were "democratic," even the "People's Choice." He insisted that "any form of entertainment which plays such an important part in the lives of so many people must contain many elements of good." Trammell praised McMillan's memo, passed it on to his coworkers, and suggested that NBC and Compton Advertising work together to promote a more positive version of the "story" of daytime radio.[13]

Between 1937 and 1942 seventy-four new dramas were created. The peak, in terms of the total number of serials, came in 1940, when "roughly sixty quarter-hours a day were devoted to serial dramas." In January 1940 serials "consumed 92 per cent of the sponsored hours" from 10:00 a.m. to 6:00 p.m.[14] Meanwhile, the attacks from "semi-intellectuals" in some of the "more literate magazines" kept coming. Merrill Denison, a Canadian playwright of some repute, published his attack on soap operas in *Harper's* magazine in April 1940. Denison concentrated on the industrial nature of the soap opera production. He cited the soap-writing team of Frank and Anne Hummert, who together produced a dozen of the most popular soap operas on the air: "[Their] joint weekly output is the equivalent of two fairly hefty novels or six full-length plays. To produce this mighty deluge of dialogue they have developed a fiction factory in which the assembly-line methods of mass-production industry have been adapted to the manufacture of radio scripts."[15]

The primary thrust of Denison's critique — that the soap operas were too constrained by commercial concerns — was in keeping with the more general critique of radio offered by the consumer movement. Denison was not alone in thinking that entertainment should be determined by more than economic concerns. Ultimately, however, it is possible that Denison felt personally threatened; he was a working playwright competing with a popular form of drama that was driven by women listeners, women writers, and, in some cases, women radio executives. He did wonder, at the conclusion of his article, what would happen if the sophisticated techniques of network radio were applied "to serve political ends" rather than the promotion of "soap, breakfast foods, and toothpaste." But Denison overlooked the fact that the promotion of soap, breakfast foods, and toothpaste had its own, often unintended, political consequences. The Westchester "I'm Not Listening" campaign was one consequence; the increasing numbers of women working in network radio was another.

In the popular press, the majority of screeds against soap operas were written by men. In 1942 the psychologist Louis Berg published two pamphlets that claimed that soap operas were harmful to the mental health of radio listeners. The first was entitled "Preliminary Report: A Study of Certain Radio Programs and Their Effects Upon the Audience, Especially Adolescents and Women at the Climacterium"; the second was called "Radio and Civilian Morale." These pamphlets claimed that mental patients treated by Dr. Berg were often made worse — more depressed, nervous, or morose — by listening to radio soaps. Berg had tested his theory by monitoring his own vital signs while he listened to radio soap operas. The results were alarming:

Dr. Berg reported the following effects: physiological: tachycardia, arrhythmia, increase in blood pressure, profuse perspiration, tremors, vasomotor instability, nocturnal frights, vertigo, and gastrointestinal disturbances; psychological: emotional irritability, malaise, insomnia, phobias, inability to concentrate, emotional instability, and varying degrees of depression.[16]

After conducting the test, Dr. Berg recommended that his female patients who were suffering from depression end their destructive addiction to the soaps.

NBC felt threatened enough by Dr. Berg to appoint a committee of physicians, headed by Dr. Morris Fishbein, to conduct its own psychological study of the effects of soap operas. Not surprisingly, these industry-approved committee members found that the serials were "helpful to listeners." They based their conclusions on the fact that, while soap operas did treat such controversial issues as "love, marriage, divorce, ambition, adoption, illness, parent-child adjustments . . . greed, envy, deceit [and] misappropriation of money," the solutions reached by the characters were "generally accepted as ethical." The committee also suggested that Dr. Berg's method of testing his own blood pressure while listening to the radio was "pseudo-scientific, uncontrolled and worse than useless" for scientific evaluation.[17]

The best rebuttal of Dr. Berg came from Max Wylie, vice-president of Blackett-Sample-Hummert — the advertising agency which produced the Hummerts' gold mine of soap operas[18]. Wylie was also a novelist and a playwright, whose annual compilations of the best radio broadcasts were influential in the field. In the advertising trade periodical *Printers Ink,* Wylie launched a humorous attack on Dr. Berg. He argued that Berg's study should have been called "A Study of Certain Radio Programs and Their Effects on Me" and charged Berg with hypocrisy, revealing that the doctor had written two salacious novels about his experiences as a prison doctor in the 1930s. Berg's 1934 novels, *Prison Doctor* and a sequel, *Prison Nurse,* according to Wylie, were full of the very conventions Berg complained of in the soap operas: "hospitals, mental institutions, jail cells, courtrooms, bedside scenes, death-bed scenes, sanitariums, and laboratories."[19]

Wylie also offered a more serious defense of soap operas in *Harper's* magazine. In that article, Wylie argued that radio soaps tapped into some truths about the miserable lives of most radio listeners: "[Radio soaps] presuppose that the great mass of all mankind — with the women worse off than the men — is cramped and poor and troubled and tired; ungifted, without a future, and insecure; adventuresome, vain, and seeking." The morbid plot twists of the daytime dramas — death, amnesia, affairs, disappearances, murder, long trials, and unwanted pregnancies — either took listeners "into their own problems" or "away from their problems." Thus, Wylie argued, soap operas offered the tired housewife the twin virtues of "participation" and "escape." "Both work," he concluded.

With this simple, two-word sentence, "Both work," Wylie addressed a conundrum that has often plagued modern-day cultural critics. Does mass culture offer some form of constructive political participation, or does it merely offer mindless escape? Wylie solved this problem with the simple proposition that soap operas functioned both as participation *and* escape. The point here is that "activity" rather than "passivity" was the operative mode for the serial listener. She was actively engaged in the story, and, quite often, actively engaged in purchasing the products advertised during her favorite quarter-hour.

Most articles attacking or defending soap operas in the popular press were written by men. However, one of the most ardent female defenders of the soap opera was also one of the most prolific authors of the genre: Irna Phillips. Educated to be a teacher, Phillips started her career in radio as an actress but was told that she had "neither the looks nor the stature to achieve professional success."[20] She *was* lacking in physical stature; at 5'3" she was a petite woman, with brown hair and flashing blue eyes. As a radio writer, however, she quickly achieved a professional stature that no one could have imagined. She began writing a serial for Chicago's WGN in 1930 called *Painted Dreams*. Eventually, she lost the rights to that show and created a new drama for WGN's competition, WMAQ. Entitled *Today's Children*, it featured an immigrant mother similar to her own. Erna Phillips had been born in 1901 (she changed the spelling of her name after consulting a psychic), the tenth child of immigrant parents who ran a small grocery in Chicago. She was a "plain, sickly, silent child" who "lived in a world of books and make-believe." She built a dramatic stage for her dolls out of old cartons, creating an imaginary family that consisted of a mother, a father, and an only child: a beautiful blonde girl with her own bathroom, friends, and ball gowns.[21]

As an adult, Phillips was a hypochondriac. Biographers have speculated that her own daily consultations with doctors might have been the inspiration for her heavy use of hospitals, doctors, and nurses as regular features on her dramas.[22] On the other hand, Phillips also created numerous stories involving marriage, childbirth, and homemaking, even though she herself never married, never carried a child to term, and never went into the kitchen "except to consult the cook."[23] Was she single by choice? She once told a *Time* magazine reporter that she would give it all up "if the right man came along."[24] But her surviving correspondence and interviews do not suggest that she was an unhappy woman. In the 1940s she adopted two children, a boy and a girl, and she had a tight-knit circle of friends in Chicago, as well as a "fiercely devoted house staff."[25]

Throughout her life, in spite of her incredible independence and professional success, Phillips did not identify herself as a feminist. She did, however, support the movement of women into the radio profession. In October 1940, she was the keynote speaker at the Vocational Information Conference for Women Students at Ohio State University. In her speech, Phillips pointed out that 90 percent of daytime programs were written by women, and that these authors made salaries that ranged from $125 to $1,000 a week (Phillips herself made $250,000 a year).[26] She explained that radio had opened the door for women in advertising agencies, mentioning the first woman radio executive at NBC, Bertha Brainard. She ended her talk with a call to the women in the audience to pursue a career in radio: "The market for trained women in radio is unlimited. When you consider that radio is primarily a commercial endeavor and that 90 percent of all purchases advertised on the air are bought by women, it really amounts to women selling to women." Because radio programs and radio products were marketed to women, Phillips argued, radio was a good field for women to enter.[27] For women, radio offered the possibility of an "active" career.

In 1943 Hobe Morrison, the drama critic for *Variety,* wrote a series of scathing attacks on soap operas, in which he attacked Phillips by name. He talked about her "stable" of writers, her high salary, and her stories of "brutal physical situations, divorces, illegitimate births, suggestions of incest and even murders." He complained that the serials were often defended with the argument that "the public wants them." A similar claim, he argued, "might be made for marijuana cigarettes."[28] Phillips was indignant in her letter of reply:

"Recently" you stated, "the current story handles the dubious setup of a spinster who wants to have a baby and is apparently going to adopt the unwanted infant of a young mother." I am a proud spinster who adopted two children in their infancy, and there is nothing dubious about such a set-up.[29]

Phillips insisted that her serials contained no references to incest ("Look up the word . . . Mr. Morrison, and decide for yourself if you have used it correctly"), and wondered what he meant by "brutal physical situations." She insisted that in her fourteen years in radio she had never lost sight of her obligation "to an unseen audience."

In 1944 Phillips was called upon to defend soap operas at the Third Annual Radio Conference, "Programming for the Home of Tomorrow," at Stephens College in Columbia, Missouri. Stephens College, which was one of the first colleges in the country to teach consumer education, was a hotbed of consumer activism. Phillips was scheduled to appear on a panel with the audience intellectual Paul Lazarsfeld and she defended the soap operas against their critics, including "educators," "psychiatrists," and "women's groups":

Do they know that we are bringing back men from overseas battle-fatigued, maimed, and trying to teach their families how to cope with their problems? That we are, through entertainment . . . preparing the American home for what is to come? Do they know the pleas that have been made through daytime radio . . . for plasma, for nurses' aides . . . ?

Phillips explained that she had cooperated with a number of nonprofit and government agencies in the construction of story lines designed to uplift American homemakers; these included the American Legion, the Association for Family Living, the Federal Council of the Churches of Christ in America, the American Medical Association, the American Red

Cross, the National Education Association, the Office of War Information, the Department of Labor, the War Department, the Navy Department, the Children's Bureau, and the Veteran's Administration. "Certainly," she argued, "this method of approaching social problems is more effective than the out and out education programs against which listeners build up a defense with the opening announcement."[30]

Phillips learned the importance of addressing social issues the hard way, when, during the war, she began to get letters complaining about a plot development in her serial *Lonely Women*. In this soap opera, a character named Elizabeth, who worked in a defense plant while her husband was working in Alaska, was accused of putting her defense job before the needs of her children. In one episode, Elizabeth's sister Bertha had just put Elizabeth's children to bed — because Elizabeth was working overtime at the factory. Bertha and her adopted sister, Maggie, complained that Elizabeth was working for the wrong reasons:

BERTHA: I hate to talk about Elizabeth — but you know as well as I do, Maggie — she doesn't have to work. Frank gets a good salary on that Alaska job and he sends home practically his entire pay check every month. After all, he doesn't have anything to spend it on up there.

MAGGIE: I think everything Elizabeth makes she puts on her back. I don't know why Ma ever suggested their living with us. Oh, it's not that I have any objection to have them here. You know I like her, but —

BERTHA: I feel the same way . . .

MAGGIE: Just wait until [Frank] finds out that Elizabeth's never with them — he'll blow his top. I've been reading in the paper — there are innumerable cases of boys like Danny who are being left alone to play in the street or turn into little hoodlums. I think it's fine for unmarried women to have these defense jobs — but when a woman neglects her own children to —

BERTHA: Maggie, I've been meaning to ask you — I don't want to go back to work in that factory. I'd like to get something — you know — something downtown. I don't suppose I have what it takes to be a model.[31]

In this dialogue Bertha and Maggie criticized Elizabeth for working at the war plant. They suggested that she was neglecting her children, and that she used the money she earned for mere adornment. In the odd conclusion to the dialogue, however, Bertha admitted that she used to work in a defense factory, but that she did not want to go back. Instead, she told Maggie that she wanted to work as a clothing model.

It did not take long for one angry listener, a Mrs. Mildred Oldenburg of Bozeman, Montana, to express her opinion of this turn of events to the sponsor of *Lonely Women*. On the same day on which the episode aired, 15 November, Oldenburg fired off a letter to General Mills:

> May one ask whether your script writers are aware of the fact that our country is involved in one of the most desperate struggles of all ages, and it will take the utmost effort on the part of all of us to bring victory to our beloved land? Are we to infer that all women who are spending their days at hard, dirty factory work are impelled purely by selfish motives instead of honest patriotism?

Oldenburg also complained about the character Bertha admitting that she preferred to work as a clothes model rather than in a defense plant. She then asked if General Mills expected to have any listeners with an I.Q. "over the age of 12?"[32]

S. C. Gale, vice-president and director of advertising at General Mills, was quick to respond. He offered the standard explanation, pointing out that some serial characters were bound to be "wholly admirable," while some were not. But he ended his letter with a promise to "discuss your letter immediately with the author." That same day, he wrote the advertising agency director for the show, H. K. "King" Painter of the Hutchinson Advertising Agency, about his and Mrs. Oldenburg's concerns. Gale expressed his concern about how the plot line for Elizabeth's character was developing: "We must under no circumstances do anything which would lead women to believe that work in a war plant is not the maximum patriotic service they can render, nor to give any women the idea that it might be proper for them to quite [*sic*] their families." Gale recognized that this was a tricky contradiction, but he asked Painter to see that the problem of women, war work, and child work was a "vital one."

Painter assured Gale that Irna Phillips had everything under control. He told Gale that he had even gone to the trouble of having one of the *Lonely Women* scripts approved by the Office of War Information, and that the plot line was in keeping with the OWI's directive that women with young children should not be encouraged to leave their children for war work. He quoted the OWI memo on "Home Life": "Women with children under ten years of age are not encouraged by the government to take employment unless the wages are necessary to their families' existence. In such cases, some arrangement must be made to care for children while their mother is at work." He explained to Gale that Phillips was "looking ahead" to the end of the war when women would return to the home. Her story line with Elizabeth, he argued, was meant to anticipate some of the conflicts that would result. Painter then forwarded both

Gale's letter and Mrs. Oldenburg's letter to Carl Wester, who handled the General Mills account, and Wester wrote Phillips, addressing her as "Snooks." He told her that they needed to "be careful" because defense plants were having a hard time retaining trained women workers. "This is one of the biggest jobs that OWI has to keep selling gals on staying with this war work."[33]

Just as these memos were being traded back and forth, Phillips decided to change the name of the serial in question from *Lonely Women* to *Today's Children,* thus reviving the title of one of her first serials. The press release announcing the name change called Irna Phillips a "trail blazer in the day-time radio field" and explained that the new title, *Today's Children* "would more closely fit the conditions following the war."[34] Meanwhile, Phillips wrote several episodes which directly responded to the "factory plot controversy." On 23 November 1943, just four days after the receipt of Mrs. Oldenburg's letter, Irna Phillips allowed the character of Elizabeth Schultz to explain her reasons for working in the defense plant to her German immigrant mother, Mama Schultz:

ELIZABETH: Mom, it may not be much but I feel as if I were doing my bit, helping out with the war . . .

MAMA: I don't feel no way — except a mama's place is with her kinder. Danny and Bess is your responsibility, liebling.

ELIZABETH: All right — but I don't know what we're going to do then. You don't just give up a defense job, Mom. I — I'd feel like a slacker if I sat home — when I know how much they need workers.

MAMA: Danny and Bess need you too, liebling. Ain't there plenty of single girls who can do your job? It don't seem right to me — married women leaving their homes and kids for someone else to look after.

ELIZABETH: But we're fighting a war, Mom. It's up to everyone to help — Look at the Russian women.[35]

With this episode, Phillips answered her fans as well as her producers. She acknowledged the thorny problem of childcare but allowed Elizabeth to show her patriotism, and even allowed Elizabeth to invoke a little international competition with the Russians. Elizabeth, Irna Phillips made clear, was not a "slacker"; she was a patriotic war worker on whose life listeners could model their own.

After the war, one Edward Morrow (likely *the* Edward R. Morrow) wrote an article for *Fortune* magazine summarizing the debate over soap operas. A *Fortune* research associate sent Phillips a working draft of the article, seeking her input. Phillips was rattled by the draft. Her copy of it was filled with questions marks in the margins and the frequent scribble, "Not true." She wrote a long letter to *Fortune* in which she responded to the article's claim that the serials rarely tried anything "new." She included testimonials from numerous social agencies that were pleased with her work, and this information was incorporated into the final draft of the article (Morrow wrote, "Some hanker to do good. Irna Phillips has asked social workers to suggest problems with which she can deal"). But other than this one change, the final version of the *Fortune* article, published in March, was not very different from the one Phillips had seen in January. The article, well written and glib, came down on the side of the anti-daytime-serialists, complaining that the genre was too commercial, too lowbrow, and too maudlin. The article concluded with a portentous nod to television: a description of a television conference in which commercials for laxatives were graphically illustrated.[36]

Phillips was offered a chance to rebut the *Fortune* article in the *Chicago Daily Times* in February 1946 and in *Variety* in the summer of 1947. In her *Variety* article, "In Defense of Daytime Serials," Phillips chided *Fortune* for ignoring the "facts" of daytime serials. Are serials an escape from reality, she asked? "No — this *is* reality — grim, stark reality — not a dream for one and frustration for millions, not a hope chest for two and frustration for millions, not a dole system, if you will, but a legitimate portrayal of American life." Life itself, Phillips argued, was like a serial drama. And storytelling was an art as old "as the history of man." She dared her critics to "escape it if you can."[37] Elizabeth Reeves of Knox Reeves Advertising wrote Phillips to congratulate her on the *Variety* article: "I think most housewives would admit that they secretly believe most of the daytime stories are true to life." Reeves also pointed out that though the networks often belittled the genre, they "haven't figured out anything better."[38]

Indeed, the soap opera made a smooth transition into the age of television, along with Phillips herself. Phillips went on to author many of the most popular soap operas of the television era, including *The Guiding Light, As the World Turns, Another World,* and *Days of Our Lives.* Though she was one of the most successful women pioneers in broadcasting, Phillips never labeled herself a feminist; in fact, she claimed that one of her television characters, Nancy Hughes from *As the World Turns,* was an antidote to Betty Friedan's critique of domesticity in *The Feminine Mystique:* "She [Nancy] finds her happiness within her home and herself, and she believes that this is woman's true function. . . . I believe that "As the World Turns" is successful because millions of women are against the feminine mystique, and Nancy is their spokeswoman."[39] On the other hand, Phillips was headstrong, independent, and tough-minded, creating plots around such social issues as abortion, adoption, and race relations. In 1967, when Phillips wanted to incorporate an interracial relationship into the plot of the soap *Love is Many a Splendored Thing*, the network refused and she quit the show.[40]

Irna Phillips was one of the most "active" defenders of soap operas in both the radio and the television age. She was an avid participant in the debate over soap operas — a debate which exposed the unpaid labor performed by women in the home. This debate also exposed the paid labor of such female soap opera authors as Irna Phillips. In the section that follows, I will turn to the letters of soap opera listeners, and specifically, to letters received by of one of the most popular soap operas of the radio age. I will consider the "work" represented by these letters, written to sponsors, as well as the work of Jane Crusinberry, who wrote *The Story of Mary Marlin*.

Jane Crusinberry and Mary Marlin

In 1935 a young woman named Mary Marlin made the move from Cedar Springs, Iowa, to Washington, D.C., along with her new baby, Davey, and her husband, Senator Joe Marlin. In 1938 Joe was sent on a diplomatic mission to China, but his plane crashed in Siberia. He was not killed, but he did suffer amnesia, and, when he failed to return to the United States, he was presumed dead. His wife, Mary Marlin, became the senator from Iowa in his stead. Of course, the story of Mary Marlin is not a true story. But it was one of the most popular radio soap operas in America, running from 1935 to 1945. The author of *The Story of Mary Marlin*, Jane Crusinberry, grew up near Chicago. At the age of eighteen she received a scholarship to study voice in Europe, but turned it down to marry the sportswriter Jim Crusinberry. They had one daughter and later divorced. Strapped for cash, Jane Crusinberry began writing *The Story of Mary Marlin* in 1934. It was first broadcast in Chicago and became so popular that it soon found a national sponsor: Kleenex.[41]

It is possible that Crusinberry modeled her senator-heroine after a real-life woman senator, Hattie Wyatt Caraway, who was appointed to serve out her husband's senate term when he died in 1931. Hattie Caraway, a Democrat from Arkansas, won her Senate seat outright in 1932, and again in 1938, but lost her third bid for the Senate in 1944. Caraway was only the second woman to serve in the U.S. Senate, and she served fourteen years — one of the longest terms of any woman senator, until Margaret Chase Smith was appointed in 1949 (Smith went on to represent the state of Maine for twenty-four years).

Crusinberry, for her part, would likely have denied any connection between Mary Marlin and real politics. She claimed she was inspired to write *The Story of Mary Marlin* after spending seven years in Europe. When she returned, Crusinberry said, she had a "new appreciation of the opportunities for achievement which have been the heritage of women as well as men in this great Republic. . . . Every girl may have her dreams, too." She named her heroine Mary "because Mary is a symbol of womanhood." She wanted to get Mary into "the world's most exclusive club, the United States Senate." But in order to get Mary into the Senate, she first had to create a husband for Mary, Joe Marlin, place them in a small town in Iowa, and then get Joe elected to the Senate:

He won the election after a stirring campaign in which he pledged himself to Young America and the Great American Dream. Once having him firmly established there, I sent him off on an important mission to China. Unfortunately, on his way across the steppes of Russian the plane crashed and Joe was believed to be dead, though in reality he was a victim of amnesia, the first in a radio serial, I believe. Then the Governor of Iowa appointed Mary to finish Joe's term in the Senate, and there she was . . .

Crusinberry claimed that she never dramatized a "real" Congressional situation, and that she avoided politics in her writing, making the romance of the plot more important than the political intrigue. But she insisted that her listeners liked the fact that Mary was a Senator: "In the last election they were so afraid my villain, Daniel Burke, was going to win that they wrote they would not listen any more if he did."[42]

Why was the soap opera form so popular with women radio listeners? Male critics, like James Thurber, charged that soap operas flattered women and made men appear weak. Harping on the frequent appearance of male characters who were wounded, hospitalized, and in wheelchairs, Thurber argued that the soap opera portrayed "the American male's subordination to the female and his dependence on her great strength of heart and soul."[43] Looking more closely at *The Story of Mary Marlin,* it is possible to see some evidence for this charge. At the height of Mary Marlin's popularity, *Life* magazine published a "photo-shoot" of the soap opera, in which the actors who played the characters on the program "posed" to re-create "scenes" from the show. In one scene, Mary Marlin hovers near a hospital door. Beyond her lies a man in a hospital bed, encased in bandages. She is just about to learn that the man is her long-lost husband, Joe Marlin. Confirming Thurber's thesis, Mary appears strong and upright, whereas Joe is in bed, horizontal, in the background, and bandaged beyond recognition.[44]

The character of Mary Marlin certainly flattered women — so much so that one listener complained that Mary had become a "paragon" and needed some "human attributes." The character who rivaled Mary for Joe's love throughout much of the early years of the program, "Bunny Mitchell," the wife of the Secretary of the Interior, was also a strong woman — one bent on destroying the marriage between Mary and Joe. In one episode, Mary was warned about Bunny's intentions and she confessed her fears to a friend: "I wouldn't say this to anyone in the world but you . . . because I know that you really know Joe and you think a lot of him. It's Joe I'm afraid of . . . because he's weak . . . I know it now . . . He's weak . . . and I'm afraid for him . . ."[45]

On the other hand, even a temptress like Bunny was bound to get her due. In one altercation between Bunny and Joe, Bunny insisted that Joe was like a child. Joe, not listening to a word she said, insisted that Bunny was the one who was childish:

BUNNY: Oh, Joe (*little laugh*) sometimes it's hard to believe you're such an important person — with a chance of being so much more important — I'm so much more worldly wise than you are — You're like a boy now — a darling little boy that I should be comforting . . .

JOE: Sh! Listen to me! You're not worldly wise — you're a child —

BUNNY: You're a little boy trying to believe it —

JOE: A reckless, impulsive child who —

BUNNY: You know a child would never look at you like this —

JOE: Who doesn't realize how dangerous it is to play with fire —

BUNNY: Reckless and impulsive perhaps — but not afraid —

JOE: Bunny — I'm gong to talk very frankly to you —

BUNNY: Oh Joe — don't be so deadly serious — To look at your face one would think the world is coming to an end because one small person — who shouldn't — loves you . . .

JOE: Bunny — You know I'm fond of you — You're lovely and exciting and you know it and you know I know it — . The human mind is a very complex thing — it's susceptible to every suggestion — made by nature or art. You're making me think of you — more than I want to — . It may not be artful on your part — but I suspect that it is — .[46]

This scene was indicative of the mixed messages sent by *The Story of Mary Marlin*. Joe suggested that Bunny was childish, and the scene showed her to be, but Joe admitted, in the end, that he was nearly powerless to resist Bunny's "artful" suggestions. He was susceptible, and she was both "nature" and "art." Women ruled, or, at the very least, they were a force to be resisted.

In Crusinberry's story, women were not only sexually artful — they were also politically savvy. In one scene in which Joe and Mary discuss the marriage of Michael and Henriette, they had a thinly veiled conversation about power and gender:

> JOE: They'll be happy if Henriette understands that Michael will have to be the head of the household — he's that kind of man.
>
> MARY: Michael will consider any of Henriette's opinions — he's that kind of man, too — Joe.
>
> JOE: Well if he does give an issue serious consideration and then decides against her opinion he'll expect her to be reasonable and go along with him — and she'll do it — . Henriette is that kind of woman. . . .
>
> *(Michael enters)*
>
> JOE: Mary's getting to be more political minded every day —
>
> MICHAEL: And she has some surprisingly clear ideas of your problems with the Farm Labor Party, Joe.
>
> MARY: Joe's going to have a fight on his hands with that Labor leader — [47]

In this discussion, Joe fought for the right of the husband to make his wife "go along with him" if he disagreed with her. Mary pointed out that any good husband would consider his wife's opinions. Their friend Michael, ironically, defended Mary against Joe, arguing that she had some "surprisingly clear ideas" about politics.

In these snippets of dialogue, all taken from scripts during the month of August 1937, we can see that some of the charges of soap opera critics were on target: *The Story of Mary Marlin* did show women to be strong and men to be weak. At one point in the story, Mary complained that she wanted Joe to be a "big man" but that he would not take strength from her. Her friend disagreed: "Why — my dear, he's been taking it — for years — always. You are his strength." Thus, even when male characters were portrayed as strong, women like Mary were represented as the "real" strength behind their men.

Crusinberry did not make any claims to feminism with her portrayals of strong women. Her story was always more about romance than politics. But sometimes her female characters sounded very nearly like radicals. In one scene between Bunny and her husband, Frazer, Bunny accused her husband of spying on her: "I'm not a slave — . I have the right to do as I want to do — and I take that right as I always have and I always will." Frazer Mitchell is taken aback by her "belligerent" attitude: "Being the wife of the Secretary of the Interior is not slavery — surely — ? I have not put you in chains — I have no rings in your nose or your toes — have I?" Bunny's reply suggested that Frazer might be the one with the belligerent attitude: "Frazer — You frighten me!" The housewife listening to this dialogue knew, of course, that Frazer had a right to be suspicious of his wife; Bunny was trying to have an affair with his best friend. Even so, the dialogue suggested the very real possibility that a woman could become dissatisfied with traditional marriage roles.

Ironically, Crusinberry was not as successful as her feisty female leads in dealing with the men with whom she did business. Ellen Seiter has argued that Crusinberry was less savvy than writers like Irna Phillips when it came to making sponsors and advertisers respect her creative control.[48] Correspondence between Crusinberry and Procter and Gamble, for example, reveals the extent to which Crusinberry failed to protect her intellectual property. In the mid-1940s, when rumors abounded that *The Story of Mary Marlin* might be canceled, Crusinberry wrote Procter and Gamble to complain that she resented having to make material from her show available to listeners. She did not want her work to be duplicated without her knowledge, and she wanted Procter and Gamble to tell listeners that the work was copyrighted and therefore not available for distribution. "Bill," writing on behalf of Procter and Gamble, tried to make Crusinberry understand the commercial implications of her refusal:

It is felt that their reaction on receiving such a reply would be something like this: "If the material is copyrighted, how can Procter and Gamble broadcast it on the air? Procter and Gamble must own the copyright and like all big business they don't think enough about people like me to go to the trouble of filling my request." When this happens these . . . women . . . tell their friends how thoughtless and unpleasant Procter and Gamble is — then one of the friends who has some other little grievance works up the story and passes it along to her circle of friends. Before very long Procter and Gamble has lost considerable good will among quite a group of people.

In this scenario, broadcasters imagined disgruntled listeners to be all-powerful, and as a result, Crusinberry could not protect her intellectual property. Her rights had to be sacrificed in order to preserve the "good-will" of the sponsor.

Procter and Gamble also complained that Crusinberry used "profanity" in her scripts, a practice they said was strictly prohibited. The company warned her that use of the words God, Christ, Jesus, Lord, devil, damn, or hell "in any sense which can be construed as profane, a curse, expletive or exclamation of anger, irritation or surprise" violated its editorial policy. Procter and Gamble was vulnerable to the offended listener, the company explained, because its products were sold to virtually every class of housewife in America:

> Our products are in over 90% of the homes of the country. . . . Every housewife who is offended or disturbed by an advertisement for . . . Ivory Soap does not simply represent the loss of an Ivory Soap consumer: it may very likely represent the loss of a consumer of several other products — P and G Naphtha, Chipso, Oxydol, Teel, Drene, Crisco, Duz, Camay or one of the others. So . . . we have to lean over backwards to avoid doing anything which will harm goodwill toward our Company where it may exist in every home.[49]

Here again, Crusinberry was being asked to keep the "goodwill" of Procter and Gamble in mind as she composed her scripts. Crusinberry, while a creative artist, was forced to subject her creative license to the selling aims of her sponsor. Ironically, Procter and Gamble argued that it was their very success — their products were in 90 percent of American homes — that made the company more "vulnerable" to the loss of goodwill.

The many representatives of the Compton Advertising Agency, which produced *The Story of Mary Marlin* for Procter and Gamble, often mediated between Crusinberry and the company. It was 1937 when Crusinberry began to get herself into trouble with her producers, her advertisers, and, finally, with the NBC executives who monitored the broadcast of her program. She had created a character named Rufus Kane — a man with flaming red hair who was described as a "human dynamo."[50] Kane was also a charismatic labor leader who brought trouble into the marriage of Mary and Joe: "When Joe learned that Rufus Kane — the new labor leader — a magnetic personage who is looming into power — would be at the Worthingtons' he flatly refused to give up the party and when Mary still refused to go he said he would go without her."[51]

NBC warned Crusinberry that Rufus Kane was too much like John. L. Lewis, but Crusinberry politely insisted that her only intention was for Rufus Kane to be "a strong potential rival for Joe a few weeks before he's out of the Washington plot." She claimed that she had no intention of going any further into politics because she "knew altogether too little about them." She was sure that the character of Rufus Kane would not offend the government because he was nothing like John L. Lewis:

He's much younger — handsomer (ahem) and fascinatin' *[sic]* and there will be no situation or action parallel to anything which occurs in real life. I'm just preparing an interesting romantic situation for Mary — when she goes back to Washington — at the next session.

However, despite Crusinberry's protests, she did seem to have some sense of the history of Midwest populist politics. Rufus Kane was not only a labor leader, he was the emerging leader of a new farm and labor political party. As Joe explained to Mary, he was interested in meeting Rufus Kane at the Worthingtons' dinner because Kane was a political rival: "The next step will be a new third party. A farmer and labor party which will ultimately try to make Rufus Kane the chief executive of these United States." This was exactly the kind of political suggestion NBC did not want Crusinberry to make. NBC's Sidney Strotz did not want *The Story of Mary Marlin* listeners to be influenced by the suggestion that a charismatic labor leader could become the president.

One year later, Compton Advertising was still meddling with Crusinberry's scripts over the issue of political references. This time, the controversy was again related to labor, and it resulted from a script in which Rufus Kane's mother, reminiscing about the past, recalled that "she and her mother used to have so much fun being in fights with miners." "John," from the Compton Advertising Agency, urged Crusinberry to delete this reference, for fear that the statement revealed a prejudice against miners. But it is clear from his letter to Crusinberry that the real issue was simply that the agency did not want *The Story of Mary Marlin* to have anything to do with labor:

Anyone who is searching for a causus belli, either for or against you and us, there is in the words "fights with miners" an implication of prejudice, however much you might deny this by saying that Mrs. Kane and her mother fought *for* the miners. . . . Each one of us dealing with public statements must remember that we are held responsible for the effect of a statement, rather than its intention. . . . We feel that you must protect yourself by completely eliminating any reference to any controversial or contentious nationally-legislated labor problem.[52]

Compton Advertising's reaction was defensive — John did not want Crusinberry to be vulnerable to the charge that she was against miners.

But his letter revealed a deeper, more insidious level of censorship: labor matters were not to be addressed in *The Story of Mary Marlin,* whether Crusinberry was for or against labor's struggle. John described the relations between miners and their employers as "strained and tragically belligerent." He did not want Crusinberry's radio show to have anything to do with them.

Crusinberry, for her part, did not relinquish her Rufus Kane plot line to please her producers and sponsors. As the election of 1940 approached and Roosevelt was feeling the heat from John L. Lewis — who was so disappointed in Roosevelt that he decided to back Wendell Willkie — Crusinberry made plans for her character Frazier Mitchell to run for President against Rufus Kane. NBC demanded that Crusinberry's soap opera election lag six months behind the national election, to avoid that "on the same Tuesday that our Mr. Willkie will be elected to the White House, that Rufus Kane is not elected." NBC also demanded that the Mitchell and Kane presidential campaigns not discuss any actual campaign issues, such as labor or war, and that the radio winner not be represented in the act of signing any bill or passing any law. Finally, NBC demanded that Crusinberry refrain from making either of her candidates either a "Democrat" or a "Republican." Not only were these demands arrogant; they were also evidence that NBC was trying to prevent Crusinberry from making her political plot lines even remotely realistic. Would not a fictional election near the time of the actual election raise interest in the show? And how could Crusinberry write a convincing political story line for an American audience without any reference to Democrats, Republicans, labor, war, bills, and/or laws? In the end, Gilbert Ralston at Compton asked Crusinberry to communicate with him via "airmail" so that he might "pin NBC down definitely on their policy."

Rufus Kane did become the president of the United States on *The Story of Mary Marlin,* and Roosevelt, of course — not Wendell Willkie — became president in the real world. Crusinberry fought for, and maintained, as much creative control as she could wrest from her meddling sponsors. At the same time, if Crusinberry's fan mail was any indication of listener loyalty to her show, it is hard to understand what the sponsors were worried about. *The Story of Mary Marlin* fans wrote hundreds of letters to NBC and Procter and Gamble — not only to express their appreciation for the show but also to praise the products that sponsored the program.

Like the fans of Mary Marlin in the radio drama, soap opera fans were uniquely dedicated letter writers. As the radio critic Charles Siepmann has observed, soap listeners were "addicts of an almost morbid character." He chastised listeners, who seemed to think that daytime drama characters were real — as in the case of a woman who knit a sweater for the fictional baby of her favorite heroine. In another case, a listener wrote Crusinberry to explain that she wanted to visit Mary Marlin's home in Alexandria, Virginia.[53] With listeners like this in mind, the audience intellectuals Hadley Cantril and Gordon W. Allport accused fan-mail writers of being "neurotic":

Many letters come from neurotics who tell the broadcasters their troubles. . . . In spite of its impressive volume, this audience mail is sent by the isolated, unorganized listeners composing only a small fraction of the total listening population. . . . The individual listener writes a letter, not because he thinks others are doing so, but because it is a sure and immediate way for him to resolve some tension the program has created. . . . Writing and mailing a letter of praise or protest achieves a rapid emotional "closure."[54]

The fan mail written by *The Story of Mary Marlin* listeners, however, contradicted the contention that listeners were "isolated" and "unorganized." Letter writers often wrote on behalf of others and expressed their belief that their letters made up only a small fraction of the many letters that would be received on a particular topic. More importantly, listeners wrote with a keen sense that their letters were more likely to be heeded if they mentioned the Procter and Gamble products that they regularly purchased. While some of the letters suggested loneliness on the part of the writer, most letters were composed with the awareness that fan mail was carefully monitored by product sponsors.

As Elena Razlogova has shown, fan mail during the early days of radio constituted the only information show producers had about how their programs were being received. Razlogova demonstrates that as radio became more corporate broadcasters continued to rely on fan mail as an important source of information about program reception.[55] Cultural critics like Theodor Adorno were also interested in the meaning of radio fan mail. He wondered: "First, are the letter-writers representative of the majority of non-writers? Second, are they neurotic? Third, has their neurosis a social meaning?"[56]

While most listeners were not neurotic, their letters reveal a great deal about the social meaning of radio soap operas. In the case of *The Story of Mary Marlin*, listener letters reveal five important truths about their relationship to the show: (1) listeners believed that flattering the sponsor would make their letters more persuasive; (2) listeners believed that threatening to boycott the sponsor's products would make their letters more effective; (3) listeners were not isolated; rather, they were conscious of, and usually referenced, their own listening community; (4) listening was bound up with patterns of housework and with the waged labor of listeners; (5) listeners identified with the creativity of Jane Crusinberry and used their letters to express their own professional and creative ambitions. These letters reveal a great deal about the social and cultural meanings of "women's work" in the 1930s and 1940s — the work of shopping, the work of patronizing the sponsor's products, the work of homemaking, and women's work outside of the home.

Of the hundreds of listeners letters in the Jane Crusinberry collection, nearly every one contains a reference to a particular sponsored product. The show had several sponsors during its ten-year run — most notably Kleenex and Procter and Gamble — and most of the letters praised Kleenex or Ivory Soap, expressing some form of gratitude that these products made *Mary Marlin* "free" to radio listeners. One listener claimed she would use "sand paper" if Mary Marlin advertised it. In a similar vein, another listener claimed that she would buy Kleenex "regardless of quality" because she loved the story so much. These letters indicate that listeners knew full well who was "paying" for the programming, and that they saw their patronage of the sponsor as part of their "contribution" to the show.[57]

Listeners usually mentioned products in a deliberate way. Many of their letters contained requests, complaints, or suggestions of some kind — in the hope that their recognition of the sponsor would give their letter more attention. Isabel Long, for example, wrote Crusinberry to request that the cast members who played certain characters not be changed. Cast changes were frequent in the radio world, leaving listeners to cope with "new voices" in the guise of old, familiar characters. At the end of her letter, Isabel Long made sure that Crusinberry knew the request was coming from a loyal consumer of Procter and Gamble products: "Please tell Procter and Gamble I use five or six of their items just because I want them, and the rest just to support your story."[58] Another listener, Anne V. Howard, upset by a casting change, begged Procter and Gamble to *"Please, please get us back the other Mary."* Then, after praising the remaining actors, she explained her preference for Ivory Soap:

I suppose whether I use Ivory Soap or Flakes is more important to you than the above. I use loads of Ivory Soap for I have two small children, one a baby, and I'm glad you're not making any changes in it. The Flakes are too expensive, for bits of Ivory Soap in a jar of water works as well as Flakes or Snow.

Howard knew what the sponsors wanted to hear. She hoped that if she provided consumer feedback, then perhaps they would honor her request for the return of the actress who had played Mary.[59]

In the spring of 1941 it was rumored that *The Story of Mary Marlin* was going to be canceled. Many listeners wrote in to express their outrage, but also to make the sponsor understand how much Mary Marlin meant to them. A Mr. and Mrs. Swearingen told Procter and Gamble that they had "just read where *The Story of Mary Marlin* is leaving the air." They speculated that if the cancellation were announced over the air, that Procter and Gamble would likely "receive a lot of letters in protest." They ended their letter with a plea to keep *Mary Marlin* on the air, and then they added a postscript: "Yes, we use Ivory Soap and Ivory Flakes." The Swearingens knew that their request to keep the show on the air would be more persuasive if they revealed themselves to be loyal customers. Their use of the word "yes" in the postscript hints at the "silent question" they imagined the sponsor to be asking: "Why should we care what you think?" "Because we use your product," was the answer implicit in the Swearingens' reply.[60]

While many *Mary Marlin* fans praised the product sponsor, other listeners threatened to take action if their requests were not granted. Sometimes an irritating plot twist was enough to elicit a threat to boycott the sponsor: "If Mary goes back to that worthless Joe I will never use Kleenex again."[61] Another listener had the opposite reaction to the same story line: "The day Sally marries Joe [I] will stop listening to [the] program and using Kleenex." Kleenex probably did not take these threats very seriously — it would have been impossible to satisfy every listener with every plot. But other complaints were more likely to make the sponsor take notice, such as this letter from Mrs. M. A. MacArthur:

Today, at the end of Mary Marlin, we were told that said program would not again appear on the air. I have followed Joe Marlin through the Steppes of Russia and Oswald to the gates of heaven. . . . I have never missed a day listening to it. . . . You simply can't do this to me. It's sabotage, that's what it is. . . . If the Ivory soap people are selling so much soap that they think they can get along without this program then I can get along without Ivory Soap. And will.

Mrs. MacArthur, who felt that canceling *Mary Marlin* was tantamount to "sabotage," was probably relieved when *Mary Marlin* continued. Her letter was stamped "HANDLED." Was Mrs. MacArthur's letter the one that finally convinced Procter and Gamble to keep *Mary Marlin* on the air?[62]

Occasionally, listeners complained about the advertising itself. Sometimes the remarks were simple, like "too much advertising," or "more story — less advertising."[63] Other listeners, like E. G. Bower, for example, were more explicit: "Use both Kleenex and Quest. Could we hear less about them on radio? Too much talk influences me against rather than for a product."[64] Still others explained that even though they liked the products advertised, they didn't like the advertising: "In spite of the fact we use Kleenex and Quest we resent the excessive advertising."[65] All of these responses, when combined with the many positive remarks listeners made about the products, suggest that listeners had a common-sense understanding of the economics of radio advertising. They knew that if they bought the products that were advertised, they were, in a sense, "paying" for the programming. As Mrs. A. F. Kendell wrote: "Program like the product is satisfying and never disappoints. Hope sales keep program on air."[66] Listeners also knew that if they threatened *not* to buy the product, their letters would also gain attention — and maybe even action.

Listeners also knew that it was important for them to represent themselves as speaking for a group larger than themselves. Their letters — often referencing family members, neighbors, and community listening groups — sought to demonstrate that they were not alone in their opinions, whether they were offering praise or complaint. One listener, concerned about the rumor that *Mary Marlin* would be canceled, hoped that Procter and Gamble would not "scoff" at her letter: "I could tell you of at least twenty of my neighbors and friends, including an invalid, and a lady almost deaf, whose only pleasure in life seems to be your daytime programs."[67] Listeners wrote with the authority of community leaders. Marilyn Hoffman, for example, complained when one of the two daily *Mary Marlin* broadcasts was about to be discontinued. She wrote that "she could just weep with indignation": "This letter is not only expressing my personal opinion, but the very definite opinion of numerous friends and listeners who have been just as faithful to 'Ivory' and 'Mary Marlin' . . . as I have . . . and I'll wager a few more thousand young housewives."[68] She ended with a plea for consideration: "We earnestly hope that you will consider our opinions." Marilyn Hoffman, in writing for her entire neighborhood, hoped fervently that her request would be heeded.

In some cases, entire groups of women wrote letters to the product sponsor. In New Haven, Connecticut, for example, a group of sixteen women signed a letter explaining that the signal from radio station WELI was drowning out the signal of WABC — the station which carried *Mary Marlin*. The sponsor at the time, Kleenex, recorded an additional twenty-four letters — all complaining about the same problem.[69] Not all group letters were positive, however. In 1942 the Sewing Club of Terre Haute, Indiana, wondered if Jane Crusinberry was sick or on vacation:

This morning as forty women worked over Red Cross sewing we listened to your program of *Mary Marlin* and it was voted the poorest program on the air. . . . This has been going on for weeks and each day it has been getting worse. . . . Surely Procter and Gamble with all its millions could find a better story to run. This is war time and we have to save ELECTRICITY.

Procter and Gamble used this letter, with its touches of caustic humor, to urge Crusinberry to alter the plot: "A COPY FOR JANE. P.S. WE ARE ALL TIRED OF THE TRIAL." One of the most powerful images in the letter from the Sewing Club was that of "forty women work[ing] over Red Cross sewing" while they listened to the radio. Radio listening was intimately bound up in women's work, and the letters to Procter and Gamble reveal the diversity of women's work lives in this period — as well as the drudgery.

Of the hundreds of letters received by Crusinberry and her sponsors, at least a third made some request that the broadcast time of *Mary Marlin* be changed in order to accommodate the listener's work habits — both inside and outside the home. One writer was upset because the program time was being changed from the morning — when most women did their household chores — to the afternoon. "Everyone knows that the American housewife spends her mornings at home doing the household chores. This affords excellent opportunity for listening in on our favorite programs while we work. And — everyone knows that *very few* healthy people spend their afternoons at home."[70] Another writer was also upset about the afternoon broadcast, complaining that her "children and husband" were "swarming all over [the] house" at that time.[71] Yet another complaint about the time of the broadcast made a distinction between city and country housewives: "Is [the] story for city people only? Dinner has to be on the table at that time and men do not want to listen to it."[72] This "country woman," as she signed her letter, not only had her chores to worry about, but also the resentment of her husband.

An even greater number of requests came from women who had to work during the day and could no longer listen to *Mary Marlin*. Mayme Maillet wrote to say that she had "enjoyed the program while unemployed. Working now. Can it be broadcast in evening?"[73] A listener from Tacoma wanted the program to be broadcast "1.5 hours earlier so working girls and school girls can listen."[74] One listener liked the program so much she knew she would be "disappointed if [she] got a job and could not hear it."[75] Theresa Lepich, an unmarried listener, asked for a copy of the script because she had "started to work a month ago" and could no longer listen to *Mary Marlin* at home.[76] Some listeners, of course, had no work at all during the Depression. Mrs. Mary Buechele wrote to say that she was very poor because her husband was out of work and that her only enjoyment was "listening to Mary Marlin."[77] Another listener, who was concerned that *Mary Marlin* was going to be canceled, asked the sponsor not to "take away this great pleasure that the poor man's wife as well as the rich man's wife may enjoy."[78] Radio had a special meaning for working-class listeners — especially those who could not afford other forms of entertainment.

Crusinberry recognized that an increasing number of her listeners were starting to work during the day — especially during the war. She suggested to Bill Ramsey at Procter and Gamble that a new audience had been created because of the war, and that this audience was being neglected. "There are millions of people who are winding up their day between midnight and two a.m. who are seeking recreation at those hours." She proposed that *Mary Marlin* be rebroadcast after midnight to take advantage of this new audience: "I believe that the first radio show that does this is going to make a hit, not only with the war workers but will benefit from the publicity attained by it. I'd like to hear what you think about this."[79]

Ramsey dismissed Crusinberry's suggestion with the argument that "this audience is still so new that no one has found a way of measuring it or figuring out what it would cost." Ramsey was not willing to take a risk on this new audience because it had not been properly "measured." Ramsey claimed that "great corporations like ours can't very well afford to jump into something blindly on the chance . . . it will pay out from a business standpoint." Of course, Procter and Gamble was exactly the kind of company that could have taken such a risk; and, as Crusinberry pointed out, movie theaters and bowling alleys that were staying open late to accommodate war workers were already profiting from the "new audience" created by the war.

Though Crusinberry was rarely successful in convincing her sponsors to take risks with her program, the ten-year run of *Mary Marlin* inspired many of her listeners to pursue creative endeavors of their own. Many listeners described the projects they were working on in the hope that Crusinberry could help them in their efforts. One listener even requested money: Mrs. A. C. Bowersox asked that since "Mary Marlin has done so much for others," could she give her a loan of $110 for a hotel training course?[80] Other letters were less demanding; one listener claimed she had lived a "very interesting and perplexing life" and would sell her story to

Crusinberry if she thought it would be useful for the show.[81] Another listener wrote to say that she had written a song and a poem that she wanted to submit to the program.[82] Still another listener, thinking like an advertiser, suggested that Crusinberry name the "new yacht" in the program after one of the sponsor's products: "Why not name the new yacht *The Quest?*"[83] Another listener wrote in to say that she had crocheted the words "Mary Marlin" into a bed quilt and was now at work on a tablecloth.[84]

In their creative enterprises listeners showed that they identified with Crusinberry and with Mary Marlin as role models for their own lives. One listener claimed that though she was not ordinarily a "fan writer," she wanted Crusinberry to know how much she appreciated the show. She also wrote that she was "off to play the part of an old maid in a one act play called 'You can never trust a man.'" She added, "Ha, ha, ever heard of it?" Likewise, another listener wrote to tell Crusinberry that she, too, was a playwright and had written a little pageant, "very little, I assure you," that was based on the "dream of the condemned man" that she heard on *Mary Marlin*. For many of these listeners, Crusinberry represented the successful, worldly, woman author whom they could only dream of becoming.

Conclusion

In the radio age, soap operas helped to produce a unique dialectic between advertising and activism. Soap operas, like the conservative commentary of Boake Carter, activated listener boycotts organized by influential clubwomen in New York. For most listeners, however, the advertisements heard over the air achieved their goal: they sold soap. At the same time, broadcasters treated women as active consumers of products and active listeners of soap operas. Broadcasters knew that a woman who knit a sweater for her favorite heroine's fictional new baby would be more likely to buy the soap advertised during the commercial break. Broadcasters also knew that consumption was an active rather than a passive process, and that to get women to buy, women needed to be motivated, stimulated, and engaged. While soap operas might have eased the housewife's workload, they also served to engage her attention, and, perhaps, a collective unconscious.

Radio activity was not always negative. In the case of Irna Phillips, for example, radio activity consisted of defending the daytime serial. In the case of *Mary Marlin* fans, some listeners wrote to complain, but most listeners wrote in order to urge the sponsor to preserve the show, or to change its time slot. And, while audience intellectuals saw soap opera fans as "neurotic" and "isolated," the fan letters written by *Mary Marlin* fans suggest that soap opera listeners were savvy about the economics of radio, organized into informal listening groups, and interested in pursuing the kind of "radio activity" which Jane Crusinberry had the privilege of enjoying: radio writing.

Women may have even found new social power in their enjoyment of the soap opera. While Michael Denning and Janice Winship have argued that female individuality has been constructed through the act of consumption (hence the frequent rhetoric of emancipation in advertising: "You've Come A Long Way, Baby,"), consumption is also a realm in which women's collective identity has been formed. It is as consumers that women have organized into various kinds of leagues, clubs, and consumer watchdog organizations. Upper-middle-class clubwomen, under the guise of wanting more radio programming geared toward home economics, protested the glut of soap operas. At the same time, soap opera listeners wrote letters individually — and collectively — arguing that their right to comment on sponsors' programs derived from their consumption of the sponsors' products.[85] Their power to act, their "radio activity," derived from their status as the consumers who mattered the most to radio sponsors.

CHAPTER FIVE

"I Won't Buy You Anything But Love, Baby"

NBC, Donald Montgomery,
and the Postwar Consumer Revolt

Yolanda Mero-Irion. This "radio-activist" had an unusual name, and, from the point of view of the broadcast industry, she also had the annoying habit of launching frequent attacks on radio — especially on soap operas and radio advertising. But she did not act alone. Rather, she was one of the representatives of the Women's National Radio Committee, an association of women's clubs that was similar to the General Federation of Women's Clubs. These were middle-class organizations, and their members had the zeal, as well as the decorum, of middle-class reformers. As Yolanda Mero-Irion explained in 1935, women were interested in the reform of radio because radio invaded women's territory: the home. Accordingly, they vowed to treat radio as they would any door-to-door salesman:

The general attitude toward radio advertising may be expressed in the following terms: Women consider that radio offers an opportunity to the manufacturer to visit every potential buyer's home in person. Having thus obtained entrée, his deportment and methods of salesmanship will determine whether he will create good-will or antagonism.[1]

NBC executive John Royal considered Yolanda Mero-Irion a nuisance. When he replaced Sidney Strotz as vice-president in charge of programs at NBC, Strotz warned him that "Mrs. Irion is one of the problems you are going to face."[2] Still, executives like Royal also worked hard to curry the favor of Mrs. Irion and her ilk. NBC's attention to such women paid off in favorable reviews: in 1936, the WNRC awarded NBC programs three out of four first places and nine out of fourteen runner-up mentions in its annual report. The radio critic Peter Morell was aghast: "Can there possibly be so many foolish women in America? Surely in order to vote awards for radio programs they must listen to the radio and must be aware of the often fraudulent and hazardous nostrums for which these programs are used as lures."[3]

In fact, the Women's National Radio Committee was aware of the "fraudulent and hazardous nostrums" that sponsored radio programming. In 1940 the executive secretary of the WNRC, Ruth Rich, wrote Niles Trammell, another NBC executive, an angry letter about the broadcaster's willingness to allow laxative manufacturers to sponsor radio programs. Her complaint was based not simply on a matter of taste, she explained — the WNRC was also worried about the health risks:

When this Committee expressed its disapproval of such advertising five years ago, it was by no means motivated entirely by the aesthetic premise that a discussion of laxatives is not accepted dinner table conversation. A far more important incentive was the fact that in its membership are representatives of the medical and allied professions, who are convinced that much of this advertising is definitely dangerous to health.[4]

Trammell passed Rich's letter on to his colleague Edgar Kobak, advising him to confer with the two NBC executives who dealt most frequently with women's organizations — Janet MacRorie and Margaret Cuthbert. Trammell, not wanting to deal with Ruth Rich himself, asked Kobak to "prepare an answer for my signature."[5]

One month later, the WNRC sent NBC a copy of its "Daytime Serial Survey." This survey, compiled from questionnaires sent to the group's twenty-four member organizations, found that WNRC members preferred daytime serial stories with "people like ourselves" rather than "fantastic happenings" and "highly fictitious characters." Members also criticized radio advertising:

In general, it was approved — in some instances even highly approved. Adverse criticism focused on the amount rather than the nature of the "Commercial." "Too prominent," "too many minutes devoted to it," "exaggerated," "chop up the program," are occasional comments. In only 2% of the cases did the listeners consider the advertising matter offensive.[6]

The WNRC got their licks in, but on the whole it was a pretty tame organization. NBC was more intimidated by the Westchester County Federation of Women, for example, when that organization resolved to launch an "I'm Not Listening" campaign for the improvement of radio. Royal and his staff paid far more attention to this threat than they did to the frequent newsletters and award-dinner invitations (many of which were refused) that NBC received from the WNRC.[7]

Margaret Cuthbert, one of the highest ranking women at NBC, often pleaded with her colleagues to work more cooperatively with women's groups such as the WNRC. In one memo, she argued that women were "more practical than men" and "could become a vast army working for us." She urged John Royal not to "antagonize" the WNRC, but to "take them in our stride." Cuthbert was frequently sent to WNRC award banquets in the place of her superiors, and she knew that these "radio active" women were tired of being slighted. As she explained in another memo, "Sending me to represent N.B.C. at the Award Luncheon . . . is just the kind of insult that will completely frustrate the Women's National Radio Committee."[8]

Another woman executive at NBC, known for her censoring blue pencil, was Janet MacRorie. She, too, urged NBC to be cautious about accepting advertising for packaged medicines because of the anti-packaged-medicine stance of the consumer movement. She acknowledged that groups like Consumers' Research and Consumers Union were "in the main rackets," but also that their claims were "readily accepted" by "many intelligent persons." "We are informed," she wrote, "that libraries having several copies of books blasting advertising are unable to supply the demand for them." She referred to Peter Morell's book *Poisons, Potions, and Profits* in particular. This consumerist tract had singled out the radio advertising of beauty treatments, quack medicines, and "dental nostrums" as harmful to listeners (see Chapter 2). It is clear from MacRorie's memo that the criticisms of the consumer movement were given weighty consideration behind the closed doors of NBC.[9]

By 1940, NBC executives were taking the "radio active" members of the consumer movement seriously — so seriously that they hatched a plot to "infiltrate" a consumerist convention at Stephens College in Columbia, Missouri. The college, founded by the Sloan Foundation in 1935, was the site of the first consumer education program in the county.[10] Conservative analysts considered that the Stephens College consumer education conference of 1939 was the event at which the "anti-business attitude" of the movement had crystallized: "There the business men of the nation, and consumers, too, saw a demonstration of hostility to business which had been generated by leaders and active workers in some sections of organized consumer activity."[11]

NBC was spurred to action when Sophie Kerr, the prolific novelist and short-story writer, attacked radio advertising at a convention of the Advertising Women of New York in February 1940. In response to Kerr's attack, Ken Dyke, an NBC executive, insisted that the network needed to monitor the consumer movement:

The ever-increasing importance of the so-called "CONSUMER MOVEMENT" and its possible effect on future operations of industry and advertising, makes it vitally important for us at NBC to keep ourselves up to date on what is going on. . . . It would seem important that a few of us sit down and discuss the Consumer Movement and what, if anything, we should do about it.

Dyke convened a meeting, which included Janet MacRorie, Margaret Cuthbert, W. G. Preston, and Judith Waller, among others, at which it was decided that Cuthbert and Preston should attend the upcoming Stephens College conference — but not as NBC executives. Rather, they were instructed to go "incognito."

In order to prepare his staff for the conference, Dyke circulated a report on the consumer movement written by the famed public relations consultant Edward Bernays. Bernays claimed that the consumer movement had "made a considerable dent on America's consciousness." He argued that the movement was an outgrowth of the Depression and that there were four factors which had led to its development:

1. The disillusionment with business and advertising in general.
2. The recession in employment and income which made it necessary for consumers to buy more cautiously.
3. A psychological reaction to high pressure selling and advertising.
4. The fact that on the outer fringe of business a limited number of manufacturers distributed products such as hair dyes, etc., which were actually harmful to the consumer who used them.

Bernays saw advertising — and specifically, the consumer's reaction to it — as one of the main causes of the consumer movement. He also observed that the consumer movement had grown during the Depression decade, even though the main channels of communication — newspapers, magazines, and radio — had been closed to it.

Bernays stressed the fact that the movement had grown through grassroots, alternative media efforts, including bulletins, books, and pamphlets. The influence of movement organizers, he argued, was "far greater than their numbers":

They permeate all groups of society. The fact that the ordinary media of communication are closed to them, has intensified their word-of-mouth carrying value. These groups include among their membership, vociferously articulate and sometimes almost fanatical adherents who use every opportunity to project the movement. It has been reported that the consumer movement sends representatives to heckle speakers at meetings such as the Town Hall of the Air, in order that their point of view may be heard on the radio and reach a wider audience.[12]

Bernays concluded his report with the statement that the consumer movement was not likely to "destroy business . . . or its advertising." But the overall thrust of his report was clear: business needed to communicate with consumer groups in order to wrest the consumer movement from the "left-wing" influences which controlled it.

To this end, NBC sent Preston and Cuthbert to spy on the Stephens College conference. Upon his return, Preston reported that the consumer movement was "confused" and "embryonic," but also "one of the most important pressure groups in the country."[13] He observed that the movement was made up of a coalition of "vertical pressure groups" from such sectors as "Religion, Education, Labor, Women's Organizations, War Veterans and Widows, Service Clubs, Health and Welfare." He argued that the "demagogues" within the movement would control it, unless business and advertising did "a more intelligent job of public relations not only directly with the consumer but more particularly with the horizontal pressure groups."[14] He was also surprised to find out that conference participants were enthusiastic about an NBC radio program called *The Next Step Forward*. Preston was pleased to learn that consumer activists approved of the program, "because we have been under terrific pressure from consumer groups to give them time on the air."[15]

NBC executives were not the only ones worried about the potential effect of the consumer movement on radio advertising. After the Stephens College conference, *Variety* reported that "radio has been placed on the defensive, along with the advertising business in general because of the New Dealish philosophy about the under-fed, ill-housed and poorly clothed lower classes." Educators at the convention had attacked advertising for its "emotional" appeal and for making consumers want things that they did not need. Pushed to its limit, *Variety* argued, this idea could bring "grief" to radio: "Obviously, any legislation stipulating that advertising statements and claims, whether spoken or printed, should be strictly literal would hurt broadcasters immediately." *Variety* also commented on the cross-class nature of the consumer attack on advertising, noting that "sociologists" who wanted to increase the spending power of the masses were aligned with "blue-noses," who found advertising for liquor and tobacco offensive.[16]

Months after the Stephens College conference Niles Trammell and Ken Dyke were still mulling over the activities of the consumer movement. Dyke sent Trammell a pamphlet prepared by the Bureau of Radio Advertising called "The Case For Distribution"; he explained that it detailed "the progress of the consumer movement and the threat which this offers to advertising . . . and radio."[17] NBC had received the pamphlet from the National Association of Broadcasters accompanied by a cover letter that exhorted NAB members of to realize that "as broadcasters, whose income is derived from advertising, we have a very clear-cut stake in . . . the future course of the consumer movement." In other words, since the consumer movement was attacking advertising, and advertising was the lifeblood of the broadcast industry, it was imperative for broadcasters to pay attention to the consumer movement.[18] In his own memo to Trammell, Dyke advised him to write a letter to the NAB praising the pamphlet but "not to waste any time reading it."[19]

Niles Trammell may not have "wasted any time" on the pamphlet, but it is clear from internal NBC correspondence that Trammell and his colleagues spent plenty of time thinking about the consumer movement. The Bureau of Radio Advertising and NBC executives saw the movement as a threat to advertising and the American way. They were not overly fearful, but they did try to influence members of the "vertical pressure groups" — such as the Women's National Radio Committee — from which the leaders of the movement were drawn. They also acknowledged, as did so many of the critics of advertising within the movement itself, that the consumer movement drew some of its inspiration from "the disillusionment with business and advertising" that was prevalent during the Depression. NBC's reaction to the movement was indicative of the dialectic between advertising and activism: radio advertising helped to provoke the consumer movement, but at the same time radio executives did not sit idly by while the movement grew in strength and influence.

Consumer Time

Even as NBC was fighting the consumer movement at its gates, the network was also broadcasting a radio program produced by one of the leaders of the movement on one of its two networks. NBC programs were aired over two networks, labeled the "Blue" and the "Red," and *Consumer Time* was broadcast on NBC's "Red" network. *Consumer Time* was produced weekly by Donald E. Montgomery, consumer's counsel for the U.S. Department of Agriculture, with input from Sadie Orr Dunbar of the General Federation of Women's Clubs. It was broadcast for fifteen minutes every Saturday as a "sustaining" show on NBC, which meant that it was not sponsored by advertising but rather by the network itself. The show was designed to help "average income" Americans "save, salvage and share," and it covered such topics as "Saving Fats," "Rent Controls," "Making Furniture," "More Heat with Less Fuel," and "Victory Gardens." From 1935 to 1947 *Consumer Time* was aired by nearly one hundred stations, in big cities like Los Angeles, New York, and Chicago, as well as in small towns like Altoona, Pennsylvania; Manchester, New Hampshire; Boseman, Montana; and Laurel, Mississippi.[20]

The USDA had been making plans for the show as early as 1933, but Montgomery put his own stamp on *Consumer Time* after he arrived at the agency in 1935.[21] Montgomery was a social activist with a strong commitment to low-income consumers and a record of government service. With a Bachelor's degree from the University of Pennsylvania and some graduate work at the University of Wisconsin, Montgomery had risen to become a high-level director of the Securities and Exchange Commission.[22] He resigned his post at the SEC to become the Consumer's Counsel, making the USDA one of the only government agencies with an "official" position devoted to the concerns of the consumer. In addition to producing *Consumer Time,* the USDA produced the widely circulated pamphlet *Consumers Guide,* and another radio program called *Consumer Flashes* which was broadcast as part of the *National Farm and Home Hour,* and which contained up-to-the-minute bulletins from such agencies as the War Production Board and the Office of Price Administration.

The USDA considered radio an essential medium for communicating with the public — especially during the war. According to Montgomery, the "stringent times" of the war and the "restrictions and hardships" made it imperative for the government to keep "open the lines of communication."[23]

Function of Radio: to inform consumers as quickly and as accurately as possible . . . of the various wartime orders on consumer goods and services, and to help consumers become more intelligent economic citizens. . . . Radio can bring an intelligent consumer understanding on rationing, price control, inflation, and various other economic policies. . . . Radio can inform consumers as to the effect of these policies on commodities. . . . Radio, used with full understanding of its tremendous possibilities of disseminating information, can and should play a major role in the educational function of both Divisions.[24]

In 1942, after producing *Consumer Time* for seven years, Montgomery believed that the program compared favorably to other government-sponsored radio programs. He was proud that, judging from the constant letters and information requests he received, that the show had become "the consumer's own."[25]

Part of what made *Consumer Time* so successful was its dramatic format. It featured an opening dialogue between male and female "consumers," which was then followed by a humorous skit. Montgomery usually ended the program with a short homily on the topic of the day. The program opened with the sound of a cash register:

> *(cash register . . . rings twice . . . close drawer)*
>
> NANCY: That's your money buying food.
>
> *(cash register)*
>
> JOHN: That's your money paying for a home.
>
> *(cash register)*
>
> NANCY: That's your money buying clothes.
>
> JOHN: Buying you a living in wartime.
>
> *(cash register . . . close drawer)*

There was a clear difference in gender roles played by John and Mrs. Nancy Freyman within the programs. Even in this opening, John and Nancy each claimed the consumer realm that was considered to be more appropriate to their sex; Nancy delivered the line about "buying food," and John delivered the line about "paying for a home."[26]

This sexual division of labor was part of the pattern of the program throughout its run. In a wartime episode on price ceilings, for example, Donald Montgomery played the "expert" while Mrs. Freyman played the uninformed consumer. Price ceilings were difficult to enforce, and the government used shows like *Consumer Time* to teach consumers — and especially, women consumers — how to confront store owners who were violating wartime price limits:

This is Don Montgomery speaking — your Consumers' Counsel, in the Department of Agriculture at Washington. And last week at this time I promised to bring you the facts on ceiling prices and how they should be posted. Mrs. Freyman, your fellow consumer, said you were all asking questions about them.

Freyman, in contrast to Montgomery, played the naïf, explaining that price supports were difficult for her to follow, what with having to "make supper, or bathe the baby." It was her role to play the hapless female consumer: "And half the time I don't even know where the ceiling prices are."[27]

The skit that followed this opening was designed to dramatize the relationship between shopkeepers and consumers as a battle of wills, opinion, and moral force. Mrs. Freyman entered one store in which the manager refused to post government price ceilings:

Well, nobody's gonna tell me how to run my business, see? I know my rights, and I'm going to charge just what I please for things — in spite of the Government and everybody else. I always have, and I always will.

Mrs. Freyman had better luck in another store, where the shopkeeper had worked hard to post the price ceilings. The shopkeeper was angry, however, because he claimed that consumers did not seem to care:

Why it took my wife and me a whole week — working every night and Sunday — to post all the ceiling prices in the store. And then nobody even bothers to look at 'em! It makes you sort of wonder. Here's America trying to win the war — and the Government trying to keep prices down to help the people — and the people themselves don't even care! Makes you sort of wonder — don't it?

Mrs. Freyman agreed with him, suggesting that maybe consumers were not interested. At that point, Montgomery reasserted himself as the authority on consumers:

I think every person in this country is interested in keeping the cost of living down. But we've got to do our job, too. Consumers I mean. It's our job to learn about price ceilings and to use them for our own protection. . . . If it doesn't work, things are going to be very bad for all of us.

Montgomery, the voice of male authority, and the voice of the government, had the last word.

Other episodes did a better job of giving credit to women as consumers — and as crucial players in the war effort. In one episode on "Fabrics," the show featured members of the WACS. Another episode on "Shoes" featured members of WAVES. In these episodes, *Consumer Time* promoted women's contribution to the military alongside their contribution to the consumer front:

Women are needed for the United States Navy just as much as fliers who patrol the Pacific or the gunners on Destroyer's Decks. This is a woman's war too, and the WAVES of the Navy handle over 200 vital jobs on shore. If you are between the ages of 20 and 36 with two years of high school or business school and with no children under 18, you are needed to maintain the fighting fleet of the United States Navy.[28]

In keeping with the corny humor of *Consumer Time,* when the program hosts asked their guests the best way to obtain top quality leather shoes, they replied that listeners would have to join up with the military: "All of the top grades of leather . . . so far as wear is concerned . . . are reserved for military use."[29]

In yet another episode on the issue of price ceilings, *Consumer Time* portrayed women as more assertive than it had in the earlier episode. This time, the skit featured a nagging wife; her henpecked husband, a grocer; and a pack of feisty "club women." It began with the grocer/husband, George, who was wearing a halo. His wife, Else, asked him how much he had paid for the halo:

GEORGE: Well, they . . . I guess, well it retails at about $4.95.

ELSE: $4.95! For a $2.95 halo! Two dollars too much. That's a black market price if I ever saw one. (Firmly) George . . .

GEORGE: *(Meekly)* Yes, dear.

ELSE: You paid more than ceiling price for it.

GEORGE: *(Still more meekly)* Yes, dear . . . but I . . .

ELSE: "But you" nothing. You're helping to bring on inflation, do you realize that? Do you remember what happened with your grocery store after the last war?

GEORGE: Yes . . . looks to me like the whole town of Centerboro has gotten together about these price lists. Yesterday afternoon about 4 o'clock, a bunch of ladies came in . . . like they'd just been to a club meeting. They had their hats on and weren't carrying no baskets nor babies . . .

WOMAN: Well, we just came from meeting, and it's all decided and written up in the minutes that we are going to read these price lists and check at least five times every shopping day.

In this episode, then, *Consumer Time* dramatized the message that club-women, if they organized around the issue of price ceilings, could prevent inflationary prices on a store-by-store basis.

Consumer Time's little skit was not far from the truth. As Meg Jacobs has argued, women organized by government agencies, and especially the Office of Price Administration, played a leading role in enforcing ceiling prices:

OPA-distributed price ceiling charts allowed volunteer housewives to check merchant compliance on each shopping trip. In turn, the Westchester Committee on Consumer Education (Westchester County, New York) published its own "feminine" version of the OPA ceiling charts, entitled "My Price Guide," which listed all the commonest purchases in an accessible format. Beatrice Gross, the chairman of the committee, expected that a hundred thousand copies of the handy booklets would find their way "into the pocketbooks of Westchester house-wives . . . so that the shopper will know the very highest price she should legally pay for a product."[30]

The women of Westchester County were among the most active women in the country when it came to consumer issues. And *Consumer Time*, which was targeted at these woman shoppers, promoted the idea that when women organized their shopping power, they could be powerful indeed.

Consumer Time also promoted a nationally diverse cast of characters. In one episode, set "back in time" during the Alaskan gold rush, an Italian miner dried winter vegetables to save his fellow miners from scurvy: "The vegetables, lasta summer, when she'sa lovely and ripa and fresca . . . I picka her. And what I no can eat . . . I fixa to dry in tha sun. Oh, she dry very nica and pretty . . . just lika a back in Italia." In an episode designed to convince consumers of the value of conserving milk for the war effort, an American housewife wanted milk to make a cream soup for her din-ner party, while in Athens, Greece, a woman tried to get milk for her baby: "In far off America, I wonder whether the people know that they feed us hope, they feed us courage, they feed us the will to go on living, when they send us milk for our babies." *Consumer Time*, while promot-ing the use of dried vegetables and milk rationing, also promoted ethnic and international sympathies.[31]

The promotion of these sympathies extended to the farthest of America's boundaries during the war. In one *Consumer Time* episode, Johnny and Mrs. Freyman conducted a telephone interview with two "Hawaiian housewives" who were "carrying on their daily tasks in the American lands closest to our Japanese enemies." In her scripted role as the naive housewife, Mrs. Freyman affirmed the link between Hawaiian and mainland housewives: "To me, Hawaii has been represented so long as a sort of picture postcard land, that I was especially glad to hear the ladies from Honolulu tell about their down-to-earth household problems . . . the same type of things that I have to face day to day." In a similar episode on "Puerto Rico and Food," *Consumer Time* promoted an all-encompassing definition of American citizenship: "Puerto Ricans are American citizens . . . and darned good citizens. As with the rest of this nation . . . it is a matter of national policy to make sure that Puerto Rico is well defended and well fed." In these episodes, *Consumer Time* tried to create a broad sense of national identification.[32]

As dramatic texts, *Consumer Time* scripts were crude, nationalistic, full of ethnic and racial stereotypes, and often condescending to women. Even so, at times the cornball humor of the show approximated clever social commentary. In one episode, a "school" of fish held a classroom session on the health benefits of eating fish. The meeting was held in secret, since of course the fish did not want humans to find out how delicious and nutritious they were. At the end of their meeting, however, the fish discovered that their proceedings had been recorded and broadcast over the radio. At the program's conclusion, Dr. Carp explained to Dr. Cod that the booklet "Fish Cookery in Wartime" was available free of charge from *Consumer Time*. Dr. Haddock objected to the premise of the cookbook: "It sounds unconstitutional to me . . . unfair to disorganized fish . . . cruel and unusual punishment."[33] This episode of *Consumer Time* poked fun at left-leaning intellectuals, and, in some ways, at itself.

Listeners appreciated the cornball drama, explaining that the dramatic form helped them to remember the lessons *Consumer Time* was trying to teach. In some cases, the target audience for *Consumer Time* included the very same clubwomen who protested daytime serials and helped to enforce ceiling prices — women like Hazel Haines from Franklin, Nebraska:

I can't say that I like extremely *emotional* radio dramas, and especially those containing nerve-racking music, but how *anyone* could dislike the fine little dramas that your staff has been putting on, on the *Consumer Time* program, is beyond me. And it is so much easier to remember the facts when they are presented in this way.

Donald Montgomery and his staff monitored the mail that listeners sent in, noting the number of requests for information elicited by each program. In 1942, for example, listeners sent in 125,200 requests for information, which included 5,380 requests generated by the program on "Coal and Sweets," 5,820 requests generated by the program "Moths and Stains Removal," and 2,730 requests generated by the program "Rubber and Spices."[34]

In 1942, in addition to sending in requests for information, listeners wrote over 2,000 letters to the producers. *Consumer Time* received letters from such unlikely listeners as a real estate broker from Brooklyn, who wrote in for the booklet "Tips on Rent Control," and a Fox Film executive, who wrote to suggest that *Consumer Time* be expanded to thirty minutes. Donald Montgomery explained in his annual reports that such letters were never solicited and that the vast majority of the letters received were positive: "Among them were letters from business men, teachers, radio stations, but most of all, and most important to us, were the majority from housewives, to whom our program is primarily aimed."[35]

Housewives — especially working-class housewives — did appreciate the program. As one woman from East Orange, New Jersey, wrote: "The program is an enlightening one for people with any intelligence and the interest to save money on buying — and who wants this more than housewives! When prices go up, and your husband's salary doesn't — I have to be alert (or have no extra money to buy Bonds)." In some cases, housewives listened together: "I am writing this letter for a group of housewives, all of us living in the same apartment. We would like you to know we enjoy your programs very much. — Mrs. R. B., Seattle, Washington." In other cases, listeners pledged to spread the word about the program: "These programs are very helpful — if only more consumers would listen to them. Doing my bit to tell folks about 'em. — Miss E. B. M., Chicago, Ill." Sometimes husbands listened, too: "When my hubby is home on Saturday he is just as interested as I. — Mrs. B. J. F, in Pearl River, New York."[36]

The reasons listeners were grateful for *Consumer Time* were as diverse as the listeners themselves. Working women appreciated the fact that the show was broadcast on the weekend: "I enjoy your program so very much! It makes up beautifully for all the helpful women's programs that I miss during the week because I am a working girl." Other listeners found that *Consumer Time* increased their appreciation of the government: "Permit me to say that this government agency is a real contribution to the people." Another listener wrote that *Consumer Time* had changed her opinion of government taxes: "I heard your program on the radio . . . and found it very instructive and entertaining. If that is the kind of thing the government is doing with our money we don't mind paying taxes. — Mrs. H. G., Howell, Michigan." In the most extreme case, a listener wrote that she was "grateful" to the government: "I think it is a wonderful program and am so grateful to our Government and to the National Broadcasting Company for this truly fine and constructive program. This is indeed Democracy. — Mrs. B. N., Los Angeles."

Consumer Time listeners, trained by a decade of writing letters to product sponsors, were effusive in their praise for the "sponsor" of *Consumer Time:* the U.S. government. One listener even wrote to "express [her] appreciation to the sponsors," perhaps not realizing that the USDA, and not Proctor and Gamble, produced *Consumer Time.* The other "sponsor" of *Consumer Time,* NBC, was only minimally involved in the show's production during the first nine years of its run. Margaret Cuthbert, in her role as director of women's and children's activities for NBC, also wrote to express her appreciation for the government's efforts: "Your scripts have been tops . . . Excellent showmanship . . . Carrying good causes forward with a light touch is one of the most effective ways." At the peak of its popularity, in 1942, *Consumer Time* even made the pages of *Variety* — an entertainment trade paper not ordinarily given to plugging government-sponsored programs:

On this hearing CONSUMER TIME was 10% concerned with advice and information for consumers, and 90% with citizen participation in and acceptance of schemes to save, salvage and share. . . . The program's style is lively. . . . Donald Montgomery, of the Consumers' Counsel Division, spoke a couple of times. Consumers learned that onions will be plentiful and should be cheap next week, and that landlords in rent control areas must not succumb to landlorditis.

Variety chided *Consumer Time* for submerging the "self-interest" of the consumer to the "nation's interest," but on the whole pronounced it a "listenable session."[37]

At the end of 1942, after collecting thousands of listener letters and hundreds of thousands of requests for information, Donald Montgomery quit his job at the USDA. His resignation came as an unwelcome surprise to many *Consumer Time* listeners, as well as to consumer groups around the country. Montgomery cited the federal government's hostility to the plight of the consumer as his reason for leaving. He explained that a new agency was being created to handle food during wartime, the War Food Administration, and that his boss, Roy F. Hendrickson, had decided that "his new organization shall not include a Consumer's Counsel to serve as spokesman and partisan for consumers in the handling of these responsibilities." Montgomery was disappointed — not only for himself, but also for the consumers he represented:

This resignation marks the end of the last, but one, of a half-dozen experiments made by the New Deal to set up offices to fight for the interest of consumers in the administration of Government programs. These have come and gone: The Consumers' Advisory Board of the NRA; the Consumer Division of the National Emergency Council; the Consumer Division of the Department of Labor; and a Special Advisor to the President on Consumer problems.[38]

When Montgomery resigned, so did many of his colleagues, including one of the scriptwriters for *Consumer Time,* Mary Taylor. She explained to her boss that her job no longer made sense: "Your rejection of Don's services as your Consumers' Counsel seems to me to be a repudiation of the work of all of us, because our work was an inseparable part of the public service he was ready and eager to do. You could find no use for it. That's why I must check out."[39]

Gordon Hubbel, another member of the Consumers' Counsel's Radio Unit, also submitted his resignation after Montgomery quit his job, explaining that without Montgomery, *Consumer Time* would no longer have the same economic and political impact:

I have been proud to be a part of an organization which had a philosophy based on an understanding of the needs of economically less fortunate citizens. . . . CONSUMER TIME, reaching an audience of nearly a million and a half consumers each week, has played a part in helping them to a better living in an economic system which has never given them an equal chance to be heard. . . . CONSUMER TIME therefore will no longer represent our basic ideals of consumer partisanship in which I believe.[40]

The USDA continued to produce both *Consumers Guide* and *Consumer Time* in the absence of Montgomery and his crew, but from Montgomery's point of view the radio program would never be the same.

Montgomery could not to mask his disappointment when he made his final speech over the air. His last *Consumer Time* broadcast came shortly after Christmas 1942. He told his listeners that he had some news that "isn't very pleasant . . . to pass along at this holiday season." He reminded his listeners of the importance of food during the war — and especially the importance of conserving and putting to good use "all the food we keep here for our own people." Montgomery asked his listeners not to forget the many lessons they had learned on *Consumer Time,* such as the dangers of wasting and hoarding food: "Sure, it will be hard at times to get the hang of it, but you can handle *your* side of the job, and I know you will." In his closing, Donald Montgomery said his good-byes: "Good-bye then, and keep tuning in *Consumer Time* because I feel sure the program will keep coming to you, and I hope you will keep on liking it."[41]

For the next five years *Consumer Time* did keep on coming, but Donald Montgomery, for one, did not "keep on liking it." Less than a year after he left the USDA, Montgomery made an angry statement to the left-leaning magazine *PM* about a change in the way *Consumer Time* was being introduced by NBC. Montgomery was angry because NBC had created a new promotional tag for the program, in which advertising, and not the government, was credited with broadcasting *Consumer Time:*

NBC has been of service to its listeners. It has provided the means to bring the radio audience of America the valuable and interesting information broadcast on *Consumer Time* programs. We can broadcast programs like this through the independent radio stations affiliated with us on the network, because broadcasting, like the free press, is supported by advertising. You the listeners may buy the goods advertised on commercial programs, or you may just listen and enjoy. This is American radio.

Montgomery disagreed, arguing that "advertisers don't give the Government the right to talk to the people over the air." Instead, he explained, the government gave broadcasting companies the right to use the air on the condition that they serve "the public interest." It was not the listeners buying "goods advertised on commercial programs" that made *Consumer Time* possible, he contended, but, rather, their tax dollars. Montgomery believed the airwaves belonged to the people.[42]

Moreover, Montgomery believed that *Consumer Time* belonged to consumers and the people who represented them. His sense of ownership over the program persisted long after he left it. He told *PM* magazine that *Consumer Time* was "our baby," and that "she was a nice girl when I last knew her but she seems to have grown up and [has] been getting around." He resented the tribute NBC offered advertisers in its preface to *Consumer Time,* since "the only help we ever got from advertisers was the occasional censoring of copy by NBC to protect the feelings of its pay clients." Montgomery believed that the government lost out when advertisers received credit for a program that was produced for the benefit of the people.

Nonetheless, *Consumer Time* represented an interesting moment in the dialectic between advertising and activism. In this unusual case, NBC offered listeners a "sustaining" program, a program paid for with the profits derived from commercially sponsored shows, which served many of the goals of the consumer movement. *Consumer Time* was often less about consuming than it was about conserving, rationing, and salvaging. In this case, a network devoted to consumption helped to subsidize the production of a program that was devoted to *under*consumption and the economic concerns of working-class listeners. *Consumer Time* was one of the few radio programs that was *designed* to make listeners "radio active."

Donald Montgomery versus Donald Duck

The bitterness Montgomery felt when he left the USDA was in sharp contrast to the idealism and excitement he exhibited when he arrived in 1935. He believed that the federal government had a responsibility to represent consumers' interests, and, at the same time, he believed that workers and farmers were also consumers. Upon his arrival at the USDA, he immediately showed his commitment to consumers by reinvigorating the county consumer councils that had been established by the National Recovery Act. In 1935 the National Recovery Administration had been declared unconstitutional by the Supreme Court and the county councils were in danger of becoming defunct. As Meg Jacobs has argued, Montgomery led the way: "He continued a program of active involvement with local councils and supplied them regularly with copies of *Consumers Guide.* His field agent, Iris Walker, traveled across the nation to help sustain a close relationship."[43]

In his role as Consumers' Counsel, Montgomery wanted to change the perception that "consumption is somehow secondary, gratuitous, sinful." Montgomery believed that consumption was part of everyday life and that it was as connected to political and social justice as production. He embraced abundance — abundance "for all the people, and not an abundance wrung out of sweated labor or dispossessed farmers." Montgomery also helped to found the Consumers National Federation, whose mission was to push the federal government to create a department solely for consumer issues. The Federation and other interested consumer groups gathered for the first time in March 1936 in New York City. One year later, Federation members met in Washington, D.C., "to acquaint national officials with what [we] are doing and how [we] are thinking in terms of consumer progress."[44]

The letterhead stationery for the Consumers National Federation was simple and bold: a group of consumers marched single-file across the page, passing first city tenements (with laundry hanging between the buildings), then smaller, single-family homes, and finally the windmills of a family farm. Their age and clothing varied: included were men, women, old people, and children, in business hats and farm hats, and clutching packages, baskets, and boxes beneath their arms. This design reflected the mood of the consumer movement of the 1930s: it showed consumers who were not only shopping, but who were also marching in unison. After the war the Consumers National Federation changed its name to the National Association of Consumers, but the letterhead design remained the same; indeed, the organization's newsletter, *Consumers on the March,* certainly took its name from the logotype design that appeared on the organization's letterhead.

Like the consumers who were represented by this graphic image, Donald Montgomery was both forward-looking and committed to the rights of housewives and low-income consumers. When he resigned from the USDA in 1942, he received dozens of letters expressing regret; they came from individuals and organizations around the country, including the Better Business Bureau of St. Louis, the American Federation of Teachers, the New York City Department of Health, the Consumer's Cooperative Society of Palo Alto, the Office of Price Administration, and even a Hollywood publicity agent. But there were also those who celebrated his resignation. Advertising and radio executives, like those at the Bureau of Radio Advertising, who prepared the pamphlet "The Case For Distribution," considered Montgomery to be one of the "Reds" behind the consumer movement:

Since his appointment to the Consumers' Counsel in 1935, Mr. Montgomery has been more active than any of his predecessors in working with various organizations called "bona fide" consumer groups. He was prominent in the activities of the Consumers National Federation, which Earl Broder, general secretary of the Communist Party, called a communistic "transmission belt."[45]

Montgomery was tagged with the communist label throughout his career. One of his more public scrapes over his political affiliations, a confrontation with practitioners of "the new science of public relations — purchased control of public thought," as Montgomery called it, took place in the spring of 1940.[46]

It started when Bruce Barton, one of the "Bs" in the advertising agency BBDO, singled out Montgomery in a vicious attack on government agencies. Addressing the Union League Club in New York, Barton claimed that "there are men in the Federal Trade Commission and the

Department of Agriculture who hate national advertising, who want to destroy it because national advertising supports the free American press and the free American radio."[47] He claimed that the Federal Trade Commission had allocated more that $80,000 for an "inquiry into distribution costs and methods," and that New Dealers were going after the advertising-sponsored press of the nation, which had opposed the "spend thrift extravagance of the New Deal."[48]

Montgomery was quick to strike back. One week later, addressing the Consumer Education Association in St. Louis, Missouri, Montgomery explained that he was not interested in attacking advertising. He called advertising "as inevitable as eating," and insisted that advertising "will last until the next to last man leaves for Mars."[49] Montgomery explained that he had nothing to do with the FTC or the Communist Party: "I don't know what Communists think about advertising." He clarified his position on advertising by explaining that the consumer movement was not against all advertising — just "bad advertising." He pointed out that advertisers themselves were often their own harshest critics.[50] Moreover, he argued, advertising, even if it was as inevitable as eating, should still be open to critique: "No institution in the country has the right to wrap itself in a sanctity that makes it immune from criticism."[51]

The fight between Bruce Barton and Donald Montgomery was covered in papers around the country, from the *New York Times* and the *Washington Post* to the *Topeka Journal*, the *New Haven Register*, and the *Albany (Ga.) Herald*. Some papers added fuel to the fire, reminding readers that Donald Montgomery was on the Dies committee's most-wanted list for being "Un-American." But many of the papers defended Montgomery, applauding his stand on consumer issues. The most strident defense of Montgomery came from a very unlikely suspect: Arthur Price, an executive for Sears Roebuck. In March 1940 Price gave a speech to the Advertising Club of Washington in which he defended Montgomery and attacked those who were deriding the consumer movement as "communist."

I believe a revolution is taking place in advertising, and has for some time — and I am not referring to communism. . . . It will do us . . . no good to confuse consumers and communists. Individual groups may be tinged with pale pink or ruddy red — but the consumer herself is just plainly and simply a customer. . . . And we had better listen to this customer, because she is asking some questions. She wants to know what it is she is buying — what grade, what quality, what value, what it will do, and what it won't!

Arthur Price compared those who attacked the consumer movement to Donald Duck: "Much loud . . . squawking — little said." Advertising's chief threat, he explained, was advertising itself: "Like everything that lives, [advertising] carries with it the seed of its own destruction."[52]

Price admitted what most advertisers only occasionally acknowledged — that their own practices led to the backlash from the consumer movement. Price understood that there was a dialectic between advertising and activism — that if advertising did not meet the needs of the consumer, the consumer was likely to act up. Montgomery understood this, too, as well as that many low-income consumers were not as concerned with advertising as they were with the fact that they could not afford the things that advertising had to sell: "With half the families of the country having earnings that allow only $2.00 a week for clothes, it is not whether advertising is the American way of the life that bothers them, but how they can cover their nakedness. Advertising is the American way if it will help them meet that problem instead of hindering them."[53]

During his seven years at the USDA Donald Montgomery frequently battled the squawking "Donald Ducks" of the advertising and broadcast industries. And while the squawkers tried to link the consumer movement to the Communist party, Donald Montgomery and his colleagues knew better: whatever the "communist front" influences within the consumer movement, the "consumer front" itself was a diverse coalition of interests and goals — an umbrella group that encompassed housewives, trade-unionists, teachers, church leaders, and even progressive business types. There were even times when Montgomery was attacked from the left. In 1939, Montgomery responded to a letter that appeared in the *Nebraskan Union Farmer* which questioned his progressive commitment. In defending himself, Montgomery quoted what Hilton Hornaday, financial editor of the *Buffalo Evening News,* had written about him: "One of the best examples in the leftist movement is Donald E. Montgomery. . . . He makes no pretense of covering up his extremely progressive views, and explains that he would rather be called a 'radical' than a 'sell-out.'"

Montgomery proved that he was more a "radical" than a "sell-out" when he left his job as the Consumers' Counsel of the USDA for a job as the Consumers' Counsel for the United Auto Workers. In this new job he had the opportunity to work toward the goal of economic democracy to which he had been so committed at the USDA:

Economic democracy requires an ever widening participation by the average man in the control of the economic forces which affect him. Most average men recognize that this can be won only through organization. Hence, the consumer movement may turn out to be the vehicle whereby breadwinning groups can give common expression to their consumer purposes.[54]

As the Consumers' Counsel for the UAW, Montgomery shaped union policy, and, more importantly, union activism on behalf of consumer issues. When he left the USDA, he explained that he was ready to exert pressure from the "outside" rather than work on the "inside."[55] And exert pressure he did. As Meg Jacobs has shown, Montgomery "played an integral role in crafting the UAW's economic brief, 'Purchasing Power for Prosperity,' and devising the 1946 'Open the Books' strike campaign against General Motors."[56]

At the end of World War II, Montgomery assumed a leading role in a series of postwar strikes, consumer boycotts, and public demonstrations. Although the war ended in 1945, the Office of Price Administration continued wartime price ceilings through the first half of 1946, with the full support of the majority of Americans. Public approval for price ceilings was high: "In March 1946, 80% thought OPA was doing a fairly good to excellent job, and 73% thought OPA should be continued. . . . In May, polls showed 75% support for another year of price controls for food, 78% for rent control, 70% for clothing ceilings, and 66% for price controls on automobiles, radios and other manufactured goods."[57] In other words, the majority of consumers supported price ceilings for every category of goods and housing.

Price ceilings were dismantled at the end of June, 1946. In response, Montgomery helped to organize a series of large and well-publicized demonstrations throughout the summer. His views on the relationship between labor and the price ceilings established by the OPA were aired on radio station WXYZ in Detroit in June. Montgomery argued that as workers fought for higher wages, it was crucial to prevent businesses from simply charging higher prices:

We . . . know that organized labor in this country must challenge *and must stop* this scheme to use every increase in the incomes of workers as an excuse for higher prices to the consumer. . . . The *people* of this country, not Wall Street, won the war. The *people* of this country, not Wall Street, must win the peace. We can win it. Congress must be made to hear our voices. Congress must be made to act for the people; not for the profiteers.

After the OPA price ceilings were lifted, the UAW called for nationwide demonstrations to take place on 16 July. UAW flyers and posters urged workers to make employers give them time off from work to participate in the demonstrations. Where permission was refused, the UAW-CIO "authorized local unions to shut down their plants."[58]

Though Montgomery was working for the UAW, his plan for action against inflation was a plan to mobilize all consumers — whether they were UAW members or not. He called on "labor unions, veterans' organizations, consumer groups, civil organizations and public minded citizens" to "unite to fight inflation."[59] He used the language of class warfare to suggest that the American people were being betrayed by an alliance of the government with big business:

Congress has surrendered to the demands of big business that price control be thrown out the window. The men representing us in Washington have turned loose on the people who elected them the gamblers, the profiteers, the speculators, the rent gougers. Prices and profits will soar. Real wages — purchasing power — will shrink. We are heading straight into another depression.

In order to pressure Congress to pass new price ceilings, the UAW offered a three-pronged plan of protest, calling for nationwide demonstrations, a national buyers strike, and collective resistance to rent increases. Organizers insisted that consumers should "buy only what you have to buy" and should "make our clothes, our household furnishings and other necessities . . . last long enough to force the profiteers . . . to stop their mad inflationary profit-buying drive."[60]

On 16 July 1946, sixty thousand UAW members and consumer activists gathered in Cadillac Square in downtown Detroit to hear an address by Walter Reuther. Reuther urged the crowd to stop buying meat for one week as a way to "terrorize profiteers" and bring prices down.[61] Similar demonstrations, organized by the CIO, veterans and women's groups, and civic groups, took place in Philadelphia, Washington, and St. Louis. *Business Week* reported on the buyers strikes with fear and loathing:

What really bothers the businessman is not the parades and the speeches — though their nuisance value is unquestioned — but the attitude that the great, inarticulate mass of consumers will adopt. Passive resistance, the club of this group, is a frightening weapon that could be wielded without fanfare or warning. Result: jerky sales — up one day, down the next — and the constant threat of losses to the seller, especially in perishables.[62]

Passive resistance was the great fear of the advertisers, whose supreme goal was to motivate consumers to buy. What would happen, *Business Week* wondered, if this passive resistance spread?

But the demonstrations were far from passive. While the majority of demonstrators gathered in Cadillac Square, the American Veterans Committee put up "friendly" pickets around the site of the Republican state convention. Everywhere they went, protesters carried signs with catchy slogans:

DON'T BUY WHILE PRICES ARE HIGH

THE PEOPLE AGAINST THE PROFITEERS

LET'S ALL HOLLER/HANG ONTO YOUR DOLLAR/FIGHT INFLATION

DON'T PAY SCAB PRICES

With such slogans, the demonstrators linked grocery shopping to the union shop by suggesting that anyone willing to pay high prices was the consumer version of a "scab." In other creative turns of phrase, demonstrators used slogans that riffed on the popular culture of the day — like "Inflation, Stay Away From My Door," which paraphrased a popular tune recorded by Kate Smith in 1932, "River Stay Away From My Door." Another slogan, "I Won't Buy You Anything But Love, Baby," was a slight variation on the popular "I Won't Give You Anything But Love, Baby," which was recorded by Una Mae Carlisle and Fats Waller in 1939.[63]

Original songs also played a role in the protests. Tom Glazer, a member of the Independent Citizens' Committee of the Arts, Professions, and Sciences, along with Pete Seeger and Butch Hawes, wrote several folksongs in honor of the fight against inflation. In addition to "A Dollar Ain't A Dollar Any More," "We Gotta Save the OPA," and "I'm a Going to Starve (If They Don't Wise Up on Capitol Hill)," Glazer wrote the catchy "Inflation Talkin' Blues." The "bad guy" in this song was the Washington lobbyist — lobbying for an end to the OPA. The "good guys" were the American people:

> . . . Well, this here feller, I'm sorry to say,
> He's trying to kill the O.P.A.
> He's trying to kill the housing bill,
> And other good things he's trying to kill.
> He's a killer. But he's only doing his job.
> He's a hard worker. Gets a bonus
> From the National Association of Manufacturers,
> From the National Association of Real Estate Boards,
> From the National Association of Dry Goods Merchants,
> Big shots . . .

. . . Now, if you don't want to spend ten dollars for a pound of steak,
And if you don't want to spend fifty dollars a pound for cake,
And if you don't want to spend twenty dollars a pound for greens,
Two hundred for rent, and Lord knows what for beans,
Write a card to your Congressman now, today,
Tell him to save that O.P.A.,
Tell him to fight just as hard as he's able
For the National Association of American People —
Biggest shots!

Glazer touched on all the key postwar consumer issues in this song: the Office of Price Administration, the rising cost (and low availability) of housing, the influence of groups like the National Association of Manufacturers, and the rising price of meat, sugar, and vegetables. In the classic folk tradition, Glazer pitted the "big shot" lobbyists against the "biggest shots" — the citizens of the United States.[64]

In addition, the catchy songs and slogans used by the protesters provided further evidence for the dialectic between advertising and activism. Although love songs and blues songs were frequently played on the radio — interspersed with commercials for consumer goods — in the postwar consumer protests, these songs became inspirational fodder for collective action. In one of the most pointed examples of this dialectic, consumer activists parodied the ubiquitous wartime advertising slogan: "Is there a Ford in your future? with the threat, "Landlord, is there a rent strike in your future?" Once a hallmark of effective advertising, the slogan was transformed into a call for a consumer's strike.[65]

The protests in Detroit were effective in securing their primary goal: they brought down the price of meat by 20 cents per pound within a week. The UAW announced over radio station WPR that consumers could resume buying meat, but that "the heat would be turned on the meat industry again, if the resumption of buying started prices on an upward trend."[66] Meanwhile, around the country, consumers followed suit. In Boston, women brought down the price of hamburger at a butcher's shop from 60 cents a pound to 45 cents a pound. In Tulsa, Oklahoma housewives waged a telephone campaign to boycott butter until the price dropped from its 79-cents-a-pound high. In St. Petersburg, Florida, the price of butter dropped from 77 cents to 19 cents a pound in one day after consumer resistance provoked a price war between two stores. In Brooklyn, in response to a well-organized picket line of a hundred women, six butcher shops closed down for the day:

An angry picket line of 100 women, many wheeling their babies, marched before the neighborhood's 25 butcher stores. Egged on by a brand-new consumer council, they ripped open the market bags of shoppers who ventured inside and successfully beat off a meat truckman trying to deliver supplies. The pickets, smarting from recent prices of as high as $1.25 a pound for steak, swore they wouldn't buy even if meat dropped to 10 cents. Within a few hours, six stores closed; others offered to dispose of steak at 55 cents a pound.[67]

Women consumers, especially organized ones, proved themselves a force to be reckoned with. These consumers were on the march.

Conclusion

Donald Montgomery's prewar organization, the Consumers National Federation, emerged in a new form after the war, with a new name, The National Association of Consumers.[68] The NAC announced that its long-range goal was "to help raise and conserve the standard of living of the American people through consumer action."[69] The NAC was indicative of a new form of consumer identity in the postwar era: if consumer activists had been smeared as communists in the 1930s, by the 1940s "everyone" was supposed to be, if not a consumer activist, then at least an *active consumer*. In 1947 NAC president Helen Hall announced the reorganization of the consumer organization in the pages of *Bread and Butter*, a consumer-oriented newsletter published by the Consumers Union. She explained that the NAC had been organized to combat the rocketing prices of basic food items after the war, such as bread, butter, and milk: "Consumers have been the forgotten people of the last six months, but they have learned a lesson every time the price of bread or milk went up." In this same issue of *Bread and Butter*, the former head of the OPA, Chester Bowles, argued that the consumer movement could unite the nation after the war: "The role of the consumer is the one economic role which all share in common — workers, farmers, and business people. A vigorous consumer movement in America could be a strong uniting force at a time when we need unity badly."[70] *Bread and Butter* urged its readers to join the NAC.

The consumer movement continued to grow after the war. Sixty consumer organizations joined the NAC in 1947, and another fifty-three joined in 1948. After 1948 the rate of new organizations joining the NAC dropped off sharply, but membership grew again in 1952.[71] In 1949 the NAC got a favorable review from a progressive publication. In an item headlined, "The Consumer — Yes" (which echoed the 1930s slogan, "The People — Yes"),

The Survey applauded the efforts of the NAC: "The National Association of Consumers, defender of one of the major efforts of us all, is continuing its campaign for a Department or Division of Consumer Protection in Washington." In 1949 the NAC had representatives in twenty-four communities in fifteen states, as well as fifteen official "chapters" and nineteen subscription groups.[72] Its newsletter, *Consumers on the March,* was received in nearly a thousand communities across the United States.[73]

After just more than a decade, in 1957, the NAC folded for good, leaving a modest legacy of immediate postwar radicalism and a series of failed efforts to pass new consumer protection legislation. The legislative failures of the consumer movement in this period were remarkable: between 1952 and 1967 there were 114 measures introduced in Congress to protect consumers, yet, as one consumer-movement historian has noted, "These bills were never enacted into law."[74] The rhetorical strength of the NAC claim — that "we are all consumers" — was also its Achilles' heel: it was difficult to organize "everyone." In fact, it was this very slogan that some politicians used against the NAC's efforts to expand consumer representation on a federal level. In 1952, when Senator Guy M. Gillette, a Democrat from Iowa, tried to create a select committee on consumer interests, his efforts were shot down: "The glib reason against Gillette's idea is this: Granted, everybody's a consumer — but first he's a farmer, a manufacturer, a merchant, a school teacher, a doctor, a builder, a banker, or a factory hand. . . . As such he's represented before Congress by an organization."[75] Gillette's proposal was endorsed by the General Federation of Women's Clubs, by the AFL, and by the National Grange. It was opposed, however, by the Senate Banking Committee. "Everyone" may have been a consumer, but not everyone was as powerful as the members of the Senate Banking Committee.

As part of its legacy, however, the National Association of Consumers helped to reinforce the idea that women were the most important consumers in the domestic economy and therefore should wield the greatest "power" in the consumer movement. The consumer movement had a high proportion of women leaders, who articulated consumption as a uniquely "female" realm of power and responsibility. Indeed, the NAC had been formed, in part, to make sure that women's "consuming" power would be recognized at a national level:

The whole drama of production and distribution is directed toward the moment when a housewife puts her money on the counter and takes away a loaf of bread or pair of shoes. She may be the heroine of the drama but she has little to say about what she takes home; about what its fair price should be; or what kind of information should be on the label to protect her purse and her family.[76]

The NAC wanted women to have more say in "what she takes home," in pricing, and in labeling, which is why the NAC organized activities like congressional write-in campaigns and a consumer's march on Washington in 1947.

In the immediate postwar period, politicians recognized the power that women wielded as consumers. President Truman acknowledged as much in 1948:

Women's organizations have at hand a ready weapon which they have not yet used to its full capacity — the power of the consumer. . . . It has been said over and over again that women control the bulk of the nation's wealth; they certainly channel its day-to-day spending for food, for clothing, for education, for all the things that make for better living. . . . This is a weapon which you can use together to combat one of the enemies that now threaten us — the high cost of living.[77]

Truman may not have intended to encourage housewives to engage in a nationwide "buyer's strike" against the meat industry, but they did just that in a 1948 protest that *Newsweek* called "The Revolt of the Housewives." Indeed, the NAC used Truman's words to challenge its readers to "refrain from buying unnecessary items," to join the NAC, and to organize local consumer chapters.[78] The history of the NAC, which was started, in part, by the "radio activity" of Donald Montgomery, reminds us that women were not only important as consumers, they were also important as consumer activists.

The "pivot point" in the dialectic between radio advertising and consumer activism in this case study was Donald Montgomery's positive use of radio programming. While radio rarely served the consumer movement in a constructive way, Montgomery found a way to broadcast his vision for a more democratic consumer society. Montgomery saw the powerful effect that *Consumer Time* had on its loyal listeners, but he also saw the limitations of radio; he quit his job with the USDA to activate a wider pool of worker/consumers under the auspices of the UAW. Still, Donald Montgomery was "radio active": he took the lessons he learned as a producer of a popular radio program — lessons about the importance of culture to mass movements — and helped to make an active consumer movement. Radio also played a role during the protests, as Montgomery addressed protesters directly on radio stations WXYZ and WPR. In addition, the consumer organization Montgomery helped to start, the NAC — with its emphasis on the importance of women as consumers — helped to sow the seeds of a feminist revival that would emerge just as the NAC itself was collapsing in the 1960s.

High-Class Hucksters

The Rise and Fall of a Radio Republic

In 1946, when radio was at the peak of its power and influence, a popular novel was published that reminded listeners, advertisers, and network executives that Americans were still unhappy with the commercials they heard over the airwaves. The author of the novel was not a radical, and neither were its many readers members of an organized front. But the novel left its mark on the radio age, reminding Americans that criticism was possible and that radio could be linked, not only to passive conformity, but, more importantly, to action.

In this book, I have told the story of how radio, from the mid-1930s to the late 1940s, helped to create a culture of "radio-activity" — of how listeners organized for and against the popular medium, forming listening clubs, reform organizations, and the consumer movement. While cultural historians have seen the period of the 1930s and 1940s as one of failed reform — focusing on the failure of activists to win significant changes for commercial radio, I have argued that radio criticism continued, and even crescendoed, during the peak years of the radio age. The story told here ends in the immediate postwar period, at a time when radio executives believed radio was impervious to popular critique. As it turned out, they were very wrong.

The Hucksters: A Perfect Farce

There's no need to caricature radio. All you have to do is listen to it. Or if you were writing about it, you'd simply report with fidelity what goes on behind the scenes. It'd make a perfect farce.[1]

Frederic Wakeman, author of the 1946 best-selling radio farce, *The Hucksters,* assigned these prophetic lines to his novel's main character — the wisecracking, cynical, advertising hustler Victor Norman. Wakeman's barely fictional account of the postwar radio and advertising industries did make a perfect farce, or at least a very profitable one. Released in May 1946, Wakeman's tale of eccentric sponsors, neurotic account executives, shameless starlets, and grating radio jingles sold over 700,000 copies in its first six months in print. It became a Book-of-the-Month Club selection, was condensed for *Reader's Digest,* and in 1947 was made into a film starring Clark Gable, Ava Gardner, Sidney Greenstreet, and Deborah Kerr. The novel was rumored to have captured such true-to-life portraits of certain advertising personalities that advance copies were "bootlegged" for between $50 and $100.[2] Outside the advertising world, *The Hucksters* tapped into the frustration that radio listeners felt when advertisers increased the number — and the irritation level — of radio commercials after the war. The book was so popular that one *New York Herald Tribune* columnist claimed in June 1946 that "every other person you meet along Broadway is carrying with him a copy of . . . *The Hucksters.*"[3]

The Hucksters told the story of Vic Norman, a radio executive who was looking for a job in New York after having served in the Office of War Information. Vic spent his last $35 on a hand-painted tie for his job interview with the advertising agency Kimberly and Maag. He got the job, but he was assigned a tough case. Vic's task was to mollify a blustering, temperamental ogre of a sponsor — the president of the Beautee Soap Company, Evan Llewelyn Evans. In their first meeting, Evans spit on the conference table to teach Vic a lesson. "'Mr. Norman,'" he said, "shouting in a deep bass. 'You have just seen me do a disgusting thing. Ugly word, spit. But you know, you will always remember what I just did. . . . Mr. Norman, if nobody remembers your brand, then you ain't going to sell soap.'"[4] Evans was a genius at selling soap, in part because of his faith in object lessons; he poured water on the table, pulled out his dentures, set a book of matches on fire, and threw his hat out the window, all to illustrate a point. Meanwhile, his cowed staff wiped up the water, fetched his hat, and put out the fire, always with smiles, bows, and choruses of "Right!" and "Check!"

Vic Norman impressed the old man by refusing to succumb to The Fear he inspired. In their first meeting, Norman pitched a radio commercial that featured a dialogue between a famous actress and her black maid. Everyone who worked for Evans thought he would reject the ad because the maid was "colored." The maid was central to the advertisement, however, since she repeated the phrase "Love that soap," in a heavy dialect, throughout the commercial. Contrary to expectation, Evans loved the ad, the commercial went on the air, and soon everyone in town was repeating the phrase "Love that soap." Vic was a hit. But he was unhappy being a "high-class huckster," with "a station wagon instead of a pushcart."[5] He delivered several long, preachy monologues condemning radio advertising, and especially the role of the sponsor. His boss sent him to Hollywood on the "Superchief," the train that shuttled radio and television industry types from coast to coast. Vic's mission in Hollywood was to create a Beautee Soap radio show, which was supposed to showcase an aging vaudeville comedian named Buddy Hare. Hare was terrible, but Evan Llewelyn Evans thought he was a combination of "Bob Hope and Jack Benny" and insisted that Hare star in a "family comedy."

On the train, however, Vic was distracted by an elegant married woman, Mrs. Kay Dorrance, and her two adorable children. Kay was traveling alone because her husband was fighting overseas. Vic and Kay fell in love. They had an affair. They exchanged lines such as "Holding you made me love-drunk" and "Oh, my love. I want you to tick like a clock."[6] The Buddy Hare show fell through. Evans was angry. Full of love for Mrs. Kay Dorrance, Vic Norman returned to New York for a stormy meeting with Evans, determined to get a partnership in the agency and bring Kay to New York. But Evans behaved like a tyrant, and Vic realized that no woman could be worth the humiliation of working for a man like Evans. He quit his job, called Kay, and broke off the affair. The End.

Though the faltering love story provided a jarring end to the novel, the moral of Wakeman's story was more about radio than it was about romance. Wakeman wanted his critique of commercial radio in *The Hucksters* to make two points very clear: (1) advertising sponsors had too much control over the entertainment content of radio shows; (2) there were too many ads per hour in commercial broadcasting. Reviewers got the message, acknowledging that *The Hucksters* tapped into a long-standing debate about the role of the sponsor in the over-commercialization of radio:

There is a controversy now mildly raging in the press as to whether the public or the people who devise radio programs and advertising plugs are most to blame for what the American people have to listen to over the air morning, noon, and night. . . . The widespread interest that this book has already aroused indicates the displeasure and annoyance with current radio practices by a very large public.[7]

Although Wakeman's story tended to lay some of the blame for radio's ills on the "public," he placed most of the blame for radio's irritating commercialism squarely on the shoulders of the broadcasting industry.

In fact, Wakeman's third — and more subtle — argument in *The Hucksters* was that modern capitalism was fueled by the businessman's sense of obligation to the domestic family unit. Many of the reviewers missed — or misunderstood — this argument because they dismissed the novel's romantic subplot. Wolcott Gibb, writing in the *New Yorker,* called *The Hucksters* a "remarkably silly book."[8] But Wakeman did not include the romance simply to attract women readers. Wakeman's strategy, which involved placing Vic Norman in a vice-grip between Kay Dorrance and her children, on the one hand, and Evan Llewelyn Evans, on the other, made Vic Norman realize that if he wanted to keep the family he had to endure the tyrant. As Frederic Wakeman himself explained years later, "The romance was supposed to be just desirable enough to become tied to the idea of a large salary." Diana Trilling was one of the few reviewers who understood this: "In other words, the economic-moral principle on which Vic operates is that unless you are fortunate enough to inherit the gifts of the truly good life you must either sell your soul to acquire them or be denied them forever. Thus is economic reality at odds with idealism."[9] Trilling lamented the fact that Vic Norman only seemed to value what he could not have; she implied that if Vic's standards for the good life had not been quite so high (Vic coveted paintings by El Greco), he could have had a family *and* a job he enjoyed.

Trilling's critique was right on target, but it is still likely that, for many of Wakeman's readers, economic reality (the need to make a living to support a family) was at odds with idealism (the desire to have a meaningful, manly, high-paying job), even if they were not in the market for El Grecos. Wakeman acknowledged them in the dedication of the book, which read "To those who sometimes awake suddenly to stare into the leisure of the night and consider with brief terror how their lives are spent."[10] If holding down an unsatisfactory white-collar job was part of the "terror" to which Wakeman referred, then *The Hucksters* struck a chord. According to Wakeman, of the "thousands of [approving] letters received from readers of the book, at least four hundred were from men stating in different ways the same idea; *I read The Hucksters and quit my job.*[11] This is powerful testimony, suggesting that what readers found in *The Hucksters* was not only a condemnation of jangling radio commercials and tasteless sponsors, but also a critique of the emerging consumer society that linked tedious, white-collar jobs, new families, and the purchasing of postwar consumer goods.

Frederic Wakeman was luckier than his protagonist when it came to having it all. At the time of the novel's publication, Wakeman was married with two children who were the same age as Kay Dorrence's youngsters in *The Hucksters*. Born in Scranton, Kansas, in 1909, and married in 1934, Wakeman had worked in advertising for most of his adult life. He took a leave from the New York advertising agency Lord and Thomas to serve in the Navy from 1942 to 1943.[12] After spending time in a Naval hospital in California, Wakeman returned to advertising (this time to Foote, Cone, and Belding) and wrote his first novel, *Shore Leave,* which was well reviewed and produced off Broadway as "Kiss Them For Me."[13] This success led to Wakeman's seven-year writer/director contract with MGM. At the same time, he also received a hefty advance from Rinehart to write *The Hucksters,* and so in 1945 he skipped out on his MGM contract and went to Mexico. Wakeman claims that he wrote the novel in twenty-nine days and placated MGM by giving them the first option on the film.[14] But unlike his protagonist, Vic, when Wakeman ditched New York for Mexico, he took his family with him. His financial success as a best-selling author allowed him to quit the huckstering business, eschew Hollywood, and travel the globe — family in tow.

Wakeman did not mean for his book to be interpreted as an attack on the American Way. He was certainly not left-leaning in his political orientation (Wakeman's spokesman, Vic Norman, had some choice words for leftish intellectuals in *The Hucksters*). In fact, Wakeman was a strong advocate of the commercial broadcasting system. He was simply hopeful that if radio reformed itself of its own free will then no "mass movement" would demand a government-sponsored form of broadcasting. But his critique of commercial radio — in both its novel and screenplay form — was *interpreted* as an attack on capitalism by broadcasting insiders. Wakeman's book was feared by broadcasting executives like NBC's Niles Trammell, who, according to several internal memos he exchanged with other executives at NBC, thought that the film version of *The Hucksters* would be welcomed by "Soviet propagandists in Moscow."[15]

The controversy surrounding radio advertising following the publication of *The Hucksters* provides a unique window onto the sudden outbreak of "active listening" in the postwar era. Disgruntled radio listeners bought Wakeman's book, saw the movie, and read the deluge of published reviews of the book. They responded to surveys of listener opinion, wrote letters to the editor, and wrote to their radio stations. Importantly, however, it was the "radio activity" of journalists, critics, and intellectuals that frightened network executives the most. In the immediate postwar period, critics who had little direct affiliation with the consumer movement exhibited new forms of "radio activity": they published reviews, criticisms, screeds, attacks, cartoons, and books that attacked radio with a tone which resonated with the consumerist attacks of the 1930s.

The year 1946 marked the peak of radio's profit and popularity — but also the beginning of its demise as the dominant mass-medium in American culture. The war was over and television was just coming into view, but somehow the volume and the vehemence of radio criticism after World War II took the commercial broadcasting industry by surprise. Advertisers, thinking that they had safely distanced themselves from the protests against radio advertising that had dominated the 1930s and early 1940s, greeted the end of the war with new commercials that were longer, louder, and more frequent. But when the war ended in 1945, the broadcast industry faced a radio listening audience that seemed more vocal, and more angry, than ever before. As one *New York Times* media critic noted: "The year of 1946 found radio subjected to more obverse and insistent criticism than the industry had experienced in the whole of its previous twenty-five years, the main burden of the complaint against the ethereal art being excessive commercialism."[16]

In March 1946 the first major blow against "excessive commercialism" came from the Federal Communications Commission, a relatively timid government agency that had the power to grant and renew station licenses. The FCC was also charged with the vague responsibility of guarding the "public interest." With this authority in mind, the FCC issued a report on radio that addressed the problem of over-commercialism — thereby setting off a wave of angry speeches and editorials from leaders of the National Association of Broadcasters. The FCC's report, *Public Service Responsibility of Broadcast Licensees,* nicknamed the "Blue Book" for its "cerulescent" blue cover, was seen by broadcast professionals as a serious threat to commercial radio.[17]

The Blue Book was not an all-out attack on commercial radio. It argued that advertising was "essential" to radio's support.[18] But the Blue Book did condemn the practice of "advertising excesses," such as "the number of commercials presented in a given hour; the piling up of commercials; the time between commercials; the middle commercial . . . and the intermixture of program and advertising."[19] The report suggested that if stations wanted their licenses renewed, they would have to eliminate these advertising excesses. The report also urged stations to carry more "sustaining" (meaning non-commercial) programs, more local live programs, and more programs devoted to public issues.[20]

The Blue Book drew a lot of angry ink from broadcasting insiders. As Richard Meyer has argued, "To say that the 1946 [Blue Book] created a furor is perhaps an understatement." From March until June, even as articles published in *Broadcasting Magazine,* the primary trade magazine for the industry, insisted that the report was "nothing to get alarmed about," the magazine's editorial page published angry opinions , often comparing the tactics of the FCC to those of fascist regimes.[21] *Variety,* a strikingly more liberal organ, applauded the Blue Book, complaining that "over the past few years over commercialization has won out," and that "good taste . . . and cognizance of public service programming have gone by the boards." *Variety* called the report a "blessing in disguise." *Variety* also quoted a broadcasting insider who admitted that fear was gripping the industry: "It's probable that never before have so many broadcasters been frightened at one time."[22]

In April 1946 a second blow was dealt to the broadcast industry. Charles Siepmann, one of the FCC's chief consultants during the researching and writing of the Blue Book, published his own attack on radio, *Radio's Second Chance.* Siepmann, born and raised in England, and a long-time employee of the BBC before coming to America, was also an old friend of John Angell, one of the top brass at NBC. Angell helped Siepmann get a teaching post at Harvard, and the two of them corresponded about the possibility of Siepmann working for NBC in the late 1930s.[23] But by the time Siepmann published *Radio's Second Chance,* he had staked out a position against the networks. Siepmann did not advocate the elimination of commercial sponsorship, but he went much further than the Blue Book in his critique of commercialism in radio, calling for listener activism to reform the medium. Like the Blue Book, *Radio's Second Chance* attacked radio for its advertising "excesses" and exhorted broadcasters to address their programming to the interests of local communities rather than those of national advertisers. Siepmann resented the fact that radio had become, in his words, "the drudge of advertising," and thought that if listeners organized to protest radio's dependence on advertising, the medium could be improved.

Broadcast industry insiders saw Siepmann's book and the FCC Blue Book as a threat to commercial radio and accused Siepmann of wanting to "BBC-ize" American radio.[24] Siepmann bore the brunt of the attack for both documents after he was identified as one of the authors of the Blue Book. *Variety,* again, applauded Siepmann's work and noted that he was fast becoming the "plumed knight" of "radio's critical contingent." Meanwhile, Siepmann came under attack by Justin Miller, president of the National Association of Broadcasters, who was "stump[ing] the country" calling those who wrote the Blue Book "stooges for the Communists," "obfuscators," "professional appeasers," "guileful men," and "astigmatic perverts."[25] The controversy might have been a boon, however, for Siepmann's career; in April 1946 he became a full professor at New York University and Director of its Communications Center.[26]

Siepmann's book was not a best seller, but it did get a favorable review in *Time* magazine for daring to propose a solution to radio's problems — fewer commercials and more listener activism:

Many doctors have diagnosed radio's ills; few have prescribed a cure. . . . Siepmann told radio how it could get well if it only half tried. Like any competent physician . . . Siepmann began with a documented case history of his patient. For many a suffering listener, it was the best analysis of radio's excesses.[27]

Time praised Siepmann's vision for a more organized listening public, as well as his suggestion that radio stations should limit the number of commercials per hour.

In May 1946, immediately following the broadcast industry's furor over the Blue Book and *Radio's Second Chance,* Rinehart published *The Hucksters.* By June, the book had been adopted by the Book-of-the-Month Club and the debate over commercial radio expanded beyond the purview of government pamphlets, industry insider homilies, and vengeful editorials in *Broadcasting Magazine.* With the publication of *The Hucksters,* the fight over commercial radio went public. Critics like Wakeman and Siepmann were not consumer activists, radicals, or working-class heroes.[28] They did not seek the overthrow of capitalism — or even the elimination of the radio sponsor. But their criticisms of commercial radio resonated with the public — and received more popular attention than the consumerist criticisms that had been leveled at commercial radio from its inception, and that had mounted dangerously before the war. Though Wakeman and Siepmann were not affiliated with the consumer movement, they sounded very much like their more radical predecessors: activists like James Rorty, Ruth Brindze, and Peter Morell.

Wakeman's dominant argument in *The Hucksters* — that the broadcast industry should reduce the number of "irritating" commercials — won widespread reviewer sympathy. As one reviewer suggested, "The reader should be warned that if he reads 'The Hucksters,' it will be a long time before he listens to his radio with his usual complacency."[29] Others who reviewed the novel differed, at times, over the question of who was to blame for radio's advertising excesses. Wakeman blamed the broadcast industry for refusing to stand up to advertising sponsors. In Wakeman's critique, sponsors were at the heart of advertising's evils. His derogatory label "huckster" was used by Wakeman in a radio interview to describe radio sponsors:

Since advertising's chief interest is in products, it should not be permitted to control the program material of radio, whose chief interest must be not in customers but in listeners. . . . You radio people should take back your programs from the hucksters. Take back your networks. Take back your stations and do your own programming without the benefit of what any sponsor thinks any program should be. . . . Commercials can then be sold to advertisers on a dignified, properly controlled basis that will protect the program, not destroy it.[30]

Wakeman's plan of action betrayed a certain amount of naiveté about the business of radio. He argued that radio should be interested in "listeners," not "customers," but from the point of view of the product sponsor, listeners *were* customers. And, as long as sponsors paid the entire cost of producing the program and the commercial, it would be difficult for broadcasters to challenge their tyrannical whims.

Some station owners heeded Wakeman's plea, increasing the number of "public interest" programs. But the effectiveness of these reforms was debated. Russell Maloney, writing for the *New York Times Book Review*, noted an increase in "sustaining" programming, but he was not convinced that it would change radio's emphasis on the bottom line: "Programs abounding in culture and what is loosely called 'public service' are lavishly tucked into all possible crevices of the day's schedule — anywhere they won't interfere with the bread-and-butter, sponsored programs, that is. As for the sponsors voluntarily improving the quality of their programs — well, I offer in evidence 'The Hucksters,' with the humble request that it be read into the FCC records."[31] Maloney, who loved *The Hucksters*, joined Wakeman to defend the book in a conversation with Carlos Franco, vice-president of the ad agency Young and Rubicom, on the radio station WQXR.[32]

In response to the critical praise for Wakeman's book, advertising industry professionals like Carlos Franco denied that *The Hucksters*'s depiction of their industry was based on reality, claiming instead that it offered an exaggerated portrait. The advertising trade magazine *Tide* found that only 5 percent of "leading" advertising men found the book to be a faithful rendition of the industry.[33] Wakeman insisted that the book was accurate, asking, "Is 'Love that soap' any more penetrating or irritating and nauseating than a combination of foghorns, jingle bells, whistles, toots and so on that your hear over the radio practically 20 hours a day?" He pointed to the book's success — a record 700,000 copies sold in six months — as evidence of the public's dissatisfaction with radio.

Wakeman's novel was even taken as a call to action by some of his reviewers. As one suggested, "Long-suffering radio audiences may also hope that *The Hucksters'* venom indicates a growing rebellion against the sins of the advertisers. It might be what Evan Evans would call (tossing his hat out of the window, to illustrate) 'a straw in the wind.'"[34] Wakeman himself did not advocate a "rebellion," or even the dismantling of the commercial broadcasting system. Rather, he wanted to protect the commercial system of broadcasting and believed that reform was the radio industry's best hope for defending itself from full-scale listener revolt:

I think that radio advertisers had better start changing some of the sounds that come out of the loudspeakers, or the American public is going to rise up in protest against it, and we might get a BBC type of radio.[35]

Thus, while some listeners may have interpreted *The Hucksters* as a radical critique of commercial radio, Wakeman himself rejected the model of state-sponsorship for broadcasting and was suspicious of "mass movements."[36] Ironically, perhaps, Wakeman was naive enough to believe that listener criticism, and even the popularity of his own novel, might be enough to scare broadcasters into cutting down on the number of commercials they broadcast each day.

On the other hand, the cacophony of anti-advertising voices did make an impact on some broadcasters. William Paley, president of CBS, was probably the most outspoken network executive to admit that broadcasters were responsible for advertising "excesses." Paley delivered a "mea culpa" address to the National Association of Broadcasters in 1946:

I have been reading and hearing . . . a growing volume of criticism of American broadcasting. . . . We cannot ignore its scope and its destructive effect. . . . I believe this rising tide of criticism . . . constitute[s] the most urgent single problem of our industry. . . . I believe part of the criticism is justified. . . .

The most persistently repeated charge against broadcasters is that we permit advertising excesses. Are we guilty or not? It is my opinion that we are. . . . This type of operation is bad radio. More than that, it is bad advertising. Certainly it is not the advertiser's fault, but the broadcaster's.[37]

Paley, like many network executives, believed that any advertising that drew the anger of consumer listeners was "bad advertising," which is why he delivered his apology and why the broadcast industry invested so much time and money in figuring out what listeners thought about radio advertising. Paley refocused the debate on the question of "advertising excesses." This was an attempt to bring critics back from the brink of considering whether or not free enterprise was the right system for the support of radio altogether.

In the end, even Frederic Wakeman succumbed to some of the advertising practices he sought to expose. His critique of postwar radio was complicated by the fact that the same marketing techniques that he condemned in the novel were used to sell his book. Rinehart broadcast a series of radio commercials that used the catch-phrase, "Love Dat Book," spoken in black dialect, just as "Love That Soap" is spoken in the novel:

> Freddie Wakeman who wrote "Shore Leave"
> Has another book today;
> Advertising folks should read it,
> Learn what Wakeman has to say

Un-Um! Love Dat Book! I'm talking about *"The Hucksters"* — that new novel by Frederic Wakeman that is just about the creamiest, crunchiest literary dish ever served between the covers of a book.

Yes, folks, read *"The Hucksters,"* and no matter what ails you, you'll feel better instantly. *"The Hucksters"* is all about the radio business and about all those bright people who entertain you from dawn to dark and from dark to dawn — or do they?

> Un-Um! Love Dat Book!
> Every listener should read it,
> Learn what Wakeman has to say.

Ask your bookseller today for the mild, mellow, chocolate-coated bombshell, *"The Hucksters."* It's the Book-of-the-Month Club choice for June and published by Rinehart and Co., who are paying through the nose for this commercial. Aren't they foolish?[38]

Though the commercial pokes fun at its own form, and even takes a jab at Rinehart, the advertising campaign was successful in securing more press for the book, and probably more sales. Even Llewelyn Evans would have been proud.

The Control of the Sponsor

Sponsors had more control over broadcasting in the radio age than at any other time. After the mid-1950s broadcasting adopted the "magazine" style of advertising, in which the networks produced the shows and sold airtime to advertisers. But during the radio age, corporations and their advertising agencies had unprecedented control over both the advertising and the entertainment that was broadcast over the air. The control of a single sponsor, however, also made radio more vulnerable to listener resistance. As we have seen, when listeners wanted to target a radio program or a radio sponsor, a boycott, while difficult to organize, was one way to make a direct attack on the bottom line. Thus, during the radio age, capital had more direct control over culture, but the direct nature of this control made individual sponsors more vulnerable to public pressure.

During this period, then, it was the broadcast professionals who often felt squeezed, between listeners on the one hand and the sponsors on the other. This was especially difficult for writers, producers, and announcers who worked on news programs. They needed both enthusiastic audiences and willing sponsors to produce shows with high ratings. One such broadcast professional, Quincy Howe, described his dilemma in 1943:

> The sponsor tends to judge news shows largely on the basis of audience appeal — which in turn puts a premium on sensationalism. . . . The serious news broadcaster . . . finds himself under pressure from two quarters. On the one hand, he is tempted to play up to the widest possible audience; on the other, he is tempted to slant his interpretation the way he thinks his sponsor might like it to go. . . . In recent months we have seen . . . sponsors snap up the news programs with a conservative slant as they never snapped up the programs with a liberal slant. . . . When [the sponsor] buys a news show he will tend, nine times out of ten, to prefer the kind of analyst who at least does no violence to the National Association of Manufacturers. . . . The big wartime profits of American industry and the popular trend away from the New Deal sharpen these conflicts.[39]

While sensationalism and conservatism were not mutually exclusive, the problem described by Howe was especially acute in the radio age: the sponsor's taste was not necessarily representative of popular taste — in news, politics, or entertainment. Stubborn sponsors, like George Washington Hill or his fictional likeness, Evan Llewelyn Evans, did not appreciate the conflict of interest at work in their demands for shows that would conform to their particular preferences as well as merit a high listener rating.

The problem of the sponsor's conservative bias was not limited to radio — magazines and newspapers had their share of battles with advertisers who disliked reading articles that were pro-labor or critical of capitalism. But whereas unions could easily produce their own newspapers and newsletters, in the radio age, the business lobby succeeded in preventing labor organizations from sponsoring their own radio programming. Charles Siepmann was especially critical of the National Association of Broadcaster's policy of prohibiting radio programs from being sponsored by "controversial" interests — specifically, labor:

In 1939 membership of labor unions totaled some 13 millions. Together with their families, these union members represented nearly 40 per cent of the American public. They shared a common interest in union matters and, many of them, a common point of view on a number of social, economic, and political questions besides. Yet in 1944 "Labor for Victory" was the only nationwide program on the air representing labor interests.[40]

Thus, sponsors not only exerted editorial control over individual shows, they also prevented organized labor from itself sponsoring radio programs.

Listeners shared the critics' view of the sponsor. One 1947 survey of New York residents found that 52.8 percent of listeners blamed the sponsor for radio's excessive commercialism, and 27 percent blamed the advertising agency. Fewer than 10 percent blamed the station. This widespread resentment against the advertising sponsor was, in part, what made *The Hucksters* so popular. Moreover, Wakeman's biting critique of the role of the sponsor hit home because of the real-life radio sponsor he had elected to spoof. Wakeman's tyrant, Evan Llewelyn Evans, was modeled on the tobacco giant George Washington Hill, president of the American Tobacco Company, and one of the premier sponsor/tyrants of the radio age.

George Washington Hill acquired his reputation for being eccentric and irritating when he began to use radio to advertise cigarettes in the late 1920s. He advertised Lucky Strikes on the radio throughout the Depression, with such slogans as "Nature in the raw is seldom mild," "Spit is a horrible word," "There's no spit in Cremo!" (referring to the process used to make Cremo cigars), "Be happy — Go Lucky," and the cryptic "LS/MFT" (Lucky Strike Means Fine Tobacco).[41] The American Tobacco Company was one of the first large companies to use radio, making Lord and Thomas one of the first agencies to produce nationally broadcast radio shows, such as the popular "Lucky Strike Orchestra," which first aired in 1928.[42] Hill tested the advertising power of the radio orchestra by suspending all of his other advertising: using radio alone he found that his sales increased by 47 percent.[43] One contemporary writer noted that the business of the American Tobacco Company for the "first five months of 1930 [had] surpassed all records for corresponding periods."[44] In 1948 another critic claimed that LS/MFT was "possibly the most inane combination of noises ever inflicted on a helpless public."[45] Irritation, it seems, sold cigarettes. By the time George Washington Hill died in 1946, he had taken the American Tobacco Company from $153 million in annual sales to $558 million.[46]

Frederic Wakeman had had his own close encounters with George Washington Hill, before the war, when he worked for Lord and Thomas, and after the war, when he worked for its successor, Foote, Cone, and Belding. Surely the similarities between George Washington Hill and Evan Llewelyn Evans were no coincidence. In the novel, Wakeman describes Evan Llewelyn Evans as "a small man, almost dainty," who "wore an old straw field hat, indoors and out, winter and summer."[47] This compares closely with a posthumous description of George Washington Hill written by one of his acquaintances in 1960:

He was a raw-boned, smallish man, who looked like a cowboy; he wore a big tilted sombrero, and, as a rule, kept it on while at work in his office. The hat was a symbol — his crown. . . . As business grew, so did his idiosyncrasies. He liked to drive up Fifth Avenue in an open Cadillac, with a bodyguard prominently on show; the windshield of the car was festooned with packages of Lucky Strikes.[48]

With similar bravado, the fictional character Evan Llewelyn Evans sends each of his secretaries a dozen bottles of Beautee toilet water every Christmas and even insists that his prostitutes keep bars of Beautee soap in their bathrooms.[49]

The psychological similarities between the two men were also striking. Like the fictional Evans, George Washington Hill was a fan of object lessons:

Once, the story goes, he commanded a new agency man to follow him from his office, drove wordlessly down Fifth Avenue to Tiffany's and demanded that a clerk show him a $150,000 necklace. Hill picked it up, shook it in the face of the astounded adman and boomed: "That's what I mean. Give me finished copy — not rough layouts!" Then he handed the necklace back to the clerk and walked out.[50]

Hill was also famous for browbeating his account handlers. He often lectured them on the craft of advertising, using his pocket knife, his watch, and his dental bridge for illustration. According to another legend, Hill once told Raymond Rubicam (of the agency Young and Rubicam), "The public reaction to entertainment and advertising is no different. . . . You just don't understand the advertising business."[51] This outburst came after Hill had rejected Rubicam's fourth Pall Mall advertising team. When Rubicam finally dumped Hill as a client, along with his $3 million Pall Mall account, agency employees were said to have "danced in the aisles."[52]

The advertising mogul who made Hill into the premier tobacco pusher in the interwar years was Albert Lasker, head of the Lord and Thomas advertising agency. Hill and Lasker worked closely on the Lucky Strike account, and Lasker put up with Hill's many interferences and outbursts, including his close monitoring of the radio shows produced by the agency on Hill's behalf. Hill, like Evan Llewelyn Evans, liked to impose his own taste in music on the radio public. At a 1928 audition for the Lucky Strike Orchestra, George Washington Hill ordered the orchestra to stretch songs out for eight minutes so that radio listeners could dance:

I want real dance music that people will like to dance by . . . and I don't want their attention diverted by French horn gymnastics. Let's give the public what the public wants and not try to educate them. We should not be concerned about introducing new numbers and novelties.[53]

Lasker handled Hill by "let[ting] him be the agency and pretend[ing] that I'm the client."[54] After Lord and Thomas became Foote, Cone, and Belding, Emerson Foote played a similar role as the main "handler" of George Washington Hill. Wakeman modeled the neurotic character of Kim Kimberly — the head of the agency that handled Evan Llewelyn Evans — loosely on Emerson Foote. Foote was a manic depressive, loathed the tobacco industry, and left advertising, ultimately, to become an anti-tobacco activist. And what did the real-life tyrant/sponsor think of Wakeman's novel? As Wakeman liked to tell the story, George Washington Hill was interrupted one evening by Pat Weaver and Robert Sarnoff, a couple of the top brass at NBC, who found him at home reading *The Hucksters*. When they expressed surprise that he was reading Wakeman's novel, given its unflattering portrait of the eccentric sponsor, Hill exclaimed: " 'You just got to read it, Pat . . . what that guy does to Emerson Foote!' "[55]

Though George Washington Hill's taste was crass, his sponsored shows *were* popular. This was true despite the fact that he invested more money in the commercials that sponsored the shows than in the shows themselves. In reference to one of his most popular shows, the *Lucky Strike Hit Parade,* Hill explained the reasoning behind this strategy:

"Taking 100% as the total value, we give 90% to the commercials and 10% to the show. . . . I don't have the right to spend the stockholder's money just to entertain the public."[56] This attitude, expressed so bluntly by George Washington Hill, was the attitude that Wakeman sought to reform by writing *The Hucksters*. Wakeman thought that network broadcasters, not sponsors, should be the ones in charge:

Apply the publishing technique to radio, by throwing the program responsibility back to the stations and networks, taking all of same away from agencies and sponsors and talent agencies. Then advertising time is sold next to "editorial and program matter" just as it is done in our newspapers and magazines.[57]

Wakeman believed that if broadcast advertising used this system, then sponsors would not be "bamboozled" by the glamour of Hollywood; admen could make ads, and broadcasters could make entertainment. As the ad agency copy chief says to Vic Norman in *The Hucksters*, "Goddammit, we're admakers not talent agents."

Hill died in September 1946, just five months after the publication of *The Hucksters*. Though there were rumors that the novel led to Hill's demise, Wakeman insists that it was tobacco, and not the novel, that killed the old man: "[In 1943] he was in very bad shape with emphysema and indeed used a throat spray three to four times for every cigarette he smoked. I judged he was a 2½ pack-a-day man."[58] Hill's death coincided with the rise of television and decline of radio as America's favorite mass medium, and, ultimately, with the decline of the sponsor's vise-grip control over individual programs. As Eric Barnouw has argued, the sponsor continued to play an influential role in early television programming. The real "death" of the sponsor did not occur until after the quiz scandals of the mid-1950s. In 1960, the "magazine" style of advertising, in which a single show had multiple sponsors, became the routine practice.

Frederic Wakeman — part prophet, part preacher — lived to see the day in which the sponsor's direct control over broadcasting entertainment was diminished. He believed that his novel contributed to the rejection of the sponsor system and the switch to the "magazine" style that dominates broadcast advertising today:

By showing precisely how a radio comedy show was botched by . . . product czar and sycophants, agency puppet and yes-men, radio network uncritical beavers plus Hollywood talent peddlers, the reading and listening public could get the point that programs should not be made by the ad business in the name of the sponsor. The book helped the TV take the show out of business tycoons. One goal for my side.[59]

While critics like Wakeman believed that the reform of radio's over-commercialism could come from within the industry, and, specifically, from the National Association of Broadcasters, others believed that the NAB was too dependent on sponsor revenues to do anything that would threaten the sponsor's control.

Radio critic Albert Williams dismissed both the NAB and the federal government as potential problem solvers and instead called on listeners to go directly to the source of the problem — the almighty sponsor. He argued that no matter how much listeners complained, their complaints would fall on deaf ears unless they targeted the big money behind the commercialism itself:

[The listeners] can publish pamphlets, issue statements, stage rallies, to their heart's content, but so long as they cudgel the poor broadcaster instead of the advertiser, they will accomplish nothing. However, a simple resolution in an annual convention of women against the product of an individual sponsor as punishment for his crass merchandising methods would bring an overnight catharsis. This bull against one advertiser would cause every other advertiser who has misused radio to have his advertising agent on the carpet the following morning, applying the proper remedy. The fear of bad publicity is a stronger deterrent to unpleasant action than the most powerful Directives, Injunctions, and Decisions.[60]

This suggestion to boycott specific sponsors was more radical than anything Frederic Wakeman, or even Charles Siepmann, proposed. Williams believed that if housewives directed their boycotts and bad publicity at "crass" sponsors, they would attack over-commercialism at its source. Williams understood that the control of the sponsor made capital more vulnerable to organized public attack; he called for consumers to use the marketplace to oppose the very logic on which the marketplace was founded.

Why 1946? Golden Age and Listener Rage

In 1946, after the war, and in some ways because of the war, the American radio industry was at its absolute peak in terms of power and profitability. According to one report, radio revenues "rose from $22,600,000 in 1937 to $90,300,000 in 1944" — an increase of 400 percent. At the same time, the ratio of income to revenues also rose, from 19.8 percent to 32.8 percent. According to a report by the Federal Communications Commission, this was because "the industry has progressively retained a larger and larger proportion of each revenue dollar as profit and has spent a smaller

TABLE 8. Radio Advertising as a Percentage of All Advertising, 1934–1955

1934	6%	1940	10%	1946	14%	1952	9%
1935	7%	1941	11%	1947	12%	1953	8%
1936	7%	1942	12%	1947	12%	1954	7%
1937	8%	1943	13%	1949	11%	1955	6%
1938	9%	1944	14%	1950	11%		
1939	9%	1945	15%	1951	10%		

SOURCE: Sterling and Kitross, *Stay Tuned,* 638–39.

and smaller proportion for serving the public."[61] The last year of the war, 1945, was also the year that radio gained the greatest share of the total advertising market: 15 percent (see Table 8). It was in these years — the age of radio — that radio advertising expenditures first began to climb. From 1940–1945 spending on radio represented a growing share of the total monies spent on advertising before it dropped down to its current level — around 6 percent.[62] During radio's peak, which coincided with World War II, radio was one of the most useful vehicles for the dissemination of news, war-related information, and propaganda. As Charles Siepmann observed, "Radio has taught us, to our cost, that ideas are weapons."[63] And it was through radio, perhaps more than through any other medium, that the Second World War of ideas was fought.

During the early years of World War II, when the consumer movement was at its peak strength, one advertising industry leader exhorted his colleagues to take the problem of advertising criticism seriously. He argued that "capitalism is definitely on a spot. It will totter and disappear unless we who know and talk to the American public awaken to the sales job this problem presents."[64] At a conference of advertisers in 1942, just after the attack on Pearl Harbor, industry professionals agreed to band together for common defense. By the end of the war they had succeeded in defending themselves against consumerist and legislative attacks and, according to their own puffery, they had helped America to win the war *and* make the world safe for capitalist expansion. By protecting themselves, they believed, they had also saved free enterprise.

At a practical level, advertisers won two victories during the war. The first was a legislative one: advertisers exploited a loophole in the "excess profit" tax. This wartime tax was levied on all corporate profits at a rate of 90 percent. After some wrangling, companies won the right to deduct from their profits any money spent on advertising which was "ordinary and necessary." This reduced the amount of profit that was taxed and allowed companies to keep their name in front of the public even during a time of rationed consumption. The second victory for advertising during the war was organizational. Advertisers formed the War Advertising Council, which oversaw the production and dissemination of public-service campaigns. In part because of these efforts, advertising expenditures grew, rather than shrank, during the war.[65]

The backlash against radio advertising after the war was thus, in part, a backlash against radio's new cultural power. Listeners and critics responded to three major changes in radio programming: the postwar return of the advertising industry to the business of selling goods, the perceived "low" quality of radio programming, and increased control over radio programming by advertisers. During the war, according to one radio industry professional, the country had became more "idealistic" and "anything that smacked of crass commercialism in the midst of an all-out battle for survival was exposed to severe public and government criticism" — sentiments to which advertisers paid heed.[66] But after the war, when the floodgates were lifted on buying and selling, advertisers "increased the number, length, and stridency of commercials, and brought back much of the 'pawnshop' atmosphere of the early 1930s."[67] According to a leading ad-man, "The war is over and the words that sold ideas . . . and ideals . . . must once again sell merchandise . . . in ever increasing quantities."[68] Advertising may have helped to win the war in Europe and Japan, but in 1946 listeners began to feel like the new battleground was being staked out over their eardrums.

Some of the angriest attacks against advertising came, in fact, from returning soldiers. For these men, as for returning veteran Frederic Wakeman, radio advertising seemed more offensive than when they had left for the war. One soldier testified:

The aspect of home-front life which most disgusted me on return was radio. . . . The first evening that I sat by a radio at home, I heard one long parade of headaches, coughs, aching muscles, stained teeth, "unpleasant full feeling," and gastric hyperacidity. . . . Our radio evenings are a sick parade of sicknesses and if they haven't yet made us a sick nation, I wonder why.[69]

Another returning veteran felt that most returning soldiers would prefer the Armed Forces Network to postwar commercial radio: "Most GIs would take the AFN in preference to American radio simply because they are fed up with commercials. . . . When I returned . . . I was shocked at the poor taste." The experience of fighting, for many of these veterans, put the postwar commercial frenzy into dark perspective.[70]

One advertising historian has argued that soldiers resented the ads they heard on the radio after the war because large corporations seemed to be taking credit for winning the war. "The servicemen thought they had something to do with it. They were annoyed with promises of new and shinier products in the postwar world."[71] A poem published in the *Saturday Review* captured this resentment. The poem was written in the voice of a fictional seller of alcoholic beverages:

> All during this war we at Gugleheimer-Botts
> Distillers of Old Bushwah a blend
> Composed of 15% straight whiskies thirty days old
> And 85% neutral spirits
> Said we'd stand by you
> And we did
>
> We stood by you at Guadalcanal, the Solomons, New Guinea,
> New Britain, St. Lo and the Battle of the Bulge.
> Names as famous in American history
> As that of Old Bushwah itself . . .
>
> We've kept the faith. We've fought the good fight.
> You in your way. We in ours.
> Now you can lay down your rifle
> And we can take up our typewriter
> After four years in Hell![72]

The four years in Hell for advertisers — four years of restricted selling — were decidedly different from the four years in Hell experienced by returning soldiers. This poem is so mockingly solemn, and so understated in its use of advertising clichés ("We've kept the faith. We've fought the good fight."), that it reads like actual advertising copy. But "Old Bushwah," merely a fictional concoction, surely was not at "Guadalcanal" or the "Battle of the Bulge." The poem was actually a bitter parody of the corporate tendency to take credit for winning the war.

Radio, already vulnerable to listener resentment, was also vulnerable to the increasing influence and power of rival media. Television was the next big thing, and even Niles Trammell, one of radio's biggest boosters, predicted that "when television comes in, sound broadcasting is finished."[73] The newspaper and film industries also posed a threat to radio. After the war, with the relaxing of the newsprint shortage, newspapers regained their size and status, whereas radio was plagued by the increased cost of radio talent, as well as by strikes and material shortages. Compounding these troubles, sponsors now had less incentive to pump their excess profits into advertising; in January 1946 the "excess profit" tax was repealed.[74] All of these threats prompted the broadcast industry to spend its advertising revenues more efficiently — which led to an increase in shows that were cheap to produce, such as soap operas and quiz shows.

Another rival of the broadcast industry was the film industry. While both industries profited during the war, movie attendance dropped after 1945. Between 1946 and 1949, "admission sales fell by 14.2%."[75] Perhaps this is one reason MGM was willing to take on the radio industry by producing *The Hucksters,* seeing the movie as one way to needle the broadcast industry for its dependence on advertising. While much of the satire about radio advertising that appeared in the book was watered down for the film version of *The Hucksters,* one scene got the attention of NBC executives. In it, Vic Norman, played with a certain lackluster smugness by Clark Gable, gave a speech about the evils of advertising while dictating a memo to his boss:

For four years I haven't been listening to the radio much. . . . In that time it's gotten worse, if possible. More irritating. More commercials per minute. More spelling out of words as if no one in the audience had gotten past the first grade. . . . We've pushed and badgered the listeners. We've sung to them and screamed at them. We've insulted them, cheated them and angered them . . . turned their homes into a combination grocery store, crap game and midway. . . . Some day 50,000,000 people are going to just reach out and turn off their radios. Snap. Just like that. And that's the end of the gravy for you and me — and Evans.

At NBC, Niles Trammell and Syd Eiges exchanged a few memos about this scene from the film. In one, Eiges complained that "Gable, in a very dramatic speech, claims that the audience has nothing to do with what it hears over the radio. . . . Regarded in its sum total this picture could do nothing but harm the radio industry."[76]

Most film reviewers anticipated that radio executives would interpret *The Hucksters* as an attack on the medium. One writer for *Advertising Age* described the film as a "conga-line of commercials" that were "brisk, funny and only slightly exaggerated." The *Advertising Age* writer remarked that it was something of a "paradox" that "the screen writers wrote better commercials than ex-adman Wakeman, and that Wakeman's book was probably a better script for a movie than what M-G-M actually used."[77] Indeed, the commercial parodies in the film were funny, from the long version of "Love That Soap," a spoken testimonial with characters from every region in the country, to the soap-opera parodies (*Just Plain Jane* and *Wife in Name Only*), to the singing commercials:

Wanna learn how to spell?
Well,
B-E-A-U-T-double-E
B-E-A-U-T-double-E
B-E-A-U-T-E-E
Spells,
Whew-hoo [whistle]
Beautee Soap

This radio ad was featured in the movie during a scene in which Jean Ogilvie, while cooking dinner for Vic, tried to find some soothing music. Instead, she found a commercial for cemetery plots; the commercial presented here, for Beautee Soap; and a commercial with the ear-piercing sound of glass breaking, for a breakfast cereal called Wham! No matter where she turned the dial, she found an ad. This was another one of the scenes that angered NBC executives, who complained that there was "an entirely uncalled for and untrue scene where Miss Ogilvie is awaiting Gable in her apartment."[78]

The scene that really riled NBC executives, however, was one during which the main character delivered a diatribe on the evils of the radio industry. Clark Gable, as Vic Norman, dictated a memo in which he complained that advertising agencies let sponsors have "their own way" too often: "[The listeners] have some rights. . . . It's their homes we go into. . . . I want to go on record as saying that I think radio has to turn over a new leaf." After finishing this memo, which he signed "Love and Kisses, Vic," Norman is approached timidly by his secretary, a severe woman with a sharp face and a prim dress:

MISS HAMMER:	Oh, Mr. Norman, sir . . .
VIC:	What's the matter, you think I'm wrong?
MISS HAMMER:	I wouldn't say.
VIC:	Do you ever listen to the radio?
MISS HAMMER:	Yes sir.
VIC:	And?
MISS HAMMER:	Well I get back at it.
VIC:	How?
MISS HAMMER:	It may sound silly, but I make it a point of honor — a point of honor — never to buy anything that's advertised that way.
VIC:	Even Beautee soap?
MISS HAMMER:	Particularly Beautee soap.
VIC:	*(Laughing)* Good for you Miss Hammer, good for you.

The appropriately named "Miss Hammer," then, by threatening to boy-cott products that were advertised with annoying commercials, revealed her devious plans. NBC executive Charles Hammond wrote to Trammell complaining that the character of Miss Hammer was meant to typify "the little people in the country" and that the "entire note [was] taken right out of the consumer movement book." He called the scene the "most dan-gerous part of the entire film," and charged that MGM had stepped on a "soapbox" and was doing a "crusading job" similar to that of the "New Republic, Consumers Union, etc." He hoped that Trammell could get the scene pulled from the film.[79]

Meanwhile, as Charles Hammond was fuming over this scene, Syd Eiges was making plans to retaliate against the entire film industry for making *The Hucksters*. He suggested to Trammell that NBC start a new radio series called "Spotlight on Hollywood." Series topics might include: an exposé of the stockholder suits "now pending against the leading movie companies"; the ineffectiveness of the censorship provided by the Johnston office; and a weekly update of the films which were banned by the "Legion of Decency."[80] Eiges also prepared three sample drafts of a press release in response to *The Hucksters*. The first draft was so overblown it seemed like a parody of red-baiting. And, yet, in the cover memo, Eiges described it as "the sharpest and hardest hitting":

If I were the commissar of propaganda for the Soviet Russian government I would pay any price for copies of the film of 'The Hucksters.' . . . In my many years in radio I have encountered no more vicious and untruthful attack on our American system of advertising which is generally recognized by all except left wingers as the bulwark of the American system of free enterprise. I predict now that no matter what any American critic may say about this picture it will receive its warmest review in "The Daily Worker."

In this draft, Eiges attacked the motion picture industry for "huckstering" sex. He urged Americans to look at the illustrations for movies in the newspaper if they had any doubts: "The American people know only too well who the real hucksters are."

It is difficult to understand why *The Hucksters,* which the *New York Times* pronounced "dull," and which *Advertising Age* said lacked the "shock power" of the novel, would incite such rage from Eiges, Hammond, and Trammell. But their reaction makes more sense when one considers: (1) the threat to radio represented by the consumer move-ment — which had been growing in power and influence just before America's entrance into the war; (2) the advent of television and the anticipation of an inter-industry battle over film and television as to which form, advertising-sponsored media or film, would be the most affordable and/or respectable. Even more galling to the brass at NBC, perhaps, was the source of the threat represented by *The Hucksters*. Whereas the books and pamphlets of the consumer movement had reached an audience of about one million, *The Hucksters* was estimated to have reached sixty million movie-goers.[81]

The consumer movement lost considerable steam after the war. It never became the threat to commercially sponsored radio (or television) that NBC executives imagined. *The Hucksters,* however, did contribute to the postwar backlash against network radio. As the audience intellectual Paul Lazarsfeld found in his 1948 study, *Radio Listening in America,* the novel and the movie did have an effect on those who were exposed to it: those who had read or seen *The Hucksters,* he discovered, were more critical of advertising than those who had not.[82]

Conclusion

The film version of *The Hucksters,* however, had a different message about women, consumption, and class ambition than did the novel. The explicit sex scenes of the novel were written out entirely, and so was Vic's illicit affair. In the film version, Vic Norman met Kay Dorrance when he sought her out in order to ask her to endorse Beautee Soap in exchange for a donation to her favorite charity.[83] In the film, Kay (Deborah Kerr) was a wealthy war widow, instead of a married woman about to cheat on her husband, and she and Vic started their romance with a clean conscience. But then Vic invited her to a seedy weekend retreat and his impropriety cooled their romance. He subsequently tried to "sell himself" on a singer named Jean Ogilvie, played lusciously by Ava Gardner. But a class dame is what he wanted, and when Kay Dorrance flew out to California to win him back, they made plans to marry. As in the novel, this made Vic into something of a company stooge, but only for one brief scene. In his last meeting with Evan Llewellyn Evans (played by Sidney Greenstreet), Vic poured water over the head of his tyrant/boss and quit his job.

Later, he and Kay drove through the streets of New York. It was the middle of the night, nearly dawn, and they found themselves driving through Fulton Market, at the base of the Brooklyn Bridge. It was there that Vic told Kay that he quit his job — in case she "wanted out." But she told him that she did not care about money and that he should sell things with "dignity and taste" that "he could believe in." They kissed, the music swelled, and the camera panned upward to capture the fog-shrouded beauty of the Brooklyn Bridge. This ending was distinct from the novel's, not only because it was "happy," in the Hollywood sense, but also because of the way in which it was happy. The Vic Norman of the novel version of *The Hucksters* was a cynic who fell embarrassingly in love and then became a cynic again. He quit both his job and his romance at the end of the book. In the movie, however, Vic was able to keep his dignity *and* live happily ever after. He did not have to sell his soul to buy into the American dream of home, family, or self-respect.

One of the striking elements of this scene was the fact that Kay, and not Vic, was driving the car. She was also the "real adult" in the scene. When Vic told her they could not get married because he needed to get a good job and make "big money," she chided him: "You're such a child, darling, you've come to hate the business that you're in and you just want to drop it and go live on a beach in Tahiti somewhere." Vic agreed: "That's not a bad idea." But Kay ignored Vic's comment and insisted that he trade his high-class aspirations for true love:

When you say money you mean big money. And that just doesn't matter, Vic. That's not something you base a life on. If you do then you're Kimberly. But us? Oh Vic, you wonderful dope. You and I are going to get married just as soon as we can get a license. And then you're going to do what you want to do. That's what matters, doing what you want to, not money.

After this speech, Vic took some change out of his pocket and threw it out of the car in the direction of a Fulton Market "hawker," who had been placed in the scene to highlight the theme of "huckstering." The hawker dove for the change, and Vic told Kay that they would start their lives with an "even nothing. . . . It's neater that way."

This scene offered a counterintuitive vision of the immediate postwar era. The message was not about conspicuous consumption or material aspiration; instead, Kay defended a life of modest means and ambitions. She placed love over money and seemed to mean it. Kay also controlled both the physical action and the dialogue in the scene. She was driving the car, just as women in general were starting to "drive" the postwar economy. And, while the novel ended cynically, almost flippantly, the movie closed with the woman in control, in a romantic embrace with the man she wanted, and espousing working-class sentiments.

The movie version of *The Hucksters* is one of many reminders that the most active of the "radio activists" of the radio age were women. While the consumer movement that came of age during the 1930s and 1940s certainly had its share of male leaders, most of the grassroots members of that movement were women. In addition, women bought 85 percent of household goods and made up the most important audience for most radio programming. The radio age appears hazy to us now; it is hard to imagine a national mass culture based on the ear rather than the eye. Perhaps the difficulty we have remembering the radio age also has to do with the importance of women to the story. Our common-sense disdain for all things consumer-oriented may have much to do with the feminization of consumption as a process. Perhaps, in the twenty-first century, production will be feminized and consumption will be masculinized, and the poles of good and evil will be reversed.

In this book, I have argued that radio activated rather than pacified its mostly women listeners. First and foremost, radio activated women to buy: the "act" of shopping was the number one goal of all commercially sponsored radio programming, and in achieving this, radio was often successful. But, at times, listeners were motivated to protest rather than purchase. The targets of their protests were varied: sometimes it was the "low" quality of the washboard weeper, sometimes it was the ideology of the pitchman, sometimes it was a prurient storyline, sometimes it was the "waste" endemic to the system of consumer capitalism. Capitalism — and certainly network broadcasting — is less vulnerable to these kinds of protests today. Some of the very reforms sought by Wakeman and Siepmann have come to pass, and they have shifted the accountability for programming from the sponsor to the broadcaster. In the process, with more than one sponsor involved in a single show, each individual sponsor has become less vulnerable to organized boycotts that might seek to challenge that programming.

At the same time, I want to argue that the left can learn from the successes of corporate advertising. Advertising, sometimes without trying, helped to organize consumers into groups that eventually turned their consumer power against advertising itself. And thus if the consumer movement was one of the unintended consequences of radio advertising, then what could we on the left do with mass culture if we were actually trying? Capitalism uses the mass media to "organize" us — as consumers and producers — every day. Why don't the rest of us get involved? Why don't we try to become producers of mass culture ourselves? Why have we left mass culture to those who put profit ahead of people? The fight against advertising itself has been lost — most likely for good. But the fight for programming that reflects our values has been mostly ignored by the majority of left intellectuals for many years.

As I was finishing this book during the summer of 2002, I often had my own radio tuned to the nightly baseball games of the Pittsburgh Pirates. There were certain commercials I found so annoying that I had to lower the volume or turn off the radio altogether. (The most offensive ad, for a local grocery chain called Giant Eagle, was a corny dialogue between a man and woman in which they used fruit and vegetable puns.) Sometimes, if I failed to turn the radio volume back up in time, I missed an important play. Every time I reached for the volume control I sensed the irony of my situation; here I was, writing a book about annoying commercials in the 1930s and 1940s, and finding myself affected by their present-day counterparts. I also realized that my power to "turn off" the radio, while real, was circumscribed by the fact that I also wanted to listen to the game. The power of the individual listener is surely limited.

But I continue to be interested in the power of listeners/consumers to organize collectively. Radio may have "activated" listeners, but in virtually every case it was political leaders, church leaders, consumer leaders, union leaders, and clubwomen leaders who organized these "activated" listeners into powerful coalitions that the broadcast industry could not ignore. Radio advertising certainly provoked listener resentment. But it was grassroots organizers who turned that resentment into collective action. In the radio age, consumers were "radio active." Some attention to their stories, to their successes, and to their failures should help us in our own active efforts to grapple with mass culture today.

Notes

Introduction

1. Remington, *Lester Beall*, 74–75. Today, copies of Beall's Rural Electrification Administration posters adorn the lobby of the Roger Williams Hotel in New York City.

2. Denning, *The Cultural Front*.

3. Douglas, *Listening In*, 16.

4. Ibid., 27, 29. Likewise, Susan Smulyan argues that in the early days of radio, with the popularity of ham radio operators, "radio thus began as an active rather than passive enterprise" (Smulyan, *Selling Radio*, 13).

5. Melody, "Dallas Smythe."

6. Smythe, *Dependency Road*, 27.

7. Smythe initiated the "blindspot debate" with his 1977 article, "Communications: Blindspot of Western Marxism." A reply to the article and Smythe's rejoinder were printed in a subsequent issue (see Murdock, "Blindspots about Western Marxism"; and Smythe, "Rejoinder to Graham Murdock"). The debate continued: see Livant, "The Audience Commodity"; Jhally, "Probing the Blindspot"; and Livant, "Working at Watching." Though Jhally and Livant have had their disagreements on Smythe's work, they have also collaborated (see Jhally and Livant, "Watching as Working"). The most recent additions to the work on the audience commodity include Maxwell, "The Image Is Gold"; and Streeter, "Viewing as Property."

8. Smythe, *Dependency Road*, 51.

9. Smulyan, *Selling Radio*; McChesney, *Telecommunications, Mass Media, and Democracy*.

10. McGovern, "Sold American," 47.

11. Jacobs, "'Democracy's Third Estate,'" 29.

12. Hilmes, *Radio Voices*.

13. Fox, *The Mirror Makers,* 162.

14. Buzzard, *Chains of Gold,* 1–28 and passim.

15. Horkheimer and Adorno, "The Culture Industry."

16. Christopher and Kittross. *Stay Tuned,* 160–61.

17. Schudson. "Criticizing the Critics of Advertising," 6.

18. See Hilmes's important chapters on women and radio, "The Disembodied Woman," "Under the Cover of Daytime," and "Conclusion: Terms of Preferment," in her *Radio Voices.*

19. Williams, *Keywords,* 79; Vickery, "Women and the World of Goods."

20. Douglas, *The Feminization of American Culture;* Huyssen, "Mass Culture as Woman."

21. Lynn Spigel applies Huyssen's insights to television (see Spigel, *Make Room for TV,* 60–61). For more on the links between vaudeville audiences, shopping, and women, see Nasaw, *Going Out.* For an engaging, more contemporary account of women, mass culture, and consumption, see Douglas, *Where the Girls Are.*

22. Glickman, "The Strike in the Temple of Consumption: Consumer Activism and Twentieth Century American Political Culture"; McGovern, "Sold American"; Katz, "Consumers Union."

23. Jacqueline Dirks has written a compelling history of the National Consumers' League in her dissertation, "Righteous Goods." Dana Frank looks at women consumers in the context of Seattle labor radicalism in the 1910s and 1920s (Frank, *Purchasing Power*). Sylvie Murray has written a book that challenges the stereotype of the passive, housebound, suburban housewife (Murray, *The Progressive Housewife*).

24. One of the more powerful histories that integrates a history of boycotting into a labor history narrative is Orleck, *Common Sense and a Little Fire.*

25. Rosenzweig, *Eight Hours for What We Will;* Nasaw, *Going Out;* Kasson, *Amusing the Million;* Butsch, *For Fun and Profit;* Ross, *Working-Class Hollywood;* Godfried, *WCFL;* Fones-Wolf, "Promoting a Labour Perspective in The American Mass Media." Fones-Wolf is currently completing a book on radio and the CIO.

Chapter 1. The Psychology of Radio Advertising

1. "Study of Lux Soap Advertisement," Bureau of Applied Social Research Papers, Columbia University Archives (hereafter cited as BASR Papers), Series I, box 27, folder 5.

2. Glander, *Origins of Mass Communications Research during the American Cold War,* 86.

3. Smulyan, *Selling Radio,* 74.

4. Hettinger, *A Decade of Radio Advertising,* xii.

5. Cantril and Allport, *The Psychology of Radio,* 271.

6. Glander, *Origins of Mass Communications Research,* 84–86.

7. Lazarsfeld, "An Episode in the History of Social Research," 272.

8. Ibid.

9. Ibid., 285.

10. Ibid., 279. Charles McGovern makes the point that advertisers often linked the acts of shopping and voting, somewhat fatuously (McGovern, "Sold American," 99). In Lazarfeld's case, however, I think the comparison was more genuine.

11. Lazarsfeld, "An Episode in the History of Social Research," 275.

12. Ibid., 287.

13. Adorno, "Scientific Experiences of a European Scholar in America," 350.

14. Ibid., 342–43.

15. Ibid., 343–44.

16. Morrison, "Kultur and Culture," 340.

17. Wiggershaus, *The Frankfurt School*, 242–44.

18. "Music in Radio," BASR Papers, Series I, box 25, folder 3, 106.

19. Ibid., 108.

20. Ibid., 118.

21. Ibid.

22. Adorno, "A Social Critique of Radio Music," 219.

23. Ibid.

24. Theodor Adorno, "Das Schema der Massen Kultur," quoted in Huyssen, *After the Great Divide*, 26.

25. Oxford English Dictionary, 2d ed., s. v. "passive"; see also OED Online, http://dictionary.oed.com/cgi/entry/00172517.

26. Ibid.

27. Ohmann, *Selling Culture*, 186, 199.

28. Marchand, *Advertising the American Dream*, 206–34.

29. Hettinger, *A Decade of Radio Advertising*, 133.

30. Marchand, *Advertising the American Dream*, 223.

31. The Solitaire, Camel, Phillip Morris, and Raleigh advertisements are from *Fifty Old Time Radio Commercials*. The Vel and Super Suds advertisements are from *One Hundred and One Old Radio Commercials*.

32. "Can't Insult Other Brands," *Variety*, 31 July 1934, 31.

33. "Woman's Work," *Time*, 25 September 1950, 48.

34. Schudson, *Advertising*.

35. Lever, *Advertising and Economic Theory*, 123.

36. Marchand, *Advertising the American Dream*, 225.

37. Bauer and Greyser, *Advertising in America*, 246.

38. Lucas and Britt, *Advertising Psychology and Research*, 207.

39. Benjamin, "At the Touch of a Button."

40. Lazarsfeld, *The People Look at Radio*, 33.

41. Wolfe, *Modern Radio Advertising*, 487.

42. Memo, John F. Royal to Roy C. Witmar, 6 April 1937; memo, Niles Trammell to Roy C. Witmar, 10 March 1937; memo, Roy C. Witmar to Niles Trammell, 5 March 1937; all in National Broadcasting Company Papers, 1921–

1969, Wisconsin Historical Society, US MSS 17AF, box 56, folder 28 (hereafter cited as NBC Papers).

43. Wolfe, *Modern Radio Advertising*, 193.

44. Siepmann, *Radio's Second Chance*, 32.

45. Jhally, *The Codes of Advertising*, 64-121.

46. Dunlap, *Radio in Advertising*, 108.

47. Lucas and Britt, *Advertising Psychology and Research*, 371.

48. Wolfe, *Modern Radio Advertising*, 26.

49. Bauer and Greyser, *Advertising in America*, 221.

50. Lazarsfeld, *The People Look at Radio*, 23.

51. Hattwick, *How to Use Psychology for Better Advertising*, 253-54.

52. Hettinger, *A Decade of Radio Advertising*, 8.

53. Cantril and Allport, *The Psychology of Radio*, 21.

54. "No Siesta for Chiquita: How a Synthetic Señorita Educated and Expanded the Banana Market," *Sponsor*, 13 February 1950, 20.

55. Lucas and Britt, *Advertising Psychology and Research*, 61.

56. Hattwick, *How to Use Psychology for Better Advertising*, 230.

57. *One Hundred and One Old Radio Commercials.*

58. *Fifty Old Time Radio Commercials.*

59. Hollonquist and Suchman, "Listening to the Listener," 301-2.

60. For a detailed history of the radio/television ratings race, see Buzzard, *Chains of Gold;* this history is drawn from part 1 of that volume, "Uniform Tools for Mass Measurement," 1-28.

61. Wolfe, *Modern Radio Advertising*, 89.

62. Ibid., 86.

63. Ibid., 170-71.

64. Hettinger and Neff, *Practical Radio Advertising*, 111.

65. Ibid., 112.

66. Ibid.

67. Lazarsfeld, *The People Look at Radio*, 68.

68. Ibid., 23.

69. Dunlap, *Radio in Advertising*, 93.

70. Lazarsfeld, *The People Look at Radio*, 86.

Chapter 2. "Poisons, Potions and Profits"

1. Letter, PA to PW, with a copy to PFL [Paul Lazarsfeld], 27 December 1934, BASR Papers, Series I, box 27, folder 4.

2. Ruth Brindze, "Facts for Consumers," *Nation*, 6 November 1935, 341.

3. Fox, *The Mirror Makers;* McGovern, "Sold American," [i].

4. Brobeck, *Encyclopedia of the Consumer Movement*, 619.

5. Fox, *The Mirror Makers*, 22; Marchand, *Advertising the American Dream*, 314.

6. McGovern, "Sold American," 307.

7. Stuart Chase, "An Inquiry Into Radio," *Outlook,* 18 April 1928, 616–19.

8. Glickman, "The Strike in the Temple of Consumption: Consumer Activism and Twentieth Century American Political Culture," 99–128; Gelston and Pascoe, *A Guide to the Documents of the Consumer Movement;* Glickman, "The Strike in the Temple of Consumption: Debating Consumerism in the Depression Decade."

9. Fox, *The Mirror Makers,* 168.

10. Sorenson, *The Consumer Movement,* 179.

11. Dameron, "Advertising and the Consumer Movement," 239.

12. Kenner, *The Fight for the Truth in Advertising.*

13. Fox, *The Mirror Makers,* 124–25.

14. Glickman, "The Strike in the Temple of Consumption: Consumer Activism and Twentieth-Century American Political Culture," 107–8; "Subject of CR" [Consumers' Research], 72.

15. Glickman, "The Strike in the Temple of Consumption: Consumer Activism and Twentieth-Century American Political Culture," 111.

16. Fox, *The Mirror Makers,* 126.

17. "Advertising Foes Busy: Radio Industry May Be Victim," *Variety,* 10 April 1940, 21, 24.

18. Pope, "His Master's Voice," 6, 10.

19. Ibid., 7.

20. Ibid., 8.

21. Ibid., 8–10.

22. Rorty, *Order on the Air!,* 7.

23. Rorty, *Our Master's Voice,* 44.

24. Ibid., 19.

25. "On Being Fired from a Job," n.d., James Rorty Papers, Special Collections, Knight Library, University of Oregon, AX 769, box 2, Folder: Manuscripts, Article Length, O–R (hereafter cited as Rorty Papers).

26. McGovern, "Sold American," 351.

27. Rorty, *Our Master's Voice,* 320.

28. With this passage, Rorty anticipated by many years the media criticism of Dallas Smythe, who argued in the 1970s that "attention," along with the money spent on receivers and repair, became the "cost" of the mass media to the consumer (Smythe, *Dependency Road,* 27).

29. Rorty, *Order on the Air!,* 27–28.

30. Paul Hutchinson, "The Cult of Ballyhoo," *Christian Century,* 6 June 1934, 763; Ernest Sutherland Bates, "Barnum's Babies," *New Republic* 79, 1 August 1934; "Summary of *Our Master's Voice: Advertising,* by James Rorty," *Book Review Digest 1934,* 807.

31. Durstine, "Roy Durstine on Reading Jim Rorty."

32. Glickman, "The Strike in the Temple of Consumption: Consumer Activism and Twentieth-Century American Political Culture," 8; Rorty, *Order on the Air!,* 28–30.

33. Pope, "His Master's Voice," 11, 14; Rorty and Decter, *McCarthy and the Communists.*

34. James Rorty, "Unpublished Memoirs, Version I," n.d., Rorty Papers, AX 769, box 2.

35. Pope says of Rorty's ecological criticism: "An ecological perspective could offer a perspective on American culture from the outside, as it were. It claimed to evaluate social structures and practices by standards higher than those of the particular society" (Pope, "His Master's Voice," 15).

36. McChesney, *Telecommunications, Mass Media, and Democracy,* 252–70.

37. Ruth Brindze, "Biographical Sketch," Vanguard Press Collection, Columbia University Archives, box 22, Folder: "Ruth Brindze, Trade Winds" (hereafter cited as Brindze Papers).

38. Brindze, "Autobiographical Sketch," 29–30.

39. Jim Henle, "Biographical Sketch of Ruth Brindze," Brindze Papers, box 23, Folder: "Ruth Brindze, Publicity, '42–'50."

40. Brindze, *How To Spend Money,* 12, 14.

41. Dorothy Van Doren, "Caveat Emptor: Review of *The Consumer Seeks a Way, How to Spend Money,* and *Counterfeit*," *Nation,* 3 July 1935, 23.

42. "The Nation Now Announces a New Feature Beginning Next Week — A Consumer's Column," *Nation,* 30 October 1935, iv.

43. Brindze, "Facts for Consumers" (6 November 1935); Brindze, "Facts for Consumers" (29 January 1936); Brindze, "The Consumer Front"; Brindze, "Mr. Aylesworth Moves Ahead"; Brindze, "Who Owns the Air"; Brindze, "Freedom of the Press Again"; Brindze, "Why You Pay More For Food"; Brindze, "The Radio Newspaper."

44. Brindze, *Not To Be Broadcast,* 11.

45. Ibid., 152.

46. Ibid.

47. Ibid., 181–82.

48. Ibid., 183, 177.

49. This program was so popular that Ford "gave away some 2 million copies of [Cameron's] talks in less than two years" (McGovern, "Sold American," 390).

50. Brindze, *Not To Be Broadcast,* 99, 201, 97.

51. Ibid., 82–83.

52. "Air Arguments: Radical Broadcasting Changes Asked by Ruth Brindze in New Book," *Literary Digest,* 3 April 1937, 33.

53. Brindze, "Autobiographical Sketch," 30.

54. Brindze, "Getting Your Money's Worth" (9 October 1939); Brindze, "Getting Your Money's Worth" (13 November 1939); Brindze, "Getting Your Money's Worth" (18 December 1939); Brindze, "Getting Your Money's Worth" (15 January 1940); Brindze, "Getting Your Money's Worth" (19 February 1940); Brindze, "Getting Your Money's Worth" (15 April 1940); Brindze, "Getting Your Money's Worth" (13 May 1940).

55. "Review of *Johnny Get Your Money's Worth,*" *Journal of Home Economics,* January 1939, 43.

56. Helen Woodward, "Young Shoppers," *Nation,* 31 December 1938, 17.

57. Anne T. Eaton, "Review of *Johnny Get Your Money's Worth (And Jane, Too!),*" *New York Times,* 8 January 1939, sec. 6, p. 10.

58. Letter, Evelyn Shrift to Ruth Brindze, [1959], Brindze Papers, box 23, Folder: "Ruth Brindze, 1953."

59. Wald, "Marxist Literary Resistance to the Cold War." *The Gulf Stream* won first prize in the *New York Herald Tribune* Book Festival and was also a Junior Literary Guild selection. Some of Brindze's subsequent children's books included: *Boating Is Fun* (1949), *The Story of the Totem Pole* (1951), *The Story of Gold* (1955), *All About Undersea Exploration* (1960), and *Investing Money: The Facts about Stocks and Bonds* (1968).

60. Dr. Eugenie Fribourg, personal communication, 9 July 2000. Ruth Brindze's sister-in-law, Eugenie Fribourg, was Albert Fribourg's sister. Today she is in her nineties and is still a practicing medical doctor. As for Ruth's nickname, "Jim," Brindze signed much of her publishing correspondence in this manner, which makes her correspondence records very confusing since one of her most frequent editors was also "Jim" — Jim Henle.

61. Brindze, *Seamanship Below Deck.*

62. Dr. Eugenie Fribourg, personal communication, 9 July 2000; Dr. Anne Fribourg, personal communication, 28 June 2000. Dr. Anne Fribourg is the daughter of Eugenie Fribourg and the niece of Ruth Brindze.

63. L.N., "The Play: Pine Forest," *New York Times,* 27 June 1936, 21.

64. Buttitta and Witham, *Uncle Sam Presents,* 72; Philip Stevenson, "Turpentine Workers," *New Theatre,* August 1936, 18.

65. Fraden, *Blueprints for a Black Federal Theatre;* O'Conner and Brown, *Free, Adult, Uncensored;* Houseman, *Run-Through;* Bond, *The Negro and the Drama.* Morell is mistakenly included in Arata, *More Black American Playwrights,* 158.

66. Morell, *Poisons, Potions, and Profits,* 239.

67. McChesney, *Telecommunications, Mass Media, and Democracy,* 58–59.

68. Morell, *Poisons, Potions, and Profits,* i–ii.

69. Ibid., 212–13.

70. Ibid., 253.

71. Ibid., 254.

72. Ibid., 258.

73. Ibid., 258–59.

74. "Review of *Poisons, Potions, Profits: The Antidote to Radio Advertising,*" *Forum,* October 1937, iv.

75. Brindze, "Consumer's Progress."

76. "Who's a Guniea Pig," UAW Washington Office, Legislative Department, Donald Montgomery Papers, Walter Reuther Library, Detroit, box 1, folder 17.

77. Valdi Morell, personal communication, 8 July 2000.

78. Meyer, "The 'Blue Book,'" 203.

79. Land, *Active Radio;* Donna Greene, "The Fight for Civil Rights on the Air," *New York Times,* 19 September 1993, sec. 13, p. 3.

Chapter 3. The Consumer Revolt of "Mr. Average Man"

1. Marchand, "National Stage, Local Participation."

2. "Paster Leads Boycott of Bowes," *Variety,* 4 March 1936, 48; "Clergymen Ask Bowes Time Switch," *Variety,* 25 March 1936, 41; Marchand, "National Stage, Local Participation," 14.

3. Memo, Frank Russell to John F. Royal, 30 June 1936, NBC Papers, US MSS 17AF, box 92 folder 4.

4. Memo, L. J. Fitzgerald (agent for Alexander Woollcott) to Mr. Engles, 17 January 1936, NBC Papers, box 51, folder 30.

5. Siepmann, *Radio's Second Chance,* 92.

6. Warren, *Radio Priest;* Brinkley, *Voices of Protest.*

7. Marlow, *Captain Boycott and the Irish,* 13.

8. Laidler, *Boycotts and the Labor Struggle;* Glickman, "Workers of the World Consume"; Glickman, *A Living Wage.*

9. Glickman, *A Living Wage.*

10. Laidler, *Boycotts and the Labor Struggle,* 7.

11. Ibid., 57.

12. Ibid., 82–97.

13. James Rorty, "Radio Comes Through," *Nation* (1938), NBC Papers, box 63, folder 87.

14. Memo, Vance Babb to James Rorty, 6 October 1938, NBC Papers, box 63, folder 87.

15. CBS broadcast, 18 November 1936, reprinted in Culbert, *News For Everyman,* 45.

16. Wolkonowicz, "The Philco Corporation," 11, 29, 37.

17. Liebling, "Boake Carter," 7.

18. Ibid., 10.

19. Ibid.

20. Ibid., 11.

21. FDR quoted in Culbert, *News For Everyman,* 35.

22. Carter quoted in Culbert, *News For Everyman,* 34.

23. "From Mike to Type: Boake Carter is Latest Radio Oracle to Start Press Column," *Literary Digest,* 17 April 1937, 30.

24. Ibid., 29–30.

25. Carter, *I Talk as I Like;* Carter, *Johnny Q. Public Speaks.*

26. Liebling, "Boake Carter," 52.

27. "Bars Picketing of WCAU," *New York Times,* 21 October 1937, sec. 17, p. 6.

28. "CIO Won't Lift Boycott Threat," *Variety,* 2 February 1938, 35.

29. Culbert, *News For Everyman,* 47; Fang, *Those Radio Commentators!,* 114.

30. The game was available until the early 1960s, though only the first edition bore Carter's name. Today, it is one of the most highly valued board games among collectors.

31. "Boake Carter See New Deal 'Plot,'" *Variety*, 16 March 1938, 26.

32. Culbert, *News For Everyman*, 53.

33. Horowitz, *Thirty-three Candles*.

34. Culbert, *News For Everyman*, 54–59; Horowitz, *Thirty-three Candles;* "Lost four great men so far this year," letter, Alfred de Grazia to Jill Oppenheim, http://www.grazian-archive.com/, accessed 10 May 2001.

35. Summers, "Miscellaneous: The Boake Carter Case," 258.

36. Ibid., 256.

37. Culbert, *News For Everyman*, 49; Summers, "Miscellaneous: The Boake Carter Case," 257. Carter became a naturalized citizen on 28 November 1934 ("Boake Carter See New Deal 'Plot,'" *Variety*, 16 March 1938, 26).

38. Culbert, *News For Everyman*, 52.

39. "Labor Leaders, New Dealers Blame Radio Commentators for Fostering Passage of Anti-Strike Measure," *Variety*, 30 June 1943, quoted in Fones-Wolf, "Creating a Favorable Business Climate."

40. Liebling, "Boake Carter," 53.

41. Balderston, "'Philco,'" 9.

42. Ibid., 10.

43. Wolkonowicz, "The Philco Corporation," 10.

44. Balderston, "'Philco,'" 10.

45. Wolkonowicz, "The Philco Corporation," 23.

46. Balderston, "'Philco,'" 11.

47. Wolkonowicz, "The Philco Corporation," 25, 27.

48. Ibid., 34.

49. Beville, *Social Stratification of the Radio Audience*, 17–23.

50. Culbert, *News For Everyman*, 40.

51. "Philco Radio Time . . . Boake Carter Speaking!" *Time*, 31 August 1936.

52. Culbert, *News For Everyman*, 40.

53. Jerry Doyle, "No Squat, No Stoop, No Squint," *New York Post*, 18 August 1937.

54. Filippelli, "UE," 352–53.

55. Filippelli and McColloch, *Cold War in the Working Class*, 18.

56. Ibid., 18–33.

57. Fones-Wolf, "Promoting a Labor Perspective in the American Mass Media," 287.

58. Letter, Eleanor Fowler to James Carey, 31 October 1936, and letter James Carey to Eleanor Fowler, 2 November 1936, UE Papers, Archive Service Center, University of Pittsburgh, box 41 (hereafter cited as UE Papers).

59. Letter, James Carey to Boake Carter, 2 November 1936, UE Papers, box 41.

60. Carter, *I Talk As I Like*, 125.

61. Boake Carter, "But —," *Boston Globe*, 14 April 1937, 19 April 1937.

62. Few of Carter's broadcasts from this period are extant, and thus these quotes are drawn from Carter's newspaper column. His columns provide an accurate barometer of what Carter was covering on a daily basis.

63. Boake Carter, "But —," *Boston Globe,* 9 July 1937.

64. Boake Carter, "But —," *Boston Globe,* 12 July 1937, 14 July 1937, 16 July 1937.

65. Letter, UE Local #101 to Boake Carter, 29 July 1937, UE Papers, box 41; letter, James Carey to James Skinner, 29 July 1937, UE Papers, box 41.

66. Letter, UE Local #101 to John C. Martin (editor of the Philadelphia Evening Ledger), 29 July 1937; letter, UE Local #101 to Dr. Leon Levy, 29 July 1937, both in UE Papers, box 41.

67. Letter, UE Local #101 to Boake Carter, 29 July 1937, UE Papers, box 41.

68. Letter, James Carey to James Skinner, 29 July 1937, UE Papers, box 41.

69. Letter, James Skinner to James Carey, 2 August 1937, UE Papers, box 41.

70. "CIO Mouthpiece Whams Carter: Philadelphia Labor Publication Stalks Philco Commentator for Anti-Union Campaign," *Variety,* 11 August 1937. Tom Girdler was one of the officials of the Republic Steel Corporation who took a hard line against the CIO during the Little Steel Strike. According to the *Nation,* "Tom Girdler . . . is an open fascist, to whom Roosevelt, Miss Perkins, John Lewis are 'Communists.' He poses as an impulsive, plain-spoken, colorful, rough personality. But his colorfulness rests entirely on an unpicturesquely foul vocabulary. He is indeed plenty tough" (see Benjamin Stolberg, *Nation,* 31 July 1937, 119–23).

71. Culbert, *News For Everyman,* 37; "From Mike to Type: Boake Carter is Latest Radio Oracle to Start Press Column," *Literary Digest,* 17 April 1937, 30.

72. "CIO Mouthpiece Whams Carter: Philadelphia Labor Publication Stalks Philco Commentator for Anti-Union Campaign," *Variety,* 11 August 1937.

73. Boake Carter, "But —," *Boston Globe,* 11 August 1937.

74. Boake Carter, "But —," *Boston Globe,* 21 August 1937.

75. Boake Carter, "But —," *Boston Globe,* 8 September 1937.

76. Mazzocco, "Democracy, Power, and Equal Rights," 34.

77. "CIO Has CBS Summoned Before NLRB: The Stations Lined Up," *Variety,* 8 September 1937, 38; Mazzocco, 223–24.

78. "Carter May Leave Philco: Persistently Reported and Persistently Denied Labor Attacks Hurt Sales," *Variety,* 17 November 1937, 41.

79. Wolkonowicz, "The Philco Corporation," 41.

80. "Philco Stages Heavy Campaign," *New York Times,* 6 November 1937, 29.

81. Liebling, "Boake Carter," 51.

82. "CIO Won't Lift Boycott Threat," *Variety,* 2 February 1938, 35.

83. Ibid.

84. "James Farley discusses with Boake Carter the influence he expects radio will have on American political campaigns," Sound Recording, January 1936, Michigan State University.

85. Carter [Richard Sheridan Ames, pseud.], "News on the Air," 23, 36, 38.

86. Carter, *I Talk As I Like,* i–xii.

87. Ibid., xii–xiii.

88. Fones-Wolf, "Promoting a Labour Perspective in the American Mass Media," 287–88. See also Fones-Wolf, "Creating a Favorable Business Climate."

89. Congress of Industrial Organizations, Political Action Committee, *Radio Handbook,* 2–31.

90. Clark, "H.V. Kaltenborn and His Sponsors," 238.

91. Ibid., 239.

92. Fones-Wolf, "Creating a Favorable Business Climate," 241–42.

Chapter 4. Washboard Weepers

1. Letter, Sidney Strotz to Jane Crusinberry, 20 August 1937, Jane Crusinberry Papers, Wisconsin Historical Society, US MSS 199AN, box 3, folder 3 (hereafter cited as JC Papers).

2. This argument is also suggested by William Boddy in his work on the political economy of 1950s television (Boddy, *Fifties Television*).

3. Herzog, "What Do We Really Know About Day-Time Serial Listeners," 3–33.

4. Arnheim, *Radio;* Arnheim, "The World of the Daytime Serial"; Warner and Henry, "The Radio Day Time Serial."

5. Brunsdon, *The Feminist, the Housewife, and the Soap Opera,* 3.

6. Willis, "Women and the Myth of Consumerism"; Wally Seccombe, "The Housewife and Her Labor Under Capitalism," *New Left Review,* January/February 1973, 3–24; Margaret Coulson, Branka Magas, and Hilary Wainwright, "'The Housewife and Her Labor under Capitalism' — A Critique," *New Left Review,* January/February 1975, 59–71; Smith, "Domestic Labour and Marx's Theory of Value."

7. Murrow, "Soap Opera," 119.

8. Merrill Denison, "Soap Opera," *Harper's Magazine,* April 1940, 498.

9. Murrow, "Soap Opera," 120.

10. "Romance on Radio Scored by Women: Fewer Love Drams and More Programs on Moneymaking Urged by 600 at Forum," *New York Times,* 29 November 1939, 25.

11. "Women to Boycott Radio 'Love Dramas': 'I'm Not Listening Committee' Is Formed in New Rochelle," *New York Times,* 11 January 1940, 17.

12. "Radio 'Love' Held Vital to Profits: Broadcasting Officials Tell Clubwomen 'Tripe' Pays for Worth-While Programs," *New York Times,* 16 March 1940, 17.

13. Memo, Niles Trammel to John E. McMillan, 3 May 1940; memo, John E. McMillan to Niles Trammel, 29 April 1940; NBC Papers, US MSS 17AF, box 76, folder 1, 1940.

14. Stedman, "A History of the Broadcasting of Daytime Serial Dramas in the United States," 115–16.

15. Merrill Denison, "Soap Opera," *Harper's Magazine,* April 1940, 503.

16. Murrow, "Soap Opera," 146.

17. "Say Virtues of Daytime Serials Outweigh Shortcomings," *Printer's Ink,* 12 February 1943, 20.

18. "Wylie Due East to Canvass New Job," *Variety,* 5 August 1942, 40.

19. Max Wylie, "Dusting Off Dr. Berg," *Printer's Ink,* 12 February 1943, 42, 44; Berg, *Prison Doctor;* Berg, *Prison Nurse.*

20. "Every Woman's Life is a Soap Opera," *McCalls,* March 1965, 116.

21. Ibid.

22. O'Dell, *Women Pioneers in Television,* 184.

23. "Every Woman's Life is a Soap Opera," *McCalls,* March 1965, 116.

24. "Radio: Script Queen," *Time,* 10 June 1940, 68.

25. O'Dell, *Women Pioneers in Television,* 184.

26. Hobe Morrison, "Analyzing the Daytime Serials," *Variety,* 18 August 1943, 34.

27. "Vocational Information Conferences for Women Students," Irna Phillips Papers, Wisconsin Historical Society, US MSS 76AN, box 62, folder: Knox Reeves, Advertising Inc., Correspondence, 1943–November 1947 (hereafter cited as IP Papers).

28. Hobe Morrison, "Analyzing the Daytime Serials," *Variety,* 18 August 1943, 42; IP papers, Wisconsin, box 63, Biography/Miscellaneous.

29. Letter, Irna Phillips to Hobe Morrison, 23 August 1943, IP Papers, box 63, Biography/Miscellaneous.

30. "The Function of the Daytime Serial Drama," IP Papers, box 63, Biography/Miscellaneous.

31. "Lonely Women" Episode #361, 15 November 1943, p. 3, IP Papers, box 50, nos. 351–372, 1943, November.

32. Letter, Mildred Oldenburg to General Mills, 15 November 1943, IP Papers, box 50, folder "Lonely Women Correspondence," 1943–1944.

33. Letter, S. C. Gale to King Painter, 19 November 1943; letter, H. K. Painter to S. C. Gale, 22 November 1943; letter, Carl Wester and Company, Radio Advertising to Irna Phillips, 22 November 1943, all in IP Papers, box 50, folder "Lonely Women Correspondence," 1943–1944.

34. "Suggested Press Release," IP Papers, box 50, folder "Lonely Women Correspondence," 1943–1944.

35. "Lonely Women," Episode #367, 23 November, 1943, pp. 3–4, IP Papers, box 50, nos. 351–372, 1943, November.

36. Letter, Doris Pullen to Irna Phillips, 2 January 1946; letter, Irna Phillips to Doris Pullen, 5 January 1946, IP Papers, box 63; draft of Edward Morrow's "Soap Opera," *Fortune* magazine, IP Papers, box 67, Biography/Miscellaneous.

37. Irna Phillips, "In Defense of Daytime Serials," IP Papers, box 67, Biography/Miscellaneous.

38. Letter, Elizabeth Reeves to Irna Phillips, 15 July 1947, IP Papers, box 62, Knox Reeves, Advertising Inc., Correspondence, 1943–November 1947.

39. "Every Woman's Life is a Soap Opera," *McCalls,* March 1965, 168.

40. O'Dell, *Women Pioneers in Television,* 189.

41. Michele Hilmes, using the Jane Crusinberry Papers at the Wisconsin Historical Society, also writes about *The Story of Mary Marlin* (see Hilmes, *Radio Voices,* 175–81).

42. Letter, Jane Crusinberry to Martin Deane Wickett, 10 December 1944, JC Papers, box 2, folder 3.

43. Stedman, "A History of the Broadcasting of Daytime Serial Dramas in the United States," 53.

44. "The Story of Mary Marlin," *Life,* 11 September 1944, 67.

45. Fan mail summaries, JC Papers, box 4, folder 1; Jane Crusinberry, "The Story of Mary Marlin," 16 August 1937, JC Papers, box 13, folder 5.

46. Jane Crusinberry, "The Story of Mary Marlin," 26 August 1937, JC Papers, box 13, folder 5.

47. Jane Crusinberry, "The Story of Mary Marlin," 12 August 1937, JC Papers, box 13, folder 5.

48. Seiter, "To Teach and to Sell."

49. Letter, William G. Werner, Proctor and Gamble, to John McMillan, Compton Advertising, 4 October 1940, JC Papers, box 2, folder 7.

50. Jane Crusinberry, "The Story of Mary Marlin," 17 August 1937, JC Papers, box 13, folder 5.

51. Jane Crusinberry, "The Story of Mary Marlin," 16 August 1937, JC Papers, box 13, folder 5.

52. Letter, "John" to Jane Crusinberry, 7 July 1938, JC Papers, box 2, folder 5.

53. Letter, Grace Squires to Mary Marlin, 11 April 1940, JC Papers, box 3, folder 10. Note that the author addressed her letter to Mary Marlin rather than to Jane Crusinberry.

54. Cantril and Allport, *The Psychology of Radio,* 96.

55. Razlogova, "Listeners Write the Scripts."

56. Theodor Adorno, "Memorandum: Music in Radio," BASR Papers, box 25, Series I, folder 3, p. 112.

57. Mrs. Edwina Mohr, from "Fan Mail Summaries," JC Papers, box 4, folder 1.

58. Letter, Isabel G. D'Long to Jane Crusinberry, 18 June 1941, JC Papers, box 3, folder 10.

59. Letter Ann V. Howard (Mrs. James J. Howard) to Procter and Gamble, 17 November 1940, JC Papers, box 3, folder 10.

60. Letter, Mr. and Mrs. H. J. Swearingen to Procter and Gamble, 13 March 1941, JC Papers, box 3, folder 10.

61. Hallie Remington, "Fan Mail Summaries," JC Papers, box 4, folder 1.

62. Letter, Mrs. M. A. MacArthur to NBC, 10 April 1941, JC Papers, box 3, folder 10.

63. Mrs. W. Dietz and E. T. L, "Fan Mail Summaries," JC Papers, box 4, folder 1.

64. E. G. Bower, "Fan Mail Summaries," JC Papers, box 4, folder 1.

65. Iva Fitch, "Fan Mail Summaries," JC Papers, box 4, folder 1.

66. Mrs. A. F. Kendell, "Fan Mail Summaries," JC Papers, box 4, folder 1.

67. Letter, "A Deeply Grateful Listener" to Procter and Gamble 3 April 1941, JC Papers, box 3, folder 10.

68. Letter, Marilyn Hoffman (Mrs. Robert Hoffman) to Procter and Gamble, 26 March 1941, JC Papers, box 3, folder 10.

69. Faye Setero, "Fan Mail Summaries," JC Papers, box 4, folder 1.

70. Letter, Marilyn Hoffman (Mrs. Robert Hoffman) to Procter and Gamble, 26 March 1941, JC Papers, box 3, folder 10.

71. Mrs. Elsie A. Hammond, "Fan Mail Summaries," JC Papers, box 4, folder 1.

72. "A Country Woman," "Fan Mail Summaries," JC Papers, box 4, folder 1.

73. Mayme Maillet, "Fan Mail Summaries," JC Papers, box 4, folder 1.

74. M. S., "Fan Mail Summaries," JC Papers, box 4, folder 1.

75. Flora D. Stafano, "Fan Mail Summaries," JC Papers, box 4, folder 1.

76. Theresa Lepich, "Fan Mail Summaries," JC Papers, box 4, folder 1.

77. Mrs. Mary Buechele, "Fan Mail Summaries," JC Papers, box 4, folder 1.

78. Letter, "A Deeply Grateful Listener" to Procter and Gamble, 3 April 1941, JC Papers, box 3, folder 10.

79. Letter, Jane Crusinberry to Bill Ramsey, 11 December 1942, JC Papers, box 3, folder 5.

80. Mrs. A. C. Bowersox, "Fan Mail Summaries," JC Papers, box 4, folder 1.

81. Mrs. Jeanne Avram, "Fan Mail Summaries," JC Papers, box 4, folder 1.

82. Mrs. Bula M. Pithan, "Fan Mail Summaries," JC Papers, box 4, folder 1.

83. Mrs. Mari A. Wass, "Fan Mail Summaries," JC Papers, box 4, folder 1.

84. Letter, Grace Squires to Mary Marlin, 11 April 1940, JC Papers, box 3, folder 10.

85. Denning, "Advertising Womanhood," 15.

Chapter 5. "I Won't Buy You Anything But Love, Baby"

1. Yolanda Mero-Irion, "What the Women Like and Dislike about Radio," *Printer's Ink,* 21 March 1935, 67.

2. Memo, John Royal to Sidney Strotz, 22 November 1940, NBC Papers, US MSS 17AF, box 8, folder 36.

3. Morell, *Poisons, Potions, and Profits,* 231–32.

4. Letter, Ruth Rich to Niles Trammel, 3 September 1940, NBC Papers, box 8, folder 36.

5. Memo, Niles Trammel to Edgar Kobak, 9 September 1940, NBC Papers, box 8, folder 36.

6. "Daytime Serial Survey," NBC Papers, box 8, folder 36.

7. Memo, Margaret Cuthbert to John Royal, 6 May 1940, NBC Papers, box 8, folder 36. Royal passed the memo on to Niles Trammel with the handwritten note, "Very important."

8. Memo, Margaret Cuthbert to John Royal, 27 March 1939, NBC Papers,

box 68 folder 51; memo, Margaret Cuthbert to John Royal, 29 March 1937, NBC Papers, box 58 folder 12.

9. Memo, Janet MacRorie to Roy C. Witmar, 29 September 1937, NBC Papers, box 92, folder 43.

10. Brobeck, *Encyclopedia of the Consumer Movement*, 141.

11. Bureau of Radio Advertising, "The Case for Distribution," NBC Papers, box 76, folder 11.

12. "Evaluation of the Consumer Movement," NBC Papers, box 77, folder 11. In this same folder are two additional reports on the consumer movement, including one prepared by George Gallup.

13. Memo, W. G. Preston to Ken Dyke, 12 April 1940, NBC Papers, box 77, folder 65.

14. Memo, W. G. Preston to Ken Dyke, 12 April 1940, NBC Papers, box 77, folder 65.

15. Memo, W. G. Preston to Ken Dyke, 12 April 1940, NBC Papers, box 77, folder 65.

16. "Advertising Foes Busy: Radio Industry May Be Victim," *Variety*, 10 April 1940, 21.

17. Memo, Ken Dyke to Niles Trammel, 27 June 1940, NBC Papers, box 76, folder 11.

18. Bureau of Radio Advertising, "The Case for Distribution," NBC Papers, box 76, folder 11.

19. Memo, Ken Dyke to Niles Trammel, 27 June 1940, NBC Papers, box 76, folder 11.

20. Consumer Time Reports, UAW Washington Office, Legislative Department, Donald Montgomery Papers, Walter Reuther Library, Detroit, box 1, folder 20 (hereafter cited as DM Papers).

21. Memo to Mr. Peek and Mr. Brand, 6 July 1933, DM Papers, box 1, folder 21: "A similar set-up is being developed for the General Federation of Women's Clubs on the NBC. Mrs. Jaffray has been detailed by that organization to make the radio arrangements and to build up continuing contacts and develop activities on part of the local branches of the Federation."

22. Biographical Description, DM Papers.

23. "Consumer Section Service — Radio," 1940, DM Papers, box 1, folder 21.

24. "Joint Radio Plan For Consumer Division, OPA, and Consumers' Counsel Division, USDA," DM Papers, box 1, folder 21.

25. "Consumer Section Service — Radio," 1940, DM Papers, box 1, folder 21.

26. *Consumer Time*, 1 January 1944, NBC Papers, Microfiche Division.

27. *Consumer Time*, 1 January 1944, NBC Papers, Microfiche Division.

28. *Consumer Time*, 29 January 1944, NBC Papers, Microfiche Division.

29. *Consumer Time*, 8 January 1944, NBC Papers, Microfiche Division.

30. Jacobs, "'How About Some Meat?'" 924.

31. *Consumer Time*, 22 January 1944; *Consumer Time*, 5 February 1944, NBC Papers, Microfiche Division.

32. *Consumer Time,* 22 April 1944; *Consumer Time,* 29 April 1944, NBC Papers, Microfiche Division.

33. *Consumer Time,* 26 February 1944, NBC Papers, Microfiche Division.

34. Consumer Time, Mail Response, 1942, DM Papers, box 1, folder 20. In a similar letter, another writer expressed her appreciation for *Consumer Time*'s "story plays": "Don't let the soap dramas or 'jive' sessions push you off the air."

35. Consumer Time, Mail Response, 1942, DM Papers, box 1, folder 20.

36. Ibid.

37. Ibid; *Variety,* 10 June 1942.

38. Donald Montgomery, "Statement On The Food Situation In 1943 By Donald Montgomery On Resigning As Consumer's Counsel Of The Agricultural Marketing Administration, Department Of Agriculture," 28 December 1942, DM Papers, box 5, folder 3.

39. Letter, Mary Taylor to Roy F. Hendrickson, n.d., DM Papers, box 5, folder 3.

40. Letter, E. Gordon Hubbel to Roy F. Hendrickosn, 30 December 1942, DM Papers, box 5, folder 3.

41. Donald Montgomery, "Final Speech for Consumer Time," DM Papers, box 5, folder 3.

42. Donald Montgomery, "Statement to PM," 14 August 1943, box 1, folder 21.

43. Jacobs, "'Democracy's Third Estate,'" 44.

44. Donald Montgomery, "Consumers Under Way," *Survey Graphics,* April 1938, 213, 217.

45. Bureau of Radio Advertising, "The Case for Distribution," NBC Papers, box 76, folder 11.

46. Montgomery, "Consumers Under Way," 215.

47. "Barton Charges Plot of New Dealers to 'Destroy' Advertising: Alleges Federal Trade Group Would Control Press and Radio," *Evening Star,* 15 February 1940, DM Papers, box 1, folder 5.

48. "New Deal Seeks to Destroy Ad, Barton Charges," *Washington Times-Herald,* 16 February 1940, DM Papers, box 1, folder 5.

49. C. F. Hughest, "The Merchant's Point of View," *New York Times,* 25 February 1940; Ernest K. Lindley, "The New 'Conspiracy,'" *Washington Post,* 23 February 1940, both in DM Papers, box 1, folder 5.

50. "Advertising is 'Everlasting' Consumer Association is Told," *Cincinnati Inquirer,* 24 February 1940, DM Papers, box 1, folder 5.

51. "Consumers Desires on Ads Discussed," *St. Louis Globe Democrat,* DM Papers, box 1, folder 5.

52. "Sears Executive in Counter Attack on FTC Detractors: Too Many Donald Ducks in Advertising, Price Insists," *Advertising Age,* 18 March 1940, DM Papers, box 1, folder 5.

53. Donald Montgomery, Speech to Labor's Non-Partisan League, Washington, D.C., 18 March 1940, DM Papers, box 1, folder 6.

54. Montgomery, "Consumers Under Way," 213.

55. Montgomery, "Rationing Is Not Enough," 37.

56. Jacobs, "'Democracy's Third Estate,'" 46.

57. Jacobs, "'How About Some Meat?'" 933.

58. Radio Talk titled "Labor and the OPA," WXYZ, Detroit, 1 June 1946, DM Papers, box 10, folder 10–3.

59. "Calling All Consumers" (rally flyer), DM Papers, box 10, folder 10–3.

60. Ibid.

61. "Unorganized Consumers Hold Key to Buyers' Strikes," *Business Week*, 20 July 1946, 16; "Buyers' Strike: Housewives and Price Tags," *Newsweek*, 29 July 1946, 15–17. *Business Week* reported that there were 40,000 people at the rally; *Newsweek* reported 60,000.

62. "Unorganized Consumers Hold Key to Buyers' Strikes," *Business Week*, 20 July 1946, 16.

63. "UAW memo to all locals," 19 July 1946, DM Papers, box 10, folder 10–3.

64. This song was covered by Bob Dylan in 1960 under the title "Talking Lobbyist."

65. "Ford held a national contest for a war time slogan and an Air Force captain named Gerald Erdahl submitted the winning entry. Ford used the slogan along side the image of a fortune teller looking into a crystal ball to see if there was, indeed, a Ford in the consumer's future" (UAW memo to all locals, 19 July 1946, DM Papers, box 10, folder 10–3).

66. UAW press release, 24 July 1946, DM Papers, box 10, folder 10–3.

67. "Buyers' Strike: Housewives and Price Tags," *Newsweek*, 29 July 1946, 15–17.

68. Gilmartin, "An Historical Analysis of the Growth of the National Consumer Movement in the United States from 1947 to 1967," 36.

69. National Association of Consumers Membership Pamphlet, [1947], pp. 1–2, Persia Campbell Collection, Consumers Union Archive, Yonkers, New York .

70. *Bread and Butter* 7, no. 4 (25 January 1947): 1–2. The Consumers' Union published *Bread and Butter* for six years, from 1941 to 1947. After 1947, the newsletter ceased publication and was absorbed as a column with the same title by *Consumer Reports*.

71. Gilmartin, "An Historical Analysis of the Growth of the National Consumer Movement in the United States from 1947 to 1967," 52.

72. "The Consumer — Yes," *The Survey*, January 1949, 57.

73. Hall, "Consumer Protection," 3.

74. Gilmartin, "An Historical Analysis of the Growth of the National Consumer Movement in the United States from 1947 to 1967," 62–63.

75. "Holding the Consumer's Hand," *Business Week*, 24 May 1952, 126–27.

76. Hall, "Consumer Protection," 4.

77. *Consumers on the March*, March 1948, 2. Truman's speech was given on

the occasion of the one-hundredth anniversary of the movement for women's rights.

78. *Consumers on the March,* March 1948, 2; "The Revolt of the Housewives," *Newsweek,* 16 August 1948, 15.

Conclusion

1. Wakeman, *The Hucksters,* 132.

2. Frederic Wakeman, personal correspondence, 2 July 1996. The story was also reported in a brief biography of Wakeman that appeared shortly after *The Hucksters* was published (see *Current Biography 1946,* s.v. "Frederic Wakeman").

3. *Current Biography 1946,* s.v. "Frederic Wakeman"; "The Best Sellers of 1946," *Publisher's Weekly,* 25 January 1947, 415. Between trade sales and Book-of-the-Month-Club sales, *The Hucksters* had sold 712,434 copies by January 1947.

4. Wakeman, *The Hucksters,* 22.

5. Ibid., 45.

6. Ibid., 265–67.

7. Harrison Smith, "No Soap," *Saturday Review,* 25 May 1946, 10.

8. Wolcott Gibb, "The Big Boffola," *New Yorker,* 1 June 1946, 88–91.

9. Diana Trilling, "Fiction in Review," *Nation,* 22 June 1946, 762.

10. "Books: Beautee and the Beast," *Time,* 3 June 1946, 106.

11. Wakeman, personal correspondence, 2 July 1996; emphasis is Wakeman's.

12. *Current Biography 1946,* s.v. "Frederic Wakeman."

13. Ibid.

14. Frederic Wakeman, personal correspondence, 2 July 1996.

15. Havig, "Frederic Wakeman's *The Hucksters* and the Postwar Debate Over Commercial Radio," 198. The quote comes from a memo from another NBC executive (Syd Eiges to Niles Trammell, 1 July 1947, with attached statements, NBC Papers, US MSS 17AF, box 115, folder 17).

16. Jack Gould, "Backward Glance: Radio in 1946 Suffered Strong Criticism," *New York Times,* 29 December 1946, sec. 2, p. 9.

17. Meyer, "The 'Blue Book,'" 199.

18. Ibid., 203.

19. Ibid.

20. White, *The American Radio,* 192.

21. Meyer, "Reaction to the 'Blue Book,'" 295–96.

22. "FCC, Industry Strip for Action," *Variety,* 13 March 1946, 35.

23. NBC Papers, box 56, folder 72, 1937; NBC Papers, box 72, folder 47, 1939.

24. Meyer, "Reaction to the 'Blue Book,'" 310; Meyer, "The Blue Book," 198.

25. Charles Siepmann, "Radio's Operation Crossroads," *Nation,* 7 December 1946, 644.

26. "Man of the Year," *Variety,* 10 April 1946, 35.

27. Meyer, "Reaction to the 'Blue Book,'" 300. The book review appeared under the headline "Cure-All" in *Time*, 22 April 1946, 62.

28. Socolow, "'Who is Doing the Kicking at the Present Time?'" 198.

29. Harrison Smith, "No Soap," *Saturday Review*, 25 May 1946, 11.

30. "The Revolt Against Radio," *Fortune*, March 1947, 102.

31. Russell Maloney, "Through Radio's Looking-Glass," *New York Times Book Review*, 26 May 1946, 1.

32. "Love Those 'Hucksters' Airy Froth," *Variety*, 24 July 1946, 34.

33. "Advertising: Love That Account," *Tide*, 9 September 1946, 87.

34. "Books: Beautee and the Beast," *Time*, 3 June 1946, 106.

35. "Love Those 'Hucksters' Airy Froth," *Variety*, 24 July 1946, 34.

36. *Current Biography 1946*, s.v. "Frederic Wakeman."

37. "Radio: The Noes Have It," *Time*, 4 November 1946, 80.

38. "'Love Dat Book' Spots to Hypo 'Hucksters' Sale," *Advertising Age*, 3 June 1946, 1, 77.

39. Siepmann, *Radio's Second Chance*, 89–90.

40. Ibid., 104–5.

41. Fox, *The Mirror Makers*, 154.

42. Dunlap, *Radio in Advertising*, 52.

43. Fox, *The Mirror Makers*, 154.

44. Dunlap, *Radio in Advertising*, 52.

45. Crosby, "Radio and Who Makes It," 29.

46. "Corporations: End of a Legend," *Time*, 23 September 1946, 84.

47. Wakeman, *The Hucksters*, 21.

48. Gunther, *Taken at the Flood*, 165.

49. Wakeman, *The Hucksters*, 15, 74.

50. "Advertising: Love That Account," *Time*, 9 September 1946, 88.

51. Fox, *The Mirror Makers*, 150.

52. Ibid.

53. Ibid., 154.

54. Gunther, *Taken at the Flood*, 166.

55. Frederic Wakeman, personal correspondence, 2 July 1996.

56. "Corporations: End of a Legend," *Time*, 23 September 1946, 86.

57. *Current Biography 1946*, s.v. "Frederic Wakeman."

58. Frederic Wakeman, personal correspondence, 2 July 1996.

59. Ibid.

60. Albert N. Williams, "Listening: Slings and Arrows," *Saturday Review*, 30 November 1946, 43.

61. "The Revolt Against Radio," *Fortune*, March 1947, 103.

62. Sterling and Kittross, *Stay Tuned*, 638–39.

63. Siepmann, *America in a World War*, 3.

64. Fox, *Madison Avenue Goes to War*, 69.

65. Ibid., 41; Fox, *The Mirror Makers*, 170.

66. Wolfe, *Modern Radio Advertising*, 22.

67. Barnouw, *The Sponsor*, 42.

68. Siepmann, "Storm in the Radio World," *American Mercury,* August 1946, 206.

69. Siepmann, *Radio's Second Chance,"* 139.

70. White, *The American Radio,* 124–25.

71. Wood, *The Story of Advertising,* 444.

72. David L. Cohn, "Advertising Greets the Homecoming Heroes and Customers," *The Saturday Review* (22 September 1945): 30.

73. John Crosby, "Radio and Who Makes It," *Atlantic Monthly* (January 1948): 29.

74. White, *The American Radio,* 65.

75. Baughman, *The Republic of Mass Culture,* 35.

76. Memo, Syd Eiges to Niles Trammell, 27 June 1947, NBC Papers, box 115, folder 17.

77. "'Hucksters' Film Lacks Shock-Power of Wakeman Novel," *Advertising Age,* 7 July 1947, 28.

78. Memo, Syd Eiges to Niles Trammell, 27 June 1947, NBC Papers, box 115, folder 17.

79. Memo, Charles P. Hammond to Niles Trammell, 26 June 1947, NBC Papers, box 115, folder 17.

80. Memo, Syd Eiges to Niles Trammell, 27 June 1947, NBC Papers, box 115, folder 17.

81. Ibid.

82. Lazarsfeld and Kendall, *Radio Listening in America,* 75–80.

83. In this scene, MGM took a page from the history of advertising. Helen Resor was the first advertising executive to use testimonials. She succeeded in convincing a "prominent" New York feminist, Mrs. O. H. P. Belmont, to endorse Pond's Cold Cream "in exchange for a donation to charity" (Fox, *The Mirror Makers,* 89).

Bibliography

Archival Sources

Ruth Brindze Papers, Vanguard Press Collection, Columbia University Archives, New York, New York

Bureau of Applied Social Research Papers, Columbia University Archives, New York [BASR Papers]

Persia Campbell Collection, Consumers Union Archive, Yonkers, New York

Jane Crusinberry Papers, Wisconsin Historical Society, Madison [JC Papers]

Paul F. Lazarsfeld Papers, Columbia University, New York

Donald Montgomery Papers, Walter Reuther Library, Detroit [DM Papers]

National Broadcasting Company Papers, 1921–1969, Wisconsin Historical Society, Madison [NBC Papers]

Irna Phillips Papers, Wisconsin Historical Society, Madison [IP Papers]

James Rorty Papers, Special Collections, Knight Library, University of Oregon, Eugene

UE Papers, Archive Service Center, University of Pittsburgh, Pittsburgh

Colston Warne Collection, Consumers Union Archive, Yonkers, New York

Newspapers and Periodicals

Bread and Butter (Weekly publication of the Consumers Union of the United States), 1941–1947

Consumer News (Newsletter of the National Association of Consumers), 1955–1956

Consumers on the March (Bulletin of the National Association of Consumers), 1946–1951

Other Published Sources

Adorno, Theodor W. "A Social Critique of Radio Music." *Kenyon Review* 9 (spring 1945): 208–19.

———. "Scientific Experiences of a European Scholar in America." In *The Intellectual Migration: Europe and America, 1930–1960,* ed. Donald Fleming and Bernard Bailyn. Cambridge, Mass.: Harvard University Press, 1969.

———. "The Culture Industry Reconsidered." In *Critical Theory and Society: A Reader,* ed. Stephen Eric Bronner and Douglas MacKay Kellner. New York: Routledge, 1989.

Agnew, Jean-Christophe. "Coming Up for Air: Consumer Culture in Historical Perspective." *Intellectual History Newsletter* 12 (1990): 3–21.

Allen, Robert C. *Speaking of Soap Operas.* Chapel Hill: University of North Carolina Press, 1985.

Anshen, Melvin. "The Rediscovery of the Consumer." *Journal of Marketing* 5, no. 3 (January 1941): 213–53.

Antler, Joyce. "Between Culture and Politics: The Emma Lazarus Federation of Jewish Women's Clubs and the Promulgation of Women's History, 1944–1989." In *U.S. History as Women's History: New Feminist Essays,* ed. Linda K. Kerber, Alice Kessler-Harris, and Kathryn Kish Sklar. Chapel Hill: University of North Carolina Press, 1995.

Arata, Esther Spring. *More Black American Playwrights: A Bibliography.* Metuchen, N.J.: Scarecrow Press, 1978.

Arnheim, Rudolph. *Radio: An Art of Sound.* Translated by Margaret Ludwig and Herbert Read. New York: Arno Press, 1971.

———. "The World of the Daytime Serial." In *Radio Research 1942–1943,* ed. Paul Lazarsfeld and Frank Stanton. New York: Duell, Sloan, and Pierce, 1944.

Balderston, William. "'Philco': Autobiography of Progress." New York: Newcomen Society in North America, 1954.

Barnouw, Eric. *The Sponsor: Notes on a Modern Potentate.* New York: Oxford University Press, 1978.

Bartos, Rena. "Ernest Dichter: Motive Interpreter." *Journal of Advertising Research* 26, no. 1 (February/March 1986): 15–20.

Bauer, Raymond A., and Stephen A. Greyser. *Advertising in America: The Consumer View.* Boston: Division of Research, Graduate School of Business Administration, Harvard University, 1968.

Baughman, James L. *The Republic of Mass Culture: Journalism, Filmmaking, and Broadcasting in America since 1941.* Baltimore: Johns Hopkins University Press, 1997.

Benjamin, Louise M. "At the Touch of a Button: A History of the Remote Control." Paper presented to the Mass Communication Division, Speech Communication Association Annual Convention, San Francisco, Calif., November 1989.

Bensman, David. *The Practice of Solidarity: American Hat Finishers in the Nineteenth Century.* Urbana: University of Illinois Press, 1985.

Berg, Louis. *Prison Doctor.* New York: Macaulay, 1932.
———. *Prison Nurse.* New York: Macaulay, 1934.
Beville, H. M., Jr. "The ABCD's of Radio Audiences." *Public Opinion Quarterly* 4, no. 2 (1940): 195–206.
———. *Social Stratification of the Radio Audience: A Study Made for the Princeton Radio Research Project.* New York: Columbia University, Office of Radio Research, 1940.
Boddy, William. *Fifties Television: The Industry and Its Critics.* Urbana: University of Illinois Press, 1990.
Bond, Frederick W. *The Negro and the Drama.* College Park, Md.: McGrath Publishing Co., 1969.
Boorstin, Daniel J. *The Decline of Radicalism: Reflections on America Today.* New York: Random House, 1969.
Borden, Neil H. *The Economic Effects of Advertising.* Chicago: Richard D. Irwin, 1942.
Breen, T. H. "Narrative of Commercial Life: Consumption, Ideology, and Community on the Eve of the American Revolution." *William and Mary Quarterly* 50, no. 3 (July 1993): 471–502.
Brindze, Ruth. "Facts for Consumers." *Nation,* 6 November 1935, 541.
———. *How To Spend Money: Everybody's Practical Guide to Buying.* New York: Vangaurd Press, 1935.
———. "The Consumer Front." *Nation,* 18 March 1936, 347.
———. "Facts for Consumers." *Nation,* 29 January 1936, 132–33.
———. "Consumer's Progress." *Nation,* 18 December 1937, 694.
———. "Freedom of the Press Again." *Nation,* 24 July 1937, 98–99.
———. "Mr. Aylesworth Moves Ahead." *Nation,* 20 February 1937, 208.
———. *Not To Be Broadcast: The Truth About Radio.* New York: Vangaurd Press, 1937.
———. "Who Owns the Air." *Nation,* 17 April 1937, 430–31.
———. "Why You Pay More For Food." *Nation,* 4 December 1937, 612–13.
———. "The Radio Newspaper." *Nation,* 5 February 1938, 154–55.
———. "Getting Your Money's Worth: A Monthly Department of Consumer Education for High School Students." *Scholastic,* 9 October 1939, 20-S.
———. "Getting Your Money's Worth: A Monthly Department of Consumer Education for High School Students." *Scholastic,* 13 November 1939, 18-S.
———. "Getting Your Money's Worth: A Monthly Department of Consumer Education for High School Students." *Scholastic,* 18 December 1939, 16-S.
———. *Seamanship Below Deck.* New York: Harcourt, 1939.
———. "Getting Your Money's Worth: A Monthly Department of Consumer Education for High School Students." *Scholastic,* 15 January 1940, 20-S.
———. "Getting Your Money's Worth: A Monthly Department of Consumer Education for High School Students." *Scholastic,* 19 February 1940, 34.
———. "Getting Your Money's Worth: A Monthly Department of Consumer Education for High School Students." *Scholastic,* 15 April 1940, 34, 39.

——. "Getting Your Money's Worth: A Monthly Department of Consumer Education for High School Students." *Scholastic,* 13 May 1940, 40, 43.

——. "Autobiographical Sketch of Ruth Brindze." *More Junior Authors.* New York: H. W. Wilson Co., 1963.

Brinkley, Alan. *Voices of Protest: Huey Long, Father Coughlin, and the Great Depression.* New York: Vintage Books, 1983.

Brobeck, Stephen, Robert N. Meyer, and Robert O. Herrman, eds. *Encyclopedia of the Consumer Movement.* Santa Barbara, Calif.: ABC-CLIO, 1997.

Brunsdon, Charlotte. *The Feminist, the Housewife, and the Soap Opera.* Oxford: Clarendon Press, 2000.

Buerkel-Rothfuss, Nancy L., and Sandra Mayes. "Soap Opera Viewing: The Cultivation Effect." *Journal of Communication* 31 (summer 1981): 108–15.

Butsch, Richard *For Fun and Profit : The Transformation of Leisure into Consumption.* Philadelphia: Temple University Press, 1990.

Buttitta, Tony, and Barry Witham. *Uncle Sam Presents: A Memoir of the Federal Theatre, 1935–1939.* Philadelphia: University of Pennsylvania Press, 1982.

Buzzard, Karen. *Chains of Gold: Marketing the Ratings and Rating the Markets.* Metuchen, N.J.: Scarecrow Press, 1990.

Campbell, Colin. *The Romantic Ethic and the Spirit of Modern Consumerism.* Oxford: Basil Blackwell, 1989.

Campbell, Persia. *The Consumer Interest: A Study in Consumer Economics.* New York: Harper, 1949.

Cantril, Hadley, and Gordon W. Allport. *The Psychology of Radio.* New York: Harper and Brothers, 1935.

Caplovitz, David. *The Poor Pay More: Consumer Practices of Low-Income Families.* New York: Free Press of Glencoe, 1963.

Carter, Boake. *Johnny Q. Public Speaks: The Nation Appraises the New Deal.* New York: Dodge Publishing Company, 1936.

——. *I Talk as I Like.* New York: Dodge Publishing Company, 1937.

—— [Richard Sheridan Ames, pseud.]. "News on the Air." *Saturday Evening Post,* 23 January 1937.

Chase, Stuart, and F. J. Schlink. *Your Money's Worth: A Study in the Waste of the Consumer's Dollar.* New York: Macmillan Co., 1927.

Christopher, Sterling H., and John M. Kittross. *Stay Tuned: A Concise History of American Broadcasting.* Belmont, Calif.: Wadsworth Publishing, 1990.

Clark, David G. "H. V. Kaltenborn and His Sponsors: Controversial Broadcasting and the Sponsor Role." In *American Broadcasting: A Source Book on the History of Radio and Television,* ed. Lawrence W. Lichty and Malachi C. Topping. New York: Hastings House, 1975.

Clark, Lincoln H. *Consumer Behavior.* Vol. 2, *The Life Cycle and Consumer Behavior.* New York: New York University Press, 1955.

Clive, Alan. *State of War: Michigan in World War II.* Ann Arbor: University of Michigan Press, 1979.

Cohen, Lizabeth. *Making a New Deal: Industrial Workers in Chicago, 1919–1939.* New York: Cambridge University Press, 1990.

——. "The Class Experience of Mass Consumption: Workers as Consumers in Interwar America." In *The Power of Culture: Critical Essays in American History,* ed. Richard Wightman Fox and T. J. Jackson Lears. Chicago: University of Chicago Press, 1993.

——. "A Middle-Class Utopia? The American Suburban Home in the 1950s." Paper presented at the Delaware Seminar in American Art, History, and Material Culture, Newark, Del., 1993.

——. "Politics, Culture, and Consumerism." Paper presented at conference on U.S. Cultures: New Conversations, University of Washington, Seattle, 10–11 May 1996.

Congress of Industrial Organizations, (U.S.) Political Action Committee. *Radio Handbook.* New York: CIO, Political Action Committee, [1944].

"The Consumer in War and Peace." *Building America* 9, no. 5 (February 1944): 130–59.

Creighton, Lucy Black. "The Consumer Movement in the United States: A Study of Efforts to Promote the Role of Consumers in the Economy." Ph.D. diss., Harvard University, 1968.

——. *Pretenders to the Throne: The Consumer Movement in the United States.* Lexington: Lexington Books, 1976.

Crosby, John. "Radio and Who Makes It." *Atlantic Monthly,* January 1948.

Culbert, David Holbrook. *News For Everyman: Radio and Foreign Affairs in Thirties America.* Westport, Conn.: Greenwood Press, 1976.

Czitrom, Daniel. *Media in the American Mind: From Morse to McLuhan.* Chapel Hill: University of North Carolina Press, 1982.

Dameron, Kenneth. "The Consumer Movement." *Harvard Business Review* 17, no. 3 (spring 1939): 271–89.

——. "Advertising and the Consumer Movement." *Journal of Marketing* 5, no. 3 (January 1941): 234–47.

Denning, Michael. *Mechanic Accents: Dime Novels and Working-Class Culture in America.* New York: Verso, 1987.

——. "The End of Mass Culture." *International Labor and Working Class History,* no. 37 (spring 1990): 4–18.

——. "The Academic Left and the Rise of Cultural Studies." *Radical History Review* 54 (fall 1992): 21–47.

——. "Proletarian Literatures: Reflections on Working-Class Reading in the Age of the CIO." *Cahiers Charles* 5, no. 14 (1992): 87–97.

——. *The Cultural Front: The Laboring of American Culture in the Twentieth Century.* New York: Verso, 1996.

——. "Advertising Womanhood." Unpublished manuscript, 1983. Photocopy.

Dereshinsky, Ralph M., Alan D. Berkowitz, and Philip A. Miscimarra, eds. *The NLRB and Secondary Boycotts.* Philadelphia: Industrial Research Unit, Wharton School, University of Pennsylvania, 1981.

Dichter, Ernest. *The Psychology of Everyday Living.* New York: Barnes and Noble, 1947.

———. "A Psychological View of Advertising Effectiveness." *Journal of Marketing* 14, no. 1 (July 1949): 61–66.

———. *The Strategy of Desire.* Garden City, N.Y.: Doubleday, 1960.

Dirks, Jacqueline K. "Righteous Goods: Women's Production, Reform Publicity, and the National Consumers' League, 1891–1919." Ph.D. diss., Yale University, 1996.

Douglas, Ann. *The Feminization of American Culture.* New York: Knopf, 1977.

Douglas, Susan. *Where the Girls Are: Growing Up Female With the Mass Media.* New York: Times Books, 1994.

———. *Listening In: Radio and the American Imagination: From Amos 'n' Andy and Edward R. Murrow to Wolfman Jack and Howard Stern.* New York: Times Books, 1999.

Dunlap, Orrin E., Jr. *Radio in Advertising.* New York: Harper, 1931.

Durstine, Roy. "Roy Durstine on Reading Jim Rorty." *Advertising and Selling* 23 (10 May 1934): 26–27.

Edsforth, Ronald. *Class Conflict and Cultural Consensus: The Making of a Mass Consumer Society in Flint, Michigan.* New Brunswick, N.J.: Rutgers University Press, 1987.

Ernst, Daniel R. *Lawyers against Labor: From Individual Rights to Corporate Liberalism.* Urbana: University of Illinois Press, 1995.

Ewen, Stuart, and Elizabeth Ewen. *Channels of Desire: Mass Images and the Shaping of American Consciousness.* Minneapolis: University of Minnesota Press, 1992.

Fang, Irving E. *Those Radio Commentators!* Ames: Iowa State University Press, 1977.

Fifty Old Time Radio Commercials. Minneapolis: Radio Reruns, 1978. Audiocassette.

Filippelli, Ronald L. "UE: The Formative Years, 1933–1937." *Labor History* 17, no. 3 (summer 1976): 351–71.

Filippelli, Ronald L., and Mark McColloch. *Cold War in the Working Class: The Rise and Decline of the United Electrical Workers.* Albany: State University of New York Press, 1995.

Fones-Wolf, Elizabeth. "Creating a Favorable Business Climate: Corporations and Radio Broadcasting, 1934–1954." *Business History Review* 73 (summer 1999): 221–55.

———. "Promoting a Labour Perspective in the American Mass Media: Unions and Radio in the CIO Era, 1936–1956." *Media, Culture, and Society* 22 (May 2000): 285–307.

Fornatale, Peter, and Joshua E. Mills. *Radio in the Television Age.* Woodstock, N.Y.: Overlook Press, 1980.

Fowles, Jib. *Advertising and Popular Culture.* Thousand Oaks, Calif.: Sage Publications, 1996.

Fox, Frank W. *Madison Avenue Goes to War: The Strange Military Career of American Advertising, 1941–1945.* Provo, Utah: Brigham Young University Press, 1975.

Fox, Stephen. *The Mirror Makers: A History of American Advertising and Its Creators.* New York: Morrow, 1984.

Fraden, Rena. *Blueprints for a Black Federal Theatre, 1935–1939.* New York: Cambridge University Press, 1994.

Frank, Dana. *Purchasing Power: Consumer Organizing, Gender, and the Seattle Labor Movement, 1919–1929.* New York: Cambridge University Press, 1994.

Friedan, Betty. *The Feminine Mystique.* New York: Norton, 1983.

Gaines, Jane M. *Contested Culture: The Image, the Voice, and the Law.* Chapel Hill: University of North Carolina Press, 1991.

Gelston, Steven W., and Peggy A. Pascoe. *A Guide to Documents of the Consumer Movement: A National Catalog of Source Material.* Mount Vernon, N.Y.: Center for the Study of the Consumer Movement, Consumers Union Foundation, 1980.

Gilmartin, Jeanine. "An Historical Analysis of the Growth of the National Consumer Movement in the United States from 1947 to 1967." Ph.D. diss., Georgetown University, 1969.

Glander, Timothy. *Origin of Mass Communications Research during the American Cold War: Educational Effects and Contemporary Implications.* Mahway, N.J.: Lawrence Erlbaum Associates, 2000.

Glickman, Lawrence B. "Workers of the World, Consume: Ira Steward and the Intellectual Origins of Labor Consumerism." Paper presented at the American Studies Association Meeting, Kansas City, Mo., November 1996.

———. *A Living Wage: American Workers and the Making of Consumer Society.* Ithaca, N.Y.: Cornell University Press, 1997.

———. "The Strike in the Temple of Consumption: Debating Consumerism in the Depression Decade." Paper presented at the American Studies Association, Montreal, Canada, October 1999.

———. "The Strike in the Temple of Consumption: Consumer Activism and Twentieth Century American Political Culture." *Journal of American History* 88, no. 1 (June 2001): 99–128.

Godfried, Nathan. *WCFL, Chicago's Voice of Labor, 1926–78.* Urbana: University of Illinois Press, 1997.

Griffith, Robert. "The Selling of America: The Advertising Council and American Politics, 1942–1960." *Business History Review* 57 (fall 1983): 388–412.

Guadet, Hazel. "Favorite Radio Programs." *Journal of Applied Psychology* 23, no. 1 (February 1939): 115–26.

Gunther, John. *Taken at the Flood: The Story of Albert D. Lasker.* New York: Harper Brothers, 1960.

Hall, Helen. "Consumer Protection." In *Social Work Year Book,* ed. Margaret B. Hodges. New York: Russell Sage Foundation, 1949.

Hall, Stuart. *The Hard Road to Renewal: Thatcherism and the Crisis of the Left.* London: Verso, 1988.

Hattwick, Melvin S. *How to Use Psychology for Better Advertising.* New York: Prentice-Hall, 1950.

Havig, Alan. "Frederic Wakeman's *The Hucksters* and the Postwar Debate over Commercial Radio." *Journal of Broadcasting* 28, no. 2 (spring 1984): 198.

Herzog, Herta. "What Do We Really Know About Day-Time Serial Listeners." In *Radio Research 1942–1943,* ed. Paul Lazarsfeld and Frank Stanton. New York: Duell, Sloan, and Pierce, 1944.

Hettinger, Herman S. *A Decade of Radio Advertising.* Chicago: University of Chicago Press, 1933.

Hettinger, Herman S., and Walter J. Neff. *Practical Radio Advertising.* New York: Prentice-Hall, 1938.

Hilmes, Michele. *Radio Voices: American Broadcasting, 1922–1952.* Minneapolis: University of Minnesota Press, 1997.

Hollonquist, Tore, and Edward A. Suchman. "Listening to the Listener: Experiences with the Lazarsfeld-Stanton Program Analyzer." In *Radio Research: 1942–1943,* ed. Paul F. Lazarsfeld and Frank N. Stanton. New York: Arno Press, 1979.

Holter, Frances. "Radio among the Unemployed." *Journal of Applied Psychology* 23, no. 1 (February 1939): 163–69.

Horkheimer, Max, and Theodor Adorno. "The Culture Industry: Enlightenment as Mass Deception." In *Dialectic of Enlightenment,* trans. John Cumming. New York: Continuum, 1997.

Horowitz, Daniel. *The Morality of Spending: Attitudes toward the Consumer Society in America, 1875–1940.* Baltimore: Johns Hopkins Press, 1985.

———. "Rethinking Betty Friedan and *The Feminine Mystique:* Labor Union Radicalism and Feminism in Cold War America." *American Quarterly* 48, no. 1 (1996): 1–42.

Horowitz, David. *Thirty-three Candles.* New York: World Union Press, 1949.

Houseman, John. *Run-Through: A Memoir.* New York: Simon and Schuster, 1972.

Hulme, Derick L., Jr. *The Political Olympics: Moscow, Afghanistan, and the 1980 U.S. Boycott.* New York: Praeger, 1990.

Huyssen, Andreas. *After the Great Divide: Modernism, Mass Culture, Postmodernism.* Bloomington: Indiana University Press, 1986.

———. "Mass Culture as Woman: Modernism's Other." In *Studies in Entertainment: Critical Approaches to Mass Culture,* ed. Tania Modleski. Bloomington: Indiana University Press, 1986.

Jacobs, Meg. "'How About Some Meat?': Office of Price Administration and Consumption Politics." *Journal of American History* 84, no. 3 (December 1997): 910–41.

———. "'Democracy's Third Estate': New Deal Politics and the Construction of a 'Consuming Public." *International Labor and Working-Class History* 5 (spring 1999): 27–51.

Jhally, Sut. "Probing the Blindspot: The Audience Commodity." *Canadian Journal of Political and Social Theory* 6, nos. 1–2 (winter/spring 1982): 204–10.

——. *The Codes of Advertising: Fetishism and the Political Economy of Meaning in the Consumer Society.* London: Routledge, 1990.

Jhally, Sut, and Bill Livant. "Watching as Working: The Valorization of the Audience Consciousness." *Journal of Communication* 3 (summer 1986): 124–36.

Kasson, John F. *Amusing the Million: Coney Island at the Turn of the Century.* New York: Hill and Wang, 1978.

Katz, David Norman. "Consumers Union: The Movement and the Magazine, 1936–1957." Ph.D. diss., Rutgers University, 1977.

Kelley, Pearce C. *Consumer Economics.* Homewood, Ill.: Richard D. Irwin, 1953.

Kelley, Robin. *Race Rebels: Culture, Politics, and the Black Working Class.* New York: Free Press, 1994.

Kendall, Patricia L., ed. *The Varied Sociology of Paul F. Lazarsfeld.* New York: Columbia University Press, 1982.

Kennedy, John F. "Strengthening of Programs for Protection of Consumer Interests." In *Caveat Emptor.* New York: Arno Press, 1976.

Kenner, H. J. *The Fight for Truth in Advertising.* New York: Round Table Press, 1936.

Kerber, Linda K., Alice Kessler-Harris, and Kathryn Kish Sklar, eds. *U.S. History as Women's History: New Feminist Essays.* Chapel Hill: University of North Carolina Press, 1995.

LaGuardia, Robert. *From Ma Perkins to Mary Hartman: The Illustrated History of Soap Operas.* New York: Ballantine Books, 1977.

Laidler, Harry W. *Boycotts and the Labor Struggle: Economic and Legal Aspects.* New York: Russell and Russell, 1968.

Land, Jeff. *Active Radio: Pacifica's Brash Experiment.* Minneapolis: University of Minnesota Press, 1999.

Landry, Robert J. *Who, What, Why Is Radio?* New York: George W. Stewart, 1942.

Lazarsfeld, Paul F. "Radio Research and Applied Psychology: Introduction by the Guest Editor." *Journal of Applied Psychology* 23, no. 1 (February 1939): 1–7.

——. *Radio and the Printed Page: An Introduction to the Study of Radio and Its Role in the Communication of Ideas.* New York: Duell, Sloan, and Pearce, 1940.

——. *The People Look at Radio.* Chapel Hill: University of North Carolina Press, 1946.

——. "Role of Criticism in Management of Mass Communications." In *Communications in Modern Society.* Urbana: University of Illinois Press, 1948.

——. "An Episode in the History of Social Research: A Memoir." In *The Intellectual Migration: Europe and America, 1930–1960,* ed. Donald Fleming and Bernard Bailyn. Cambridge, Mass.: Belknap Press of Harvard University Press, 1969.

Lazarsfeld, Paul F., and Elihu Katz. *Personal Influence: The Part Played by People in the Flow of Mass Communications.* Glencoe, Ill.: Free Press, 1955.

Lazarsfeld, Paul F., and Patricia Kendall. *Radio Listening in America*. New York: Prentice-Hall, 1948.

Lazarsfeld, Paul F., and Robert K. Merton. "Mass Communication, Popular Taste, and Organized Social Action." In *The Communication of Ideas: A Series of Addresses,* ed. Lyman Bryson. New York: Institute for Religious and Social Studies, 1948.

Lazarsfeld, Paul F., and Frank N. Stanton, eds. *Radio Research: 1942–1943*. New York: Arno Press, 1979.

Lears, T. J. Jackson. *Fables of Abundance: A Cultural History of Advertising in America*. New York: Basic Books, 1994.

Lever, E. A. *Advertising and Economic Theory*. London: Oxford University Press, 1947.

Liebling, A. J. "Boake Carter." *Scribner's Magazine,* August 1938.

Lipsitz, George. *Class and Culture in Cold War America: A Rainbow at Midnight*. New York: Praeger, 1981.

———. *Time Passages: Collective Memory and American Popular Culture*. Minneapolis: University of Minnesota Press, 1990.

Livant, Bill. "The Audience Commodity: On the 'Blindspot' Debate." *Canadian Journal of Political and Social Theory* 3, no. 1 (winter 1979): 91–106.

———. "Working at Watching: A Reply to Sut Jhally." *Canadian Journal of Political and Social Theory* 6, nos. 1–2 (winter/spring 1982): 211–15.

Lucas, Darrell Blaine, and Steuart Henderson Britt. *Advertising Psychology and Research: An Introductory Book*. New York: McGraw-Hill, 1950.

Lynn, Susan. *Progressive Women in Conservative Times: Racial Justice, Peace, and Feminism, 1945 to the 1960s*. New Brunswick, N.J.: Rutgers University Press, 1992.

MacDonald, J. Fred. *Don't Touch That Dial: Radio Programming in American Life, 1920–1960*. Chicago: Nelson-Hall, 1979.

Marchand, Roland. *Advertising the American Dream: Making Way for Modernity*. Berkeley: University of California Press, 1985.

———. "National Stage, Local Participation: The Major Bowes' Original Amateur Hour and the New 1930s Genre." Paper presented at the Annual Meeting of the Organization of American Historians, Chicago, March 1996.

Marlow, Joyce. *Captain Boycott and the Irish*. London: Andre Deutsch, 1973.

Martineau, Pierre. *Motivation in Advertising: Motives that Make People Buy*. New York: McGraw-Hill Book Company, 1957.

Mather, Loys L. *Economics of Consumer Protection*. Danville, Ill.: Printers and Publishers, 1971.

Maxwell, Richard. "The Image Is Gold: Value, the Audience Commodity, and Fetishism." *Journal of Film and Video* 43 (spring/summer 1991): 29–45.

Mazzocco, Dennis William. "Democracy, Power, and Equal Rights: The AFL vs. CIO Battle to Unionize U.S. Broadcast Technicians, 1926–1940. Ph.D. diss., University of California at San Diego, 1996.

McChesney, Robert W. *Telecommunications, Mass Media, and Democracy: The*

Battle for the Control of U.S. Broadcasting, 1928–1935. New York: Oxford University Press, 1994.

McGovern, Charles Francis. "Sold American: Inventing the Consumer, 1890–1940." Ph.D. diss., Harvard University, 1993.

Meehan, Eileen R. "Heads of Household and Ladies of the House: Gender, Genre, and Broadcast Ratings, 1929–1990." In *Ruthless Criticism: New Perspectives in U.S. Communication History,* ed. William S. Solomon and Robert W. McChesney. Minneapolis: University of Minnesota Press, 1993.

Melody, Bill. "Dallas Smythe: A Lifetime at the Frontier of Communications." *Canadian Journal of Communication* 17, no. 4 (1992). www.wlu.ca/~www-press/jrls/cjc/BackIssues/17.4/melody.html

Meyer, Richard J. "The 'Blue Book.'" *Journal of Broadcasting* 6 (summer 1962): 197–294.

———. "Reaction to the 'Blue Book.'" *Journal of Broadcasting* 6 (summer 1962): 295–312.

Meyerowitz, Joanne. "Beyond the Feminine Mystique: A Reassessment of Postwar Mass Culture, 1946–1958." *Journal of American History* 79 (March 1993): 1455–82.

———, ed. *Not June Cleaver: Women and Gender in Postwar America, 1945–1960.* Philadelphia: Temple University Press, 1994.

Meyrowitz, Alvin, and Marjorie Fiske. "The Relative Preference of Low Income Groups for Small Stations." *Journal of Applied Psychology* 23, no. 1 (February 1939): 158–61.

Montgomery, Donald. "Consumers Under Way." *Survey Graphics,* April 1938.

———. "Rationing Is Not Enough." *Survey Graphics,* February 1943.

Morell, Peter. *Poisons, Potions, and Profits: The Antidote to Radio Advertising.* New York: Knight Publishers, 1937.

Morrison, David E. "Kultur and Culture: The Case of Theodor W. Adorno and Paul F. Lazarsfeld." *Social Research* (summer 1978): 331–55.

Murdock, Graham. "Blindspots about Western Marxism: A Reply to Dallas Smythe." *Canadian Journal of Political and Social Theory* 2, no. 2 (spring/summer 1978): 109–19.

———. "Embedded Persuasions: The Fall and Rise of Integrated Advertising." In *Come On Down?: Popular Media Culture in Post-War Britain,* ed. Dominic Strinati and Stephen Wagg. London: Routledge, 1992.

Murray, Sylvie. *The Progressive Housewife: Community Activism in Suburban Queens, 1945–1965.* Philadelphia: University of Pennsylvania Press, 2003.

Murrow, Edward. "Soap Opera." *Fortune Magazine,* March 1946.

Nasaw, David. *Going Out: The Rise and Fall of Public Amusements.* New York: Basic Books, 1993.

National Broadcasting Company. *Broadcast Advertising: A Study of the Radio Medium — The Fourth Dimension of Advertising.* Vol. 1. New York: National Broadcasting Company, 1929.

Nava, Mica. "Consumerism Reconsidered: Buying and Power." *Cultural Studies* 5, no. 2 (May 1991): 157–71.

O'Conner, John, and Lorraine Brown. *Free, Adult, Uncensored: The Living History of the Federal Theatre Project.* Washington, D.C.: New Republic Books, 1978.

O'Dell, Cary. *Women Pioneers in Television: Biographies of Fifteen Industry Leaders.* Jefferson, N.C.: McFarland and Company, 1997.

Ohmann, Richard. "Where Did Mass Culture Come From? The Case of Magazines." In *Politics of Letters,* ed. Richard Ohmann. Middletown, Conn.: Wesleyan University Press, 1987.

———. *Selling Culture: Magazines, Markets, and Class at the Turn of the Century.* New York: Verso, 1996.

One Hundred and One Old Radio Commercials. Plymouth, Minn.: Metacom, 1994. Compact disc.

Orleck, Annelise. *Common Sense and a Little Fire: Women and Working-Class Politics in the United States, 1900–1965.* Chapel Hill: University of North Carolina Press, 1995.

Pease, Otis. *The Responsibilities of American Advertising: Private Control and Public Influence, 1920–1940.* New Haven, Conn.: Yale University Press, 1958.

Peterson, Esther. "Consumer Representation in the White House." In *Consumer Activists: They Made a Difference: A History of Consumer Action Related by Leaders in the Consumer Movement,* ed. National Consumers Committee for Research and Education. Mount Vernon, N.Y.: Consumers Union Foundation, 1982.

Phillips, M. C., and F. J. Schlink. *Discovering Consumers.* New York: John Day Company, 1934.

Pope, Daniel. "His Master's Voice: James Rorty and the Critique of Advertising." *Maryland Historian* 19, no. 1 (spring/summer 1988): 5–16.

Powel, Harford. "What the War Has Done to Advertising." *Public Opinion Quarterly* 31 (March 1942): 195–203.

Radway, Janice A. *Reading the Romance: Women, Patriarchy, and Popular Literature.* Chapel Hill: University of North Carolina Press, 1991.

Razlogova, Elena. "Listeners Write the Scripts: Radio Audiences and Radio Production During the 1930s and 1940s." Paper delivered at the Annual Conference of the Organization of American Historians, Washington, D.C, April 2002.

Remington, R. Roger. *Lester Beall: Trailblazer of American Graphic Design.* New York: W. W. Norton, 1996.

Rorty, James. *Order on the Air!* New York: John Day Company, 1934.

———. *Our Master's Voice: Advertising.* New York: John Day, 1934.

Rorty, James, and Moshe Decter. *McCarthy and the Communists.* Boston: Beacon Press, 1954.

Rosenzweig, Roy. *Eight Hours for What We Will: Workers and Leisure in an Industrial City, 1870–1920.* New York: Cambridge University Press, 1983.

Ross, Steven J. *Working-Class Hollywood: Silent Film and the Shaping of Class in America.* Princeton, N.J. : Princeton University Press, 1998.

Sayre, Jeanette. "A Comparison of Three Indices of Attitude Toward Radio Advertising." *Journal of Applied Psychology* 23, no. 1 (1939): 23–31.

Schudson, Michael. "Criticizing the Critics of Advertising: Towards a Sociological View of Marketing." *Media Culture and Society* 3, no. 1 (1981): 3–12.

———. *Advertising, The Uneasy Persuasion: Its Dubious Impact on American Society.* New York: Basic Books, 1984.

Seiter, Ellen. "To Teach and to Sell: Irna Phillips and Her Sponsors, 1930–1954." *Journal of Film and Video* 41 (spring 1989): 21–35.

Shurick, E. P. J. *The First Quarter-Century of American Broadcasting.* Kansas City: Midland Publishing Company, 1946.

Siepmann, Charles. *America in a World War: Radio in Wartime.* New York: Oxford University Press, 1942.

———. *Radio's Second Chance.* Boston: Little, Brown, 1946.

Silber, Norman Isaac. *Test and Protest: The Influence of the Consumers Union.* New York: Holmes and Meier, 1983.

Smith, Augustus J., and Peter Morell. *Turpentine.* Alexandria, Va.: Alexander Street Press, 2002.

Smith, N. Craig. *Morality and the Market: Consumer Pressure for Corporate Accountability.* New York: Routledge, 1990.

Smith, Paul. "Domestic Labour and Marx's Theory of Value." In *Feminism and Materialism,* ed. Annette Kuhn and Ann Marie Wolpe. Boston: Routledge, 1978.

Smulyan, Susan. *Selling Radio: The Commercialization of American Broadcasting, 1920–1934.* Washington, D.C.: Smithsonian Institution Press, 1994.

Smythe, Dallas W. "Buy Something: Five Myths of Consumerism." In *In the Marketplace: Consumerism in America,* ed. Frank Browning. San Francisco: Canfield Press, 1972.

———. "Communications: Blindspot of Western Marxism." *Canadian Journal of Political and Social Theory* 1 (fall 1977): 1–27.

———. "Rejoinder to Graham Murdock." *Canadian Journal of Political and Social Theory* 2, no. 2 (spring/summer 1978): 120–27.

———. *Dependency Road: Communications, Capitalism, Consciousness, and Canada.* Norwood, N.J.: Ablex Publishing Corporation, 1981.

Sobel, Lester A., ed. *Consumer Protection.* New York: Facts on File, 1976.

Socolow, Michael. "'Who is Doing the Kicking at the Present Time?': N.B.C., C.B.S., James Lawrence Fly, and the Politics of Chain Broadcasting Regulation, 1936–1943." Paper presented at the Annual Meeting of the Organization of American Historians, Washington D.C., April 2002.

Sorenson, Helen. *The Consumer Movement: What It Is and What It Means.* New York: Harper and Brothers, 1941.

Spigel, Lynn. *Make Room for TV: Television and the Family Ideal in Postwar America.* Chicago: University of Chicago Press, 1992.

Spigel, Lynn, and Denise Mann, eds. *Private Screenings: Television and the Female Consumer.* Minneapolis: University of Minnesota Press, 1992.

Stedman, Raymond William. "A History of the Broadcasting of Daytime Serial

Dramas in the United States." Ph.D. diss., University of Southern California, 1959.

Sterling, Christopher H., and John M. Kittross. *Stay Tuned: A Concise History of American Broadcasting.* Belmont, Calif.: Wadsworth Publishing Company, 1990.

Strauss, Lori A. "The Anti-Advertising Bias in Twentieth-Century Literature." *Journal of American Culture* 16, no. 1 (spring 1993): 81–85.

Streeter, Thomas. "Viewing as Property: Broadcasting's Audience Commodity." In *Selling the Air: A Critique of the Policy of Commercial Broadcasting in the United States,* ed. Thomas Streeter. Chicago: University of Chicago Press, 1996.

"Subject of CR" [Consumers' Research]. *The Tide of Advertising and Marketing* 9 (October 1935): 72.

Summers, Harrison Boyd. "Miscellaneous: The Boake Carter Case." *Radio Censorship.* New York, H. W. Wilson Company, 1939.

Swerdlow, Amy. "The Congress of American Women: Left-Feminist Peace Politics in the Cold War." In *U.S. History as Women's History: New Feminist Essays,* ed. Linda K. Kerber, Alice Kessler-Harris, and Kathryn Kish Sklar. Chapel Hill: University of North Carolina Press, 1995.

Tedlow, Richard S. "From Competitor to Consumer: The Changing Focus of Federal Regulation of Advertising, 1914–1938." *Business History Review* 55, no. 1 (spring 1981): 35–58.

———. *New and Improved: The Story of Mass Marketing in America.* New York: Basic Books, 1990.

Tegler, Patricia. "The Daytime Serial: A Bibliography of Scholarly Writings, 1943–1981." *Journal of Popular Culture* 16 (winter 1982). Reprinted in Mary Cassata and Thomas Skill, eds., *Life on Daytime Television: Tuning-In American Serial Drama* (Norwood, N.J.: Ablex, 1983), 187–96.

Teslik, Kennan Lee. *Congress, the Executive Branch, and Special Interests: The American Response to the Arab Boycott of Israel.* Westport, Conn.: Greenwood Press, 1982.

Tosdal, H. R. "The Consumer and Consumption in Recent Literature." *Harvard Business Review* 17, no. 4 (spring 1939): 508–13.

U.S. House. Un-American Activities Committee. *Report on the Congress of American Women.* 81st Cong., 1st sess., 1949. H. Rept.

Vickery, Amanda. "Women and the World of Goods: A Lancashire Consumer and Her Possessions." In *Consumption and the World of Goods,* ed. John Brewer and Roy Porter. New York: Routledge, 1993.

Wakeman, Frederic. *The Hucksters.* New York: Rinehart and Company, 1946.

Wald, Alan. "Marxist Literary Resistance to the Cold War." *Prospects* 20 (1995): 479–92.

Waller, Judith C. *Radio: The Fifth Estate.* Boston: Houghton Mifflin, 1946.

Warne, Clinton. "The Consumer Movement and the Labor Movement." *Journal of Economic Issues* (June 1973): 307–16.

Warne, Colston E. "Advertising: A Critic's View." In *Caveat Emptor.* New York: Arno Press, 1976.

———. "Advertising and the Consumer Movement." In *The Consumer Movement: Lectures by Colston E. Warne,* ed. Richard L. D. Morse. Manhattan, Kan.: Family Economics Trust Press, 1993.

Warner, W. Lloyd, and William E. Henry. "The Radio Day Time Serial: A Symbolic Analysis." *Genetic Psychology Monographs* 37 (1948): 3–71.

Warren, Donald I. *Radio Priest: Charles Coughlin, The Father of Hate Radio.* New York: Free Press, 1996.

Watkins, Evan. *Throwaways: Work Culture and Consumer Education.* Stanford, Calif.: Stanford University Press, 1993.

Webster, Harold Tucker. *The Best of H. T. Webster: A Memorial Collection.* New York: Simon and Schuster, 1953.

Westbrook, Robert B. "'I Want a Girl, Just Like the Girl that Married Harry James': American Women and the Problem of Political Obligation in World War II." *American Quarterly* 42, no. 4 (December 1990): 587–614.

White, Llewellyn. *The American Radio: A Report on the Broadcasting Industry in the United States from The Commission on Freedom of the Press.* Chicago: University of Chicago Press, 1947.

Wiggershaus, Rolf. *The Frankfurt School: Its History, Theories, and Political Significance.* Trans. Michael Robertson. Cambridge, Mass.: MIT Press, 1994.

Williams, Raymond. *Culture and Society, 1780–1950.* New York: Columbia University Press, 1958.

———. *Keywords: A Vocabulary of Culture and Society.* New York: Oxford University Press, 1976.

Willis, Ellen. "Women and the Myth of Consumerism." In *In the Marketplace: Consumerism in America,* ed. Frank Browning. San Francisco: Canfield Press, 1972.

Willis, Susan. *A Primer for Daily Life.* London: Routledge, 1991.

Wolfe, Charles Hull. *Modern Radio Advertising.* New York: Funk and Wagnalls, 1949.

Wolman, Leo. *The Boycott in American Trade Unions.* Baltimore: Johns Hopkins Press, 1916.

Wood, James Playsted. *The Story of Advertising.* New York: Ronald Press Company, 1958.

Woodward, Helen. *It's an Art.* New York: Harcourt, Brace and Company, 1938.

Index

Adler, Alfred, 21
Adorno, Theodor: and critique of culture industry, 7, 19; and producer/audience dialectic, 23–24, 39, 131; and resistance to capitalist communications system, 25–27
advertising: brand identification and, 41–45; capturing listeners, 37–38, 39, 43; consumer movement and, 2, 3, 40–41, 140, 142, 143, 144; content of, 29, 30, 31–33, 36–37; excesses in, 20, 87, 171–73, 174, 175–76, 178, 183–84, 186; form of, 27, 28, 29, 41–43; listener mistrust of, 17–18, 30, 31–33, 36–37; listener resentment and, 18, 28, 29, 30, 31–33, 37, 38–39, 48; negative content of, 30–37; structure of, 28, 38–39, 43–44
advertising agencies, 7–8, 27, 55, 177. *See also specific agencies*
The Advertising Agency Looks at Radio (O'Neill), 19
Advertising Age (trade magazine), 18, 56, 186, 188
AFL (American Federation of Labor), 66, 92, 95, 98, 99, 164
African Americans, 62, 70–71, 77. *See also* minority groups; racism
Africana (musical), 71
Albany (Ga.) Herald, 157
Alexander, A. L., 72–73
Allen, Fred, 19, 36–37

Allen, Ida Bailey, 113
Allport, Gordon W., 19–20, 42, 49, 131
"America First" movement, 83
American Druggist Association, 75
American Federation of Radio Artists, 112
American Federation of Teachers, 156
American Home Economics Association, 55
American Medicine Mobilizes (Rorty), 63
American Tobacco Company, 178–79
American Veterans Committee, 161
Amos 'n' Andy, 47
Angell, John, 172
Another World, 122
Arens, Egmont, 59
Armed Forces Network (AFN), 184
Arnheim, Rudolph, 111
As the World Turns, 122–23
audience: as commodities for sponsors to purchase, 4–5, 6, 8, 29, 45–46; demographic studies of, 18, 28–29, 44–50; surveys of, 17–18, 41, 44–50, 183
audience intellectuals: advertising strategies and, 27–45; European Socialist roots of, 19–21; psychological studies by, 17–27; radio rating systems and, 45–51
"Authority and the Family" (Frankfurt Institute study), 21

Bab-O cleaning supply, 40
Barnard, Mrs. Everett L., 113

Barnouw, Eric, 85, 181
Barton, Bruce, 156–57
Bauer, Otto, 22
BBC (British Broadcasting Corporation), 50, 172, 173, 175
BBDO advertising agency, 59, 60, 61, 91, 156
Beall, Lester, 1–2
Bellows, Henry Adam, 106–7
Berg, Louis, 115–16
Bernays, Edward, 142–43
Better Business Bureau, 68, 156
Beville, H. M., 47
Big Sister, 111
Blackett-Sample-Hummert advertising agency, 116
Bliss, Willard, 101
Blue Book of the FCC, 76, 171–72, 173
Bowes, Major, 47, 81–82
Bowles, Chester, 163
boycotts: consumers and, 10–13; history of, 81–84; labor and, 2–4, 86, 89–90, 92, 95–99, 100, 102
Brainard, Bertha, 117
Bread and Butter (consumer newsletter), 163, 209n.70
Brindze, Ruth: censorship and, 58, 65–67; children's books and, 68–69; as consumer advocate, 64–65, 68–70, 74–75, 173; grass-roots activism of, 53, 63–64; importance of, 76–77; personal life of, 69, 199n.60
Bristol Myers, 37
Broadcasting Magazine, 18, 172, 173
Broadcast Measurement Bureau (BMB), 45
Broder, Earl, 156
Brother Jim Crow (Rorty), 63
Brunsdon, Charlotte, 111
Buffalo Evening News, 158
Bühler, Charlotte and Karl, 21
Bureau of Radio Advertising, 144, 156
Business Week, 160
"But-" (Boake Carter), 88, 89, 90
Butsch, Richard, 11

Cadillac Square demonstrations, 160–61, 162
Camel cigarettes, 32
Cameron, William J., 66
Cantril, Hadley, 19–20, 42, 49, 131
capitalism: corporate fear of attacks on, 5, 56–57, 74–75, 156–58, 173, 178, 183;

James Rorty and, 57–58, 59–60, 61, 62–63; mass media and, 25, 56, 59–60, 67, 71, 191–92
Captain Cash, 39
Caraway, Hattie Wyatt, 123–24
Carey, James, 86, 89, 94–97, 98–99
Carlisle, Una Mae, 161
Carter, Boake: and Franklin Roosevelt, 88, 90, 91–92, 99, 101; free speech and, 89, 90, 92, 103–5; popularity of, 88–89, 90, 201n.30; rise of, 86–92; sponsor boycotts and, 86, 89–90, 92, 95–99, 100, 102. *See also* boycotts; censorship; CIO; Philco Radio
"The Case For Distribution" (Bureau of Radio Advertising), 144, 156
Catholic Church, 82, 83, 88, 107
CBS (Columbia Broadcasting System), 20, 71, 87, 90, 92, 112–13, 175
censorship: labor and, 66, 103, 105–6, 109, 127–30, 178; minorities and, 58, 62, 65–67, 71; newscasters and, 85–86, 104, 177–78; public pressure and, 89, 92, 103–5, 106–8; sponsor control and, 177–78
Charlie McCarthy program, 43
Chase, Stuart, 6, 54, 55, 57, 64
Chase and Sanborn Coffee, 43, 73, 81–82
Cheerioats, 43–44
Chester, Colby M., 89–90, 102–3
Chicago Daily Times, 122
children, 68–69
Chiquita banana song, 42–43
CIO (Congress of Industrial Organization): Boake Carter and, 86, 88, 89, 92, 95–97, 98–100; censorship of, 66, 103, 105–6; General Foods boycott by, 90, 102–3; WCAU and, 100, 101–2, 103. *See also* Carey, James; labor; Lewis, John L.; United Electrical and Radio Workers
Clark, David, 107
Clayton, Patti, 43
Cliquot Club Eskimos, 27
clubwomen, 112, 113, 115, 139–41, 148–49, 150, 192
code of ethics, NAB, 105–6
collective action, 3, 55, 56, 62, 67, 192
commercial products: consumer recognition of, 41–46, 105; dangerous or harmful, 17–18, 30, 31–33, 36–37, 56, 71–73; labeling of, 164–65

communism, 54, 59, 62–63, 101, 156–58,
    173. *See also* Marxism; socialism
Compton Advertising Agency, 109, 114,
    128–30
Connally-Smith anti-strike bill, 92
Connery, William P., 82
Consumer Advisory Board, 52
consumer backlash, 89, 158, 184
consumer commodification, 4–5, 6, 8, 11,
    29, 45
consumer conventions, 57, 118–19, 141–44
consumer cooperatives, 55
consumer education, 56, 141–42, 149
Consumer Education Association, 157
Consumer Flashes, 145
consumer movement: active future strate-
    gies for, 13, 182, 191–92; advertising's
    creation of, 52–58; corporate fear of, 5,
    30, 56–57, 141–44, 160, 173, 178, 183,
    188–89; demonstrations by, 159–63;
    grassroots activism within, 63–64, 143,
    191, 192; make-up of, 52–53, 55, 143–44,
    158, 164–65; organized labor and, 55, 57,
    73–74, 159–63, 165. *See also* Brindze,
    Ruth; Montgomery, Donald; Morell,
    Peter; Rorty, James
consumer protection legislation, 56, 63, 73,
    164
Consumer Reports, 55, 56
Consumer's Counsel, 145, 152–53
Consumer's Defender, 62–63
Consumers Guide (USDA), 145, 153, 155
Consumers on the March, 156, 164
Consumers' National Federation, 155–56
Consumers' Research, Inc., 52, 54, 55, 56, 141
Consumers Union, 55–56, 71, 74, 141, 163,
    209n.70
Consumer Time, 145–55, 165; government
    sponsorship of, 145–46, 151–52, 154; lis-
    tener letters to, 150–52. *See also*
    Montgomery, Donald
control of the airways: advertising spon-
    sors and, 5, 7–8, 127–30, 168, 177–82,
    184; censorship as result of, 58, 62, 65–
    67, 71; consumer boycotts and, 84, 89,
    90, 92, 103–8
Cooperative Analysis of Broadcasting
    (CAB), 45
Cooperative Distributors, 62
Copeland Act, 56
cosmetics in advertising, 17–18, 72
Coughlin, Father, 83, 88

county consumer councils, 64, 155
"cowcatcher" commercials, 38
Cream of Wheat, 82–83
Crossley, Archibald, 45
Crusinberry, Jane: censorship and, 109,
    127–30; fan mail to, 130–36; portrayal
    of women by, 124–27; as women's role
    model, 136–37, 138
Culbert, David, 90, 91
"Culture and the Crisis" (Rorty), 59
Cuthbert, Margaret, 140, 141, 142, 143, 152

Daily Bread and Other Foods (Brindze), 69
Davies, Joseph E., 90
Dawes, Henry May, 107–8
Days of Our Lives, 122
Debs, Eugene V., 65
A Decade of Radio Advertising (Hettinger),
    19, 20
de Grazia, Alfred, 91
Denison, Merrill, 114–15
Denning, Michael, 1, 138
The Dialectic of Enlightenment (Adorno
    and Horkheimer), 7
direct advertising, 27, 55
Dirks, Jacqueline, 9
Douglas, Ann, 9
Douglas, Susan, 3
drugs, 56, 65, 72, 73, 74, 75
Dunbar, Sadie Orr, 145
Dunlap, Orrin E., 19, 20
Durstine, Roy, 61
Duz soap, 34–35, 36
Dyke, Ken, 142, 144

Eiges, Syd, 186–88
Emspak, Julius, 95–96
Evans, S. Harry, 71
Eveready Program, 27
Ewen, Stuart, 29
excess profit tax, 183–84, 185–86

false advertising, 17–18, 56, 71–73
fan mail, 8, 130–37, 138, 150–51
Farley, James A., 103–4
Federal Bureau of Investigation (FBI), 75
Federal Communications Commission
    (FCC), 39, 63, 76, 82, 91, 171–72, 173
Federal Drug Administration (FDA), 56
Federal Radio Commission, 65–66
Federal Trade Commission (FTC), 56, 65,
    68, 156–57

The Feminine Mystique (Friedan), 122–23
feminism, 9, 10, 111, 117–18, 122–23, 165,
    191
The Fight for Truth in Advertising
    (Kenner), 56
Filippelli, Ronald L., 94–95
film industry, 185–89
Fishbein, Freda, 71
Fishbein, Morris, 62, 115
Flanagan, Hallie, 70
Fleishmann's Yeast, 56, 72
Fones-Wolf, Elizabeth, 2, 11, 96, 105, 107
Foote, Cone, and Belding advertising
    agency, 170, 179, 180
Foote, Emerson, 180
Ford, Henry, 66–67
Fortune, 121–22
Forum, 74
Fowler, Eleanor, 96
Fox, Stephen, 7, 54, 57
Franco, Carlos, 174–75
Frank, Dana, 9
Frankfurt School, 7, 19, 21
Freeman, Joseph, 59
Freyman, John and Nancy, 146–47, 149–
    50
Fribourg, Albert, 69, 199n.60
Fribourg, Eugenie, 199n.60
Friedan, Betty, 122–23

Gable, Clark, 167, 186–87
Gale, S. C., 120–21
Gardner, Ava, 167, 189
General Electric (GE), 66
General Federation of Women's Clubs, 10,
    139, 145, 164
General Foods, 52, 89–90, 92, 102–3
General Mills, 106–7, 120–21
General Motors (GM), 159
Genetic Psychology Monographs, 111
German-Americans, 83
"Getting Your Money's Worth" (Brindze),
    68
Gibb, Wolcott, 169
Gillette, Guy M., 164
Girdler, Tom, 100, 202n.70
Glander, Timothy, 19
Glazer, Tom, 161–62
Glickman, Lawrence, 10, 55, 57, 61, 83–84
Godfried, Nathan, 11
Gold, Mike, 59
Gold Medal Flour, 106–7

goodwill. *See* program sponsors
Good Will Court, 72–73
government consumer protection, 63, 73,
    145–46, 151–52, 153, 154, 156
government-sponsored radio, 48–50, 67,
    170, 175
grassroots activism, 6, 63–64, 191, 192
Greenstreet, Sydney, 167, 189
Gross, Beatrice, 149
The Guiding Light, 33, 122
Gulf Stream (Brindze), 68

Hall, Helen, 163
Hammond, Charles, 188
Happiness Boys, 27
Harper's, 114, 116
Hawes, Butch, 161–62
Hawthorne Courts (first known spoken
    commercial), 30
Hendrickson, Roy F., 152
Henle, James, 68
Henry, William, 111
Herzog, Herta, 111
Hettinger, Herman S., 19, 20, 46–47
Hill, George Washington, 177–81
Hilmes, Michelle, 9
"hitchhiker" commercials, 38
Hitler, Adolf, 7
Hooper, C. E., 45
Horgan, Margaret, 75
Horkheimer, Max, 7, 21
Hornaday, Hilton, 158
Horowitz, David, 91
Houseman, John, 70
housewives. *See* women
Howe, Quincy, 177
How To Spend Money (Brindze), 64–65
Hubbel, Gordon, 153
The Hucksters (Wakeman): advertising
    industry criticism of, 174–75; consumer
    movement and, 188–89; economic-
    moral principle in, 168–70; film version
    of, 186–91; radio industry reaction to,
    170, 186–88; women's portrayal in, 190–
    91. *See also* Wakeman, Frederic
Hummert, Frank and Anne, 114
Huyssen, Andreas, 9

"I'm Not Listening" campaign, 111, 113–14,
    115, 141
"In Defense of Daytime Serials" (Phillips),
    122

"Inflation Talkin' Blues" (Glazer), 161–62
Instantaneous Audience Measurement
   Service, 46
Ipana toothpaste, 27, 31, 32, 36
Italian-Americans, 83
I Talk as I Like (Carter), 89, 104–5
Ivory Soap, 132

Jacobs, Meg, 7, 149, 155, 159
Jenckes, Virginia E., 91
Jergen's Lotion, 43
Jhally, Sut, 40
jingles in advertising, 28, 29, 41–43
*Johnny Get Your Money's Worth (And Jane,
   Too!)* (Brindze), 68
Johnny Q. Public Speaks (Carter), 89
John Reed Club, 59
Journal of Home Economics, 68

Kallet, Arthur, 6, 54–55, 64
Kaltenborn, H. V., 86, 106–8
Kasson, John, 11
Katz, David, 10
Kenner, H. J., 56
Kerr, Deborah, 167, 189
Kerr, Sophie, 142
Kleenex, 123, 132, 133–34
Knes, Joe, 102
Knox Reeves Advertising, 122
Kobak, Edgar, 140

labor: censorship and, 65–66, 103, 105–6,
   109, 177–78; consumer organizations
   and, 55, 57, 73–74, 159–63, 165; history
   of, 83–84. *See also* AFL; CIO; United
   Electrical and Radio Workers Union
Labor Record, 99–100
Lafayette Theater, 70
Laidler, Harry, 84
Lambin, Maria, 59
Larchmont Times, 64
Lasker, Albert, 180
Lazarsfeld, Paul: active listener choice and,
   19, 21–22, 23, 26–27; advertising studies
   by, 17–18, 38, 40, 44, 52; audience strati-
   fication studies by, 22–23, 47–50, 93;
   shopping-voting link and, 21–22, 195n.10
Leader, William, 102
League of Professional Groups for Foster
   and Ford, 59, 62
Lears, T. J. Jackson, 29
Legion of Decency, 188

letters. *See* fan mail
Lever, Jack, 62–63
Levy, Ike, 100, 101
Levy, Leon, 20, 87, 98, 100, 101, 102, 103
Lewis, John L.: Boake Carter and, 86, 88,
   89, 95, 97, 100–101; soap opera charac-
   terization of, 109, 128–30
Lewis, Monica, 43
licensing of stations, 65–66, 91, 171
Life magazine, 124–25
Lindbergh, Charles, 87
Lippman, Walter, 86
Literary Digest, 67
Little Steel strike, 97
Lonely Women, 119–21
The Lone Ranger, 43–44
longshoremen strike, 96
Lord and Thomas advertising agency, 170,
   178, 179, 180
Love is Many a Splendored Thing, 123
Lucky Strike Hit Parade, 180–81
Lucky Strikes, 178–79, 180
Lux Radio Theatre, 43
Lux Soap and Flakes, 17, 18, 43, 52
Lynd, Robert, 22

McCarthy era, 62, 69, 75
McChesney, Robert, 5, 53
McCulloch, Mark, 95
McFadden, Dorothy, 10
McGovern, Charles, 6, 10, 54, 55, 60,
   195n.10
McMillin, John, 114
MacRorie, Janet, 140, 141, 142
magazine style advertising, 177, 181
Major Bowes' Amateur Hour, 47, 81–82
Maloney, Russell, 174
Marchand, Roland, 27, 29, 30, 32, 37
Maritime Unions of the Pacific Coast, 96
Marling, F. H., 107
Marmola (obesity drug), 65
Marxist consumer labor theories, 2, 4–5,
   11, 111
mass culture: battle for control of, 5–8, 13,
   191–92; labor and, 11–12; progressive
   strategies and, 13, 191–92; women and,
   8–9, 113, 191
Matthews, J. B., 55
Mazzacco, Dennis, 101
Mero-Irion, Yolanda, 139–40
MGM (Metro Goldwyn Meyer), 170, 186,
   188

middle commercial, 38, 172
Miller, Justin, 173
minority groups, 62, 67, 75, 150. *See also* African Americans; racism
Miranda, Elsa, 43
Modern Radio Advertising (Wolfe), 19
Montgomery, Donald: *Consumer Time* and, 145–55; corporate antagonism towards, 156–58; public interest radio and, 154, 165; and UAW, 158–60
Morell, Peter: consumer activism of, 71–74, 173; cultural background of, 53, 57–58, 70–73; importance of, 76–77; right-wing backlash against, 75–76; solutions offered by, 73–74
Morell, Valdi, 75–76
Morrison, Hobe, 118
Morrow, Edward, 121–22
"Mr. Average Man" (Boake Carter), 104–5
Munn, Frank, 27
Murray, Phillip, 106
Murray, Sylvia, 9
musical jingles, 29, 41–43
"Music in Radio" (Adorno), 24

Nasaw, David, 11
The Nation, 64, 65, 67, 74
National Association of Broadcasters (NAB): labor censorship and, 105–6, 178; radio reform opposition by, 144, 171, 173, 175, 182
National Association of Consumers (NAC), 156, 163–65
National Association of Manufacturers, 90, 162, 177
National Barn Dance, 47
National Committee on Education by Radio, 71
National Consumers League, 55
National Farm and Home Labor Hour, 145
National Farmer-Milk Cooperative, 55
National Federation of Women's Clubs, 55
National Grange, 164
National Labor Relations Board, 101
The National Radio Home-Maker's Club, 113
National Recovery Act, 155
National Recovery Administration, 95, 155
Nazi Germany, 7
NBC (National Broadcasting Company): boycott threats and, 82; commercial improvement and, 33, 39, 85; consumer activists and, 139–44; *Consumer Time* and, 145, 154–55; film industry and, 170, 186–88; labor censorship by, 66, 109, 130; soap operas and, 109, 112–13, 114, 115, 128–30, 140; Stephens College conference infiltration by, 141–44
Nebraskan Union Farmer, 158
negative advertising, 29, 30, 31–33, 36–37
Negro Unit of the Federal Theater Project, 70
Nervine, 31, 32, 36
New Deal. *See* Roosevelt, Franklin D.
New Haven Register, 157
New Masses, 59, 62
New Rochelle Standard Star, 64
New Rochelle Women's Club, 113
Newspaper Guild, 102
Newsweek magazine, 165
New York Bureau of Statistics of Labor, 84
New York City Department of Health, 156
New York Herald Tribune, 167
New York Times, 70, 114, 157, 171, 188
New York Times Book Review, 174
The Next Step Forward, 143
Nielsen, A. C., 45–46
Not To Be Broadcast (Brindze), 53, 63, 65, 67, 69–70

Office of Price Administration (OPA), 145, 149, 156, 159, 162
Office of Radio Research, 19, 20–21, 22, 23–24, 47, 52
Office of War Information (OWI), 120–21
Ohmann, Richard, 29
Oldenburg, Mildred, 119–21
"On Being Fired from a Job" (Rorty), 60
100,000,000 Guinea Pigs (Schlink and Kallet), 6, 55, 64, 69, 72
O'Neill, Neville, 19
Order on the Air! (Rorty), 59, 61
Our Master's Voice (Rorty), 59, 60, 61

Pacifica Radio, 76
Painted Dreams, 117
Painter, H. K. "King," 120
Paley, William, 20, 87, 175–76
Palmolive Radio Hour, 27
Parker Watch Company, 83
Penner, Joe, 92
The People Look at Radio (Lazarsfeld), 19

The People's Press, 102

Pep Boys, 87

Philadelphia Daily News, 87

Philadelphia Evening Ledger, 98

Philco Radio: Boake Carter and, 85–86, 92, 92–106; CIO boycott of, 85–86, 98–100, 102; rise of, 92–94

Phillip Morris, 32

Phillips, Bill, 1

Phillips, Irna: feminism and, 117–18, 122–23; soap opera defense by, 116, 118, 121–23; working women and, 119–21

Philrod Fishing Club, 94–95

PM magazine, 1, 154

Poisons, Potions, and Profits (Morell), 53, 71, 74, 141

Pope, Daniel, 58, 59, 62, 63, 198n.35

Post, Marjorie, 90

Pot O' Gold, 39

Preston, W. G., 24, 142, 143

Price, Arthur, 157–58

price ceilings, 146–49, 159–63, 165

Princeton Radio Project, 23, 24, 93

print advertising, 29, 30, 38

Printer's Ink, 18, 116

Procter and Gamble, 33–34, 39, 109, 110, 127–28, 130–37

program sponsors: conservative bias of, 177–78; product goodwill and, 38–40, 66–67, 84, 107, 127–28

The Psychology of Radio (Allport and Cantril), 19–20

public interest programming, 66, 154, 171–72, 174, 183

Pure Oil Company, 107–8

Quest, 133–34, 137

racism, 71, 76, 150. *See also* African Americans; minority groups

radio activity theorists, 19, 26

Radio in Advertising (Dunlap), 19, 20

Radio (Arnheim), 111

Radio Guide, 90

Radio Listening in America (Lazarsfeld), 19, 189

Radio and the Printed Page (Lazarsfeld), 19

radio ratings services, 45–46

Radio Research and Communications Research (Lazarsfeld), 19

Radio's Second Chance (Siepmann), 172–73

Radio Workers' Union, 66

Radox, 46

Raleigh cigarettes, 32

Ralston, Gilbert, 130

Ramsey, Bill, 136

Rauschenbush, Walter, 59

Rauschenbush, Winifred, 59

Razlogova, Elena, 131

RCA (Radio Corporation of America), 93–94, 96

Rea, Virginia, 27

Reader's Digest, 167

Reeves, Elizabeth, 122

religion and radio, 81–82, 83, 88, 107

repetition in advertising, 26, 41–43

Resor, Helen, 212n.83

Reuther, Walter, 160

Rich, Ruth, 140

Rinehart & Co., 170, 173, 176

The Road of Life, 34

Rockefeller Foundation, 19, 20, 22

Roosevelt, Franklin D.: Boake Carter and, 88, 90, 91–92, 99, 101, 103; consumer protection and, 63, 64, 153; corporate antagonism towards, 157, 177

Rorty, James: ecological perspective by, 63, 198n.35; politics and, 53, 57–58, 59–60, 61, 62–63; radio economics and, 58–63, 197n.28; and radio reform, 61–62, 63, 76–77, 85, 173

Rosenzweig, Roy, 11

Ross, Steven J., 11

Royal, John, 39, 82, 139–40, 141

Rubicam, Raymond, 180

Russell, Frank, 82

Sal Hepatica laxative, 36–37

Sarnoff, Robert, 180

Saturday Evening Post, 104

Saturday Review, 185

Schlink, F. J., 6, 54–55, 64

Scholastic, 68

Schudson, Michael, 8, 36

Scott, Alan, 103

Seeger, Pete, 161

Seiter, Ellen, 127

Selling Radio (Smulyan), 5

Senate Banking Committee, 164

Shore Leave (Wakeman), 170

Siepmann, Charles, 130–31, 172–73, 178, 182, 183, 191

Simon, A. L., 113
Sinatra, Frank, 81
Skinner, James M., 93, 99
Sloan, Alfred H., 57
Smith, G. Reid, 81–82
Smith, J. Augustus, 70
Smith, Kate, 19
Smulyan, Susan, 5, 20, 53, 193n.4
Smythe, Dallas, 4–5, 6, 29, 197n.28
soap operas: debate over, 111, 112–23; eco-
    nomics of, 110, 112–13, 114–15; psycho-
    logical studies and, 111, 115–16; women
    and, 111, 112–13, 115–16, 119–21, 124–27.
    See also Crusinberry, Jane; Phillips, Irna;
    specific soap operas
socialism, 19, 21, 22. See also communism;
    Marxism
Solitaire skin cream, 32, 36
"spot" announcement, 38
Steel, Johannes, 83
Stephens College, 57, 118–19, 141–44
Stokowski, Leopold, 93
The Story of Mary Marlin. See Crusinberry,
    Jane
Stretching Your Dollar in War-Time
    (Brindze), 69
Strotz, Sidney, 109, 129, 139–40
structure in advertising, 28, 37, 38–39, 41–
    43, 43–44
Super Suds, 32
The Survey, 164
sustaining programming, 14, 85–86, 154–
    55, 172, 174

Taylor, Mary, 153
Telecommunications, Mass Media, and
    Democracy (McChesney), 5
telephone coincidental ratings method, 45
television, 122, 171, 185, 188–89
testimonial advertising, 29, 212n.83
Thirty-Three Candles (Horowitz), 91
Thomas, Lowell, 86, 87
Thompson, Big Bill, 102
Thompson, Dorothy, 90
Thurber, James, 124–25
Tide magazine, 19, 57, 175
Time magazine, 94, 117, 173
Today's Children, 117, 121
Tomorrow's Food (Rorty), 63
Topeka Journal, 157
The Town Crier, 82–83

Trammell, Niles, 39, 114, 140, 144, 170,
    185–89
Trilling, Diana, 169
Truman, Harry S., 165
Turpentine (Morell), 70–71, 77

United Auto Workers (UAW), 158–62
United Electrical and Radio Workers
    Union (UE), 86, 94–96, 98–99, 101,
    102. See also Carey, James; Carter,
    Boake; CIO
United Fruit, 42
U. S. Department of Agriculture (USDA),
    1, 3, 145, 152–54, 156, 157, 158
Utility Consumers League, 66

Vanguard Press, 68, 69
Variety: radio advertising and, 33, 57, 143–
    44; radio commentary and reviews in,
    82, 152, 172, 173; soap opera debate in,
    114, 118, 122
Veblen, Thorstein, 54, 58
veterans, 10, 160, 161, 184–85

WABC (New York), 66, 134
Wakeman, Frederic: bases for The Huckster
    characters, 178–82, 186; commercial
    excesses and, 167–70, 184; radio reform
    and, 173–76, 191. See also The Hucksters
Wald, Alan, 68–69
Walker, Iris, 155
Waller, Fats, 161
Waller, Judith, 142
War Advertising Council, 184
War Food Administration, 152
Warne, Colston, 54, 55, 63, 77
Warner, Lloyd, 111
War Production Board, 145
Washington Post, 157
WCAU (Philadelphia), 20, 87, 90, 98, 100,
    101–2, 103
WCFL (Chicago), 11, 66
Weaver, Pat, 180
Webber, J. Leroy, 37
Webster, H. T., 110
WELI (New Haven), 134
We Open the Gates (Rorty), 63
Westchester County (NY), 64, 70, 113, 115,
    141, 149
Wester, Carl, 121
WEVD (New York), 65–66

WGN (Chicago), 117
WGY (Schenectady), 66
Wheeler-Lea amendments, 56
White Naphtha soap, 33–34, 36
WHN (New York), 113
Who's A Guinea Pig (American Druggist Association), 75
Wilkie, Wendell, 130
Williams, Albert, 182
Williamson, Judith, 29
Winchell, Walter, 43, 87, 90
Winship, Janice, 138
WJZ (New York), 66
WLBT (Jackson, Miss.), 76
WMAQ (Chicago), 117
WNEW (New York), 66
Wolfe, Charles, 19
Wolkonowicz, John, 102
women: clubwomen, 112, 113, 115, 139–41, 148–49, 150, 192; consumer activism by, 9–11, 55, 137–38, 139–41, 163–65, 191; *Consumer Time* and, 145, 146–48, 150;

The Hucksters movie depiction of, 190–91; mass culture and, 8–9, 113, 191; soap operas and, 110–12, 113, 119–21, 124–27, 135–36
Women League of Shoppers, 10
Women's International League for Peace and Freedom, 96
Women's National Radio Committee (WNRC), 139–41, 144
Woodward, Helen, 68
Woollcott, Alexander, 82–83
WPR (Detroit), 162, 165
WQXR (New York), 174
WXYZ (Detroit), 159, 165
Wylie, Max, 116

You Can Help Your Country Win the War (Brindze), 69
Young and Rubicam advertising agency, 174, 180
Your Money's Worth (Chase and Schlink), 6, 54–55, 64

Compositor:	BookMatters
Text:	10/13 Galliard
Display:	Galliard
Printer and Binder:	Maple-Vail Manufacturing Group